Microsoft® Office Excel® 2007

ILLUSTRATED

INTRODUCTORY

Elizabeth Eisner Reding/Lynn Wermers

COURSE TECHNOLOGY
CENGAGE Learning

Australia • Brazil • Japan • Korea • Mexico • Singapore • Spain • United Kingdom • United States

COURSE TECHNOLOGY
CENGAGE Learning™

Microsoft® Office Excel® 2007—Illustrated Introductory
Elizabeth Eisner Reding/Lynn Wermers

Senior Acquisitions Editor: Marjorie Hunt

Senior Product Manager: Christina Kling Garrett

Associate Product Manager: Rebecca Padrick

Editorial Assistant: Michelle Camisa

Senior Marketing Manager: Joy Stark

Marketing Coordinator: Jennifer Hankin

Developmental Editors: Barbara Clemens, MT Cozzola

Production Editor: Daphne Barbas

Copy Editor: Gary Michael Spahl

QA Manuscript Reviewers: Nicole Ashton, John Frietas, Jeff Schwartz, Susan Whalen

Cover Designers: Elizabeth Paquin, Kathleen Fivel

Cover Artist: Mark Hunt

Composition: GEX Publishing Services

For product information and technology assistance, contact us at
Cengage Learning Customer & Sales Support, 1-800-354-9706
For permission to use material from this text or product, submit all requests online at **cengage.com/permissions**
Further permissions questions can be emailed to
permissionrequest@cengage.com

ISBN-10: 1-4239-0521-0

ISBN-13: 978-1-4239-0521-9

Course Technology
25 Thomson Place
Boston, Massachusetts 02210
USA

Cengage Learning is a leading provider of customized learning solutions with office locations around the globe, including Singapore, the United Kingdom, Australia, Mexico, Brazil, and Japan. Locate your local office at:
international.cengage.com/region

Cengage Learning products are represented in Canada by Nelson Education, Ltd.

For your lifelong learning solutions, visit **course.cengage.com**

Purchase any of our products at your local college store or at our preferred online store **www.ichapters.com**

Trademarks:

Some of the product names and company names used in this book have been used for identification purposes only and may be trademarks or registered trademarks of their respective manufacturers and sellers.

Microsoft and the Office logo are either registered trademarks or trademarks of Microsoft Corporation in the United States and/or other countries. Course Technology is an independent entity from Microsoft Corporation, and not affiliated with Microsoft in any manner.

Printed in the United States of America
4 5 6 7 8 9 11 10 09 08

About This Book

Welcome to *Microsoft® Office Excel—Illustrated Introductory!* Since the first edition of this book was published in 1994, millions of students have used various Illustrated texts to master software skills and learn computer concepts. We are proud to bring you this new Illustrated book on the most exciting version of Microsoft Office ever to release.

As you probably have heard by now, Microsoft completely redesigned this latest version of Office from the ground up. No more menus! No more toolbars! The software changes Microsoft made were based on years of research during which they studied users' needs and work habits. The result is a phenomenal and powerful new version of the software that will make you and your students more productive and help you get better results faster.

Before we started working on this new edition, we also conducted our own research. We reached out to nearly 100 instructors like you who have used previous editions of this book and our Microsoft Office texts. Some of you responded to one of our surveys, others of you generously spent time with us on the phone, telling us your thoughts. Seven of you agreed to serve on our Advisory Board and guided our decisions.

As a result of all the feedback you gave us, we have preserved the features that you love, and made improvements that you suggested and requested. And of course we have covered all the key features of the new software. (For more details on what's new in this edition, please read the Preface.) We are confident that this book and all its available resources will help your students master Microsoft Office Excel 2007.

Advisory Board

We thank our Advisory Board who enthusiastically gave us their opinions and guided our every decision on content and design from beginning to end. They are as follows:

Kristen Callahan, Mercer County Community College

Paulette Comet, Assistant Professor, Community College of Baltimore County

Barbara Comfort, J. Sargeant Reynolds Community College

Margaret Cooksey, Tallahassee Community College

Rachelle Hall, Glendale Community College

Hazel Kates, Miami Dade College

Charles Lupico, Thomas Nelson Community College

Author Acknowledgments

Elizabeth Eisner Reding Creating a book of this magnitude is a team effort. I would like to thank my husband, Michael, as well as Christina Kling Garrett, the project manager, and my development editor, MT Cozzola, for her suggestions and corrections. I would also like to thank the production and editorial staff for all their hard work that made this project a reality.

Lynn Wermers I would like to thank Barbara Clemens for her insightful contributions, great humor, and patience. I would also like to thank Christina Kling Garrett for her encouragement and support in guiding and managing this project.

Preface

Welcome to *Microsoft Office Excel 2007, Illustrated Introductory*. If this is your first experience with the Illustrated series, you'll see that this book has a unique design: each skill is presented on two facing pages, with steps on the left and screens on the right. The layout makes it easy to digest a skill without having to read a lot of text and flip pages to see an illustration.

This book is an ideal learning tool for a wide range of learners—the rookies will find the clean design easy to follow and focused with only essential information presented, and the hotshots will appreciate being able to move quickly through the lessons to find the information they need without reading a lot of text. The design also makes this a great reference after the course is over! See the illustration on the right to learn more about the pedagogical and design elements of a typical lesson.

What's New in This Edition

We've made many changes and enhancements to this edition to make it the best ever. Here are some highlights of what's new:

- **New Getting Started with Microsoft Office 2007 Unit**—This unit begins the book and gets students up to speed on features of Office 2007 that are common to all the applications, such as the Ribbon, the Office button, and the Quick Access toolbar.

- **Real Life Independent Challenge**—The new Real Life Independent Challenge exercises offer students the opportunity to create projects that are meaningful to their lives, such as a budget for buying a house.

- **New Case Study**—A new case study featuring Quest Specialty Travel provides a practical and fun scenario that students can relate to as they learn skills. This fictional company offers a wide variety of tours around the world.

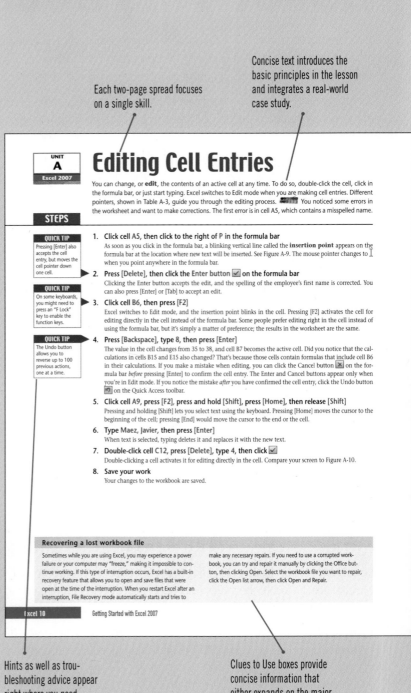

Each two-page spread focuses on a single skill.

Concise text introduces the basic principles in the lesson and integrates a real-world case study.

Hints as well as troubleshooting advice appear right where you need it—next to the step itself.

Clues to Use boxes provide concise information that either expands on the major lesson skill or describes an independent task that in some way relates to the major lesson skill.

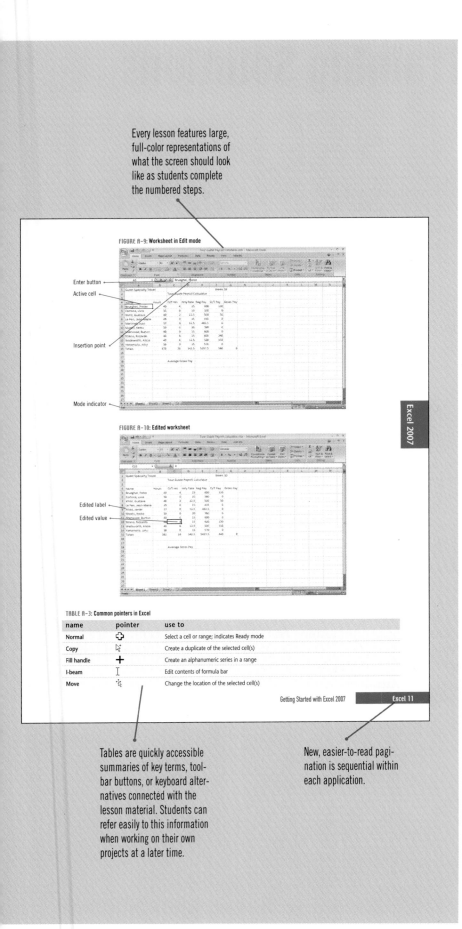

Every lesson features large, full-color representations of what the screen should look like as students complete the numbered steps.

FIGURE A-9: Worksheet in Edit mode

Enter button
Active cell
Insertion point
Mode indicator

FIGURE A-10: Edited worksheet

Edited label
Edited value

TABLE A-3: Common pointers in Excel

name	pointer	use to
Normal	⇧	Select a cell or range; indicates Ready mode
Copy	⊾	Create a duplicate of the selected cell(s)
Fill handle	+	Create an alphanumeric series in a range
I-beam	I	Edit contents of formula bar
Move	⊹	Change the location of the selected cell(s)

Getting Started with Excel 2007   Excel 11

Tables are quickly accessible summaries of key terms, tool-bar buttons, or keyboard alternatives connected with the lesson material. Students can refer easily to this information when working on their own projects at a later time.

New, easier-to-read pagination is sequential within each application.

• **Content Improvements**—All of the content in the book has been updated to cover Office 2007 and also to address instructor feedback. See the instructor resource CD for details on specific content changes for Excel.

Assignments

The lessons use Quest Specialty Travel, a fictional adventure travel company, as the case study. The assignments on the light purple pages at the end of each unit increase in difficulty. Data files and case studies provide a variety of interesting and relevant business applications. Assignments include:

• **Concepts Reviews** consist of multiple choice, matching, and screen identification questions.

• **Skills Reviews** provide additional hands-on, step-by-step reinforcement.

• **Independent Challenges** are case projects requiring critical thinking and application of the unit skills. The Independent Challenges increase in difficulty, with the first one in each unit being the easiest. Independent Challenges 2 and 3 become increasingly open-ended, requiring more independent problem solving.

• **Real Life Independent Challenges** are practical exercises in which students create documents to help them with their every day lives.

• **Advanced Challenge Exercises** set within the Independent Challenges provide optional steps for more advanced students.

• **Visual Workshops** are practical, self-graded capstone projects that require independent problem solving.

Assessment & Training Solutions

SAM 2007 helps bridge the gap between the classroom and the real world by allowing students to train and test on important computer skills in an active, hands-on environment.

SAM 2007's easy-to-use system includes powerful interactive exams, training or projects on critical applications such as Word, Excel, Access, PowerPoint, Outlook, Windows, the Internet, and much more. SAM simulates the application environment, allowing students to demonstrate their knowledge and think through the skills by performing real-world tasks.

Designed to be used with the Illustrated series, SAM 2007 includes built-in page references so students can print helpful study guides that match the Illustrated textbooks used in class. Powerful administrative options allow instructors to schedule exams and assignments, secure tests, and run reports with almost limitless flexibility.

Student Edition Labs

Our Web-based interactive labs help students master hundreds of computer concepts, including input and output devices, file management and desktop applications, computer ethics, virus protection, and much more. Featuring up-to-the-minute content, eye-popping graphics, and rich animation, the highly interactive Student Edition Labs offer students an alternative way to learn through dynamic observation, step-by-step practice, and challenging review questions. Also available on CD at an additional cost.

Online Content   Blackboard

Blackboard is the leading distance learning solution provider and class-management platform today. Course Technology has partnered with Blackboard to bring you premium online content. Instructors: Content for use with *Microsoft Office Excel 2007–Illustrated Introductory* is available in a Blackboard Course Cartridge and may include topic reviews, case projects, review questions, test banks, practice tests, custom syllabi, and more.

Course Technology also has solutions for several other learning management systems. Please visit *www.course.com* today to see what's available for this title.

Instructor Resources

The Instructor Resources CD is Course Technology's way of putting the resources and information needed to teach and learn effectively into your hands. With an integrated array of teaching and learning tools that offers you and your students a broad range of technology-based instructional options, we believe this CD represents the highest quality and most cutting edge resources available to instructors today. Many of these resources are available at *www.course.com*. The resources available with this book are:

- **Instructor's Manual**—Available as an electronic file, the Instructor's Manual includes detailed lecture topics with teaching tips for each unit.

- **Sample Syllabus**—Prepare and customize your course easily using this sample course outline.

- **PowerPoint Presentations**—Each unit has a corresponding PowerPoint presentation that you can use in lecture, distribute to your students, or customize to suit your course.

- **Figure Files**—The figures in the text are provided on the Instructor Resources CD to help you illustrate key topics or concepts. You can create traditional overhead transparencies by printing the figure files. Or you can create electronic slide shows by using the figures in a presentation program such as PowerPoint.

- **Solutions to Exercises**—Solutions to Exercises contain every file students are asked to create or modify in the lessons and end-of-unit material. Also provided in this section, there is a document outlining the solutions for the end-of-unit Concepts Review, Skills Review, and Independent Challenges. An Annotated Solution File and Grading Rubric accompany each file and can be used together for quick and easy grading.

- **Data Files for Students**—To complete most of the units in this book, your students will need Data Files. You can post the Data Files on a file server for students to copy. The Data Files are available on the Instructor Resources CD, the Review Pack, and can also be downloaded from *www.course.com*. In this edition, we have included a lesson on downloading the Data Files for this book, see page xvi.

Instruct students to use the Data Files List included on the Review Pack and the Instructor Resources CD. This list gives instructions on copying and organizing files.

- **ExamView**—ExamView is a powerful testing software package that allows you to create and administer printed, computer (LAN-based), and Internet exams. ExamView includes hundreds of questions that correspond to the topics covered in this text, enabling students to generate detailed study guides that include page references for further review. The computer-based and Internet testing components allow students to take exams at their computers, and also saves you time by grading each exam automatically.

CourseCasts—Learning on the Go. Always available...always relevant.

Want to keep up with the latest technology trends relevant to you? Visit our site to find a library of podcasts, CourseCasts, featuring a "CourseCast of the Week," and download them to your mp3 player at *http://coursecasts.course.com*.

Our fast-paced world is driven by technology. You know because you're an active participant—always on the go, always keeping up with technological trends, and always learning new ways to embrace technology to power your life.

Ken Baldauf, a faculty member of the Florida State University Computer Science Department, is responsible for teaching technology classes to thousands of FSU students each year. He knows what you know; he knows what you want to learn. He's also an expert in the latest technology and will sort through and aggregate the most pertinent news and information so you can spend your time enjoying technology, rather than trying to figure it out.

Visit us at *http://coursecasts.course.com* to learn on the go!

Brief Contents

Contents

Unit C: Formatting a Worksheet   51

Unit D: Working with Charts   79

| EXCEL 2007 | Unit G: Using Tables | 153 |

| EXCEL 2007 | Unit H: Analyzing Table Data | 177 |

Read This Before You Begin

Frequently Asked Questions

What are Data Files?

A Data File is a partially completed Excel workbook, or another type of file that you use to complete the steps in the units and exercises to create the final document that you submit to your instructor. Each unit opener page lists the Data Files that you need for that unit.

Where are the Data Files?

Your instructor will provide the Data Files to you or direct you to a location on a network drive from which you can download them. Alternatively, you can follow the instructions on the next page to download the Data Files from this book's Web page.

What software was used to write and test this book?

This book was written and tested using a typical installation of Microsoft Office 2007 installed on a computer with a typical installation of Microsoft Windows Vista.

The browser used for any steps that require a browser is Internet Explorer 7. If you are using this book on Windows XP, please see the next page "Important notes for Windows XP users." If you are using this book on Windows Vista, please see the Appendix at the end of this book.

Do I need to be connected to the Internet to complete the steps and exercises in this book?

Some of the exercises in this book assume that your computer is connected to the Internet. If you are not connected to the Internet, see your instructor for information on how to complete the exercises.

What do I do if my screen is different from the figures shown in this book?

This book was written and tested on computers with monitors set at a resolution of 1024 × 768. If your screen shows more or less information than the figures in the book, your monitor is probably set at a higher or lower resolution. If you don't see something on your screen, you might have to scroll down or up to see the object identified in the figures.

The Ribbon—the blue area at the top of the screen—in Microsoft Office 2007 adapts to different resolutions. If your monitor is set at a lower resolution than 1024 × 768, you might not see all of the buttons shown in the figures. The groups of buttons will always appear, but the entire group might be condensed into a single button that you need to click to access the buttons described in the instructions. For example, the figures and steps in this book assume that the Editing group on the Home tab in Word looks like the following:

1024 × 768 Editing Group

Editing Group on the
Home Tab of the
Ribbon at 1024 × 768

If your resolution is set to 800 × 600, the Ribbon in Word will look like the following figure, and you will need to click the Editing button to access the buttons that are visible in the Editing group.

800 × 600 Editing Group

Editing Group
on the Home Tab of the
Ribbon at 800 × 600

800 × 600 Editing Group clicked

Editing Group on the Home Tab of the Ribbon at
800 × 600 is selected to show available buttons

Important Notes for Windows XP Users

The screenshots in this book show Microsoft Office 2007 running on Windows Vista. However, if you are using Microsoft Windows XP, you can still use this book because Office 2007 runs virtually the same on both platforms. There are a few differences that you will encounter if you are using Windows XP. Read this section to understand the differences.

Dialog boxes

If you are a Windows XP user, dialog boxes shown in this book will look slightly different than what you see on your screen. Dialog boxes for Windows XP have a blue title bar, instead of a gray title bar. However, beyond this superficial difference in appearance, the options in the dialog boxes across platforms are the same. For instance, the screen shots below show the Font dialog box running on Windows XP and the Font dialog box running on Windows Vista.

FIGURE 1: Dialog box in Windows XP

FIGURE 2: Dialog box in Windows Vista

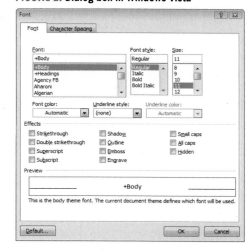

Alternate Steps for Windows XP Users

Nearly all of the steps in this book work exactly the same for Windows XP users. However, there are a few tasks that will require you to complete slightly different steps. This section provides alternate steps for a few specific skills.

Starting a program

1. Click the **Start button** on the taskbar
2. Point to **All Programs**, point to **Microsoft Office**, then click the application you want to use

FIGURE 3: Starting a program

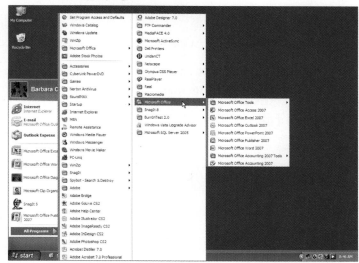

Saving a file for the first time

1. Click the **Office button**, then click **Save As**
2. Type a name for your file in the File Name text box
3. Click the **Save in list arrow**, then navigate to the drive and folder where you store your Data Files
4. Click **Save**

FIGURE 4: Save As dialog box

Opening a file

1. Click the **Office button**, then click **Open**
2. Click the **Look in list arrow**, then navigate to the drive and folder where you store your Data Files
3. Click the file you want to open
4. Click **Open**

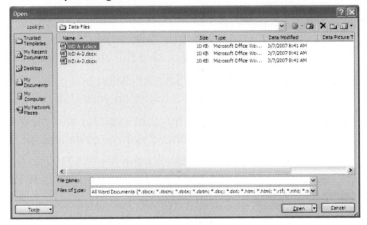

FIGURE 5: Open dialog box

Downloading Data Files for This Book

In order to complete many of the lesson steps and exercises in this book, you are asked to open and save Data Files. A Data File is a partially completed Excel workbook, or another type of file that you use as a starting point to complete the steps in the units and exercises. The benefit of using a Data File is that it saves you the time and effort needed to create a file; you can simply open a Data File, save it with a new name (so the original file remains intact), then make changes to it to complete lesson steps or an exercise. Your instructor will provide the Data Files to you or direct you to a location on a network drive from which you can download them. Alternatively, you can follow the instructions in this lesson to download the Data Files from this book's Web page.

1. Start Internet Explorer, type **www.course.com** in the address bar, then press [Enter]

2. When the Course.com Web site opens, click the Student Downloads link

3. On the Student Downloads page, click in the Search text box, type **9781423905219**, then click Go

> **QUICK TIP**
> You can also click Student Downloads on the right side of the product page.

4. When the page opens for this textbook, in the left navigation bar, click the Download Student Files link, then, on the Student Downloads page, click the Data Files link

5. If the File Download – Security Warning dialog box opens, click Save. (If no dialog box appears, skip this step and go to Step 6.)

> **TROUBLE**
> If a dialog box opens telling you that the download is complete, click Close.

6. If the Save As dialog box opens, click the Save in list arrow at the top of the dialog box, select a folder on your USB drive or hard disk to download the file to, then click Save

7. Close Internet Explorer and then open My Computer or Windows Explorer and display the contents of the drive and folder to which you downloaded the file

8. Double-click the file **905219.exe** in the drive or folder, then, if the Open File – Security Warning dialog box opens, click Run

> **QUICK TIP**
> By default, the files will extract to C:\ CourseTechnology\ 905219

9. In the WinZip Self-Extractor window, navigate to the drive and folder where you want to unzip the files to, then click Unzip

10. When the WinZip Self-Extractor displays a dialog box listing the number of files that have unzipped successfully, click OK, click Close in the WinZip Self-Extractor dialog box, then close Windows Explorer or My Computer

You are now ready to open the required files.

Getting Started with Microsoft Office 2007

Microsoft Office 2007 is a group of software programs designed to help you create documents, collaborate with co-workers, and track and analyze information. Each program is designed so you can work quickly and efficiently to create professional-looking results. You use different Office programs to accomplish specific tasks, such as writing a letter or producing a sales presentation, yet all the programs have a similar look and feel. Once you become familiar with one program, you'll find it easy to transfer your knowledge to the others.  This unit introduces you to the most frequently used programs in Office, as well as common features they all share.

OBJECTIVES

Understand the Office 2007 Suite

Start and exit an Office program

View the Office 2007 user interface

Create and save a file

Open a file and save it with a
     new name

View and print your work

Get Help and close a file

Understanding the Office 2007 Suite

Microsoft Office 2007 features an intuitive, context-sensitive user interface, so you can get up to speed faster and use advanced features with greater ease. The programs in Office are bundled together in a group called a **suite** (although you can also purchase them separately). The Office suite is available in several configurations, but all include Word and Excel. Other configurations include PowerPoint, Access, Outlook, Publisher, and/or others. ▓▓▓▓▓ Each program in Office is best suited for completing specific types of tasks, though there is some overlap in terms of their capabilities.

DETAILS

The Office programs covered in this book include:

- **Microsoft Office Word 2007**

  When you need to create any kind of text-based document, such as memos, newsletters, or multi-page reports, Word is the program to use. You can easily make your documents look great by inserting eye-catching graphics and using formatting tools such as themes. **Themes** are predesigned combinations of color and formatting attributes you can apply, and are available in most Office programs. The Word document shown in Figure A-1 was formatted with the Solstice theme.

- **Microsoft Office Excel 2007**

  Excel is the perfect solution when you need to work with numeric values and make calculations. It puts the power of formulas, functions, charts, and other analytical tools into the hands of every user, so you can analyze sales projections, figure out loan payments, and present your findings in style. The Excel worksheet shown in Figure A-1 tracks personal expenses. Because Excel automatically recalculates results whenever a value changes, the information is always up-to-date. A chart illustrates how the monthly expenses are broken down.

- **Microsoft Office PowerPoint 2007**

  Using PowerPoint, it's easy to create powerful presentations complete with graphics, transitions, and even a soundtrack. Using professionally designed themes and clip art, you can quickly and easily create dynamic slideshows such as the one shown in Figure A-1.

- **Microsoft Office Access 2007**

  Access helps you keep track of large amounts of quantitative data, such as product inventories or employee records. The form shown in Figure A-1 was created for a grocery store inventory database. Employees use the form to enter data about each item. Using Access enables employees to quickly find specific information such as price and quantity, without hunting through store shelves and stockrooms.

Microsoft Office has benefits beyond the power of each program, including:

- **Common user interface: Improving business processes**

  Because the Office suite programs have a similar **interface**, or look and feel, your experience using one program's tools makes it easy to learn those in the other programs. Office documents are **compatible** with one another, meaning that you can easily incorporate, or **integrate**, an Excel chart into a PowerPoint slide, or an Access table into a Word document.

- **Collaboration: Simplifying how people work together**

  Office recognizes the way people do business today, and supports the emphasis on communication and knowledge-sharing within companies and across the globe. All Office programs include the capability to incorporate feedback—called **online collaboration**—across the Internet or a company network.

Word document

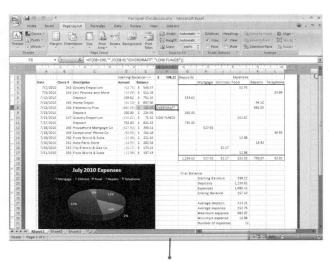

Excel worksheet

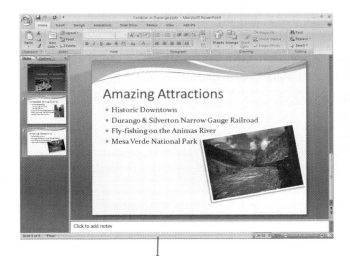

PowerPoint presentation

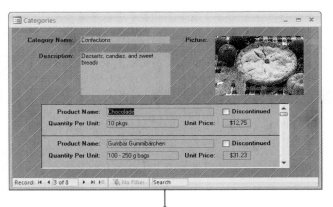

Access database form

Deciding which program to use

Every Office program includes tools that go far beyond what you might expect. For example, although Excel is primarily designed for making calculations, you can use it to create a database. So when you're planning a project, how do you decide which Office program to use? The general rule of thumb is to use the program best suited for your intended task, and make use of supporting tools in the program if you need them. Word is best for creating text-based documents, Excel is best for making mathematical calculations, PowerPoint is best for preparing presentations, and Access is best for managing quantitative data. Although the capabilities of Office are so vast that you *could* create an inventory in Excel or a budget in Word, you'll find greater flexibility and efficiency by using the program designed for the task. And remember, you can always create a file in one program, and then insert it in a document in another program when you need to, such as including sales projections (Excel) in a memo (Word).

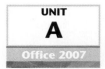

Starting and Exiting an Office Program

The first step in using an Office program is of course to open, or **launch**, it on your computer. You have a few choices for how to launch a program, but the easiest way is to click the Start button on the Windows taskbar, or to double-click an icon on your desktop. You can have multiple programs open on your computer simultaneously, and you can move between open programs by clicking the desired program or document button on the taskbar or by using the [Alt][Tab] keyboard shortcut combination. When working, you'll often want to open multiple programs in Office, and switch among them throughout the day. Begin by launching a few Office programs now.

STEPS

1. **Click the** Start button ⊕ **on the taskbar**

   The Start menu opens, as shown in Figure A-2. If the taskbar is hidden, you can display it by pointing to the bottom of the screen. Depending on your taskbar property settings, the taskbar may be displayed at all times, or only when you point to that area of the screen. For more information, or to change your taskbar properties, consult your instructor or technical support person.

2. **Point to** All Programs, **click** Microsoft Office, **then click** Microsoft Office Word 2007

   Microsoft Office Word 2007 starts and the program window opens on your screen.

3. **Click** ⊕ **on the taskbar, point to** All Programs, **click** Microsoft Office, **then click** Microsoft Office Excel 2007

   Microsoft Office Excel 2007 starts and the program window opens, as shown in Figure A-3. Word is no longer visible, but it remains open. The taskbar displays a button for each open program and document. Because this Excel document is **active**, or in front and available, the Microsoft Excel – Book1 button on the taskbar appears in a darker shade.

4. **Click** Document1 – Microsoft Word **on the taskbar**

   Clicking a button on the taskbar activates that program and document. The Word program window is now in front, and the Document1 – Microsoft Word taskbar button appears shaded.

5. **Click** ⊕ **on the taskbar, point to** All Programs, **click** Microsoft Office, **then click** Microsoft Office PowerPoint 2007

   Microsoft Office PowerPoint 2007 starts, and becomes the active program.

6. **Click** Microsoft Excel – Book1 **on the taskbar**

   Excel is now the active program.

7. **Click** ⊕ **on the taskbar, point to** All Programs, **click** Microsoft Office, **then click** Microsoft Office Access 2007

   Microsoft Office Access 2007 starts, and becomes the active program.

8. **Point to the taskbar to display it, if necessary**

   Four Office programs are open simultaneously.

9. **Click the** Office button ⊕, **then click** Exit Access, **as shown in Figure A-4**

   Access closes, leaving Excel active and Word and PowerPoint open.

FIGURE A-2: Start menu

FIGURE A-3: Excel program window and Windows taskbar

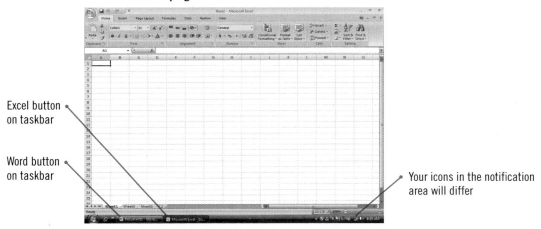

Excel button
on taskbar

Word button
on taskbar

Your icons in the notification
area will differ

FIGURE A-4: Exiting Microsoft Office Access

Microsoft
Office button

Exit Access
button

Mouse pointer

Using shortcut keys to move between Office programs

As an alternative to the Windows taskbar, you can use a keyboard shortcut to move among open Office programs. The [Alt][Tab] keyboard combination lets you either switch quickly to the next open program, or choose one from a palette. To switch immediately to the next open program, press [Alt][Tab]. To choose from all open programs, press and hold [Alt], then press and release [Tab] without releasing [Alt]. A palette opens on screen, displaying the icon and filename of each open program and file. Each time you press [Tab] while holding [Alt], the selection cycles to the next open file. Release [Alt] when the program/file you want to activate is selected.

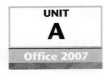
Viewing the Office 2007 User Interface

One of the benefits of using Office is that the programs have much in common, making them easy to learn and making it simple to move from one to another. Individual Office programs have always shared many features, but the innovations in the Office 2007 user interface mean even greater similarity among them all. That means you can also use your knowledge of one program to get up to speed in another. A **user interface** is a collective term for all the ways you interact with a software program. The user interface in Office 2007 includes a more intuitive way of choosing commands, working with files, and navigating in the program window. ▰▰▰ Familiarize yourself with some of the common interface elements in Office by examining the PowerPoint program window.

STEPS

1. **Click Microsoft PowerPoint – [Presentation1] on the taskbar**

    PowerPoint becomes the active program. Refer to Figure A-5 to identify common elements of the Office user interface. The **document window** occupies most of the screen. In PowerPoint, a blank slide appears in the document window, so you can build your slide show. At the top of every Office program window is a **title bar**, which displays the document and program name. Below the title bar is the **Ribbon**, which displays commands you're likely to need for the current task. Commands are organized into **tabs**. The tab names appear at the top of the Ribbon, and the active tab appears in front with its name highlighted. The Ribbon in every Office program includes tabs specific to the program, but all include a Home tab on the far left, for the most popular tasks in that program.

2. **Click the Office button** 🔘

    The Office menu opens. This menu contains commands common to most Office programs, such as opening a file, saving a file, and closing the current program. Next to the Office button is the **Quick Access toolbar**, which includes buttons for common Office commands.

3. **Click** 🔘 **again to close it, then point to the Save button** 💾 **on the Quick Access toolbar, *but do not click it***

    You can point to any button in Office to see a description; this is a good way to learn the available choices.

4. **Click the Design tab on the Ribbon**

    To display a different tab, you click its name on the Ribbon. Each tab arranges related commands into **groups** to make features easy to find. The Themes group displays available themes in a **gallery**, or palette of choices you can browse. Many groups contain a **dialog box launcher**, an icon you can click to open a dialog box or task pane for the current group, which offers an alternative way to choose commands.

5. **Move the mouse pointer** ⬉ **over the Aspect theme in the Themes group as shown in Figure A-6, *but do not click the mouse button***

    Because you have not clicked the theme, you have not actually made any changes to the slide. With the **Live Preview** feature, you can point to a choice, see the results right in the document, and then decide whether you want to make the change.

6. **Move** ⬉ **away from the Ribbon and towards the slide**

    If you clicked the Aspect theme, it would be applied to this slide. Instead, the slide remains unchanged.

7. **Point to the Zoom slider** 🔽 **on the status bar, then drag** 🔽 **to the right until the Zoom percentage reads 166%**

    The slide display is enlarged. Zoom tools are located on the status bar. You can drag the slider or click the plus and minus buttons to zoom in/out on an area of interest. The percentage tells you the zoom effect.

8. **Drag the Zoom slider** 🔽 **on the status bar to the left until the Zoom percentage reads 73%**

FIGURE A-5: PowerPoint program window

Quick Access toolbar

Title bar

Tabs

Ribbon

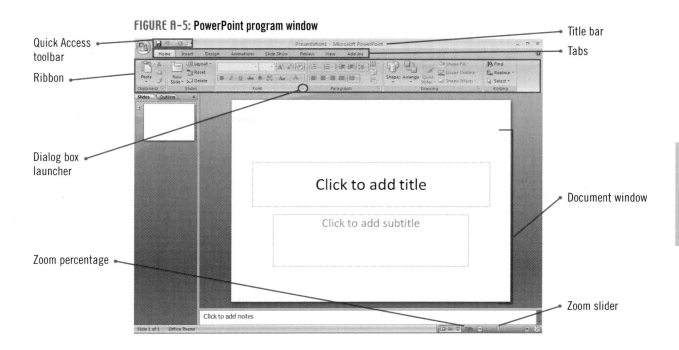

Dialog box launcher

Document window

Zoom percentage

Click to add title

Click to add subtitle

Zoom slider

Click to add notes

FIGURE A-6: Viewing a theme with Live Preview

Aspect theme

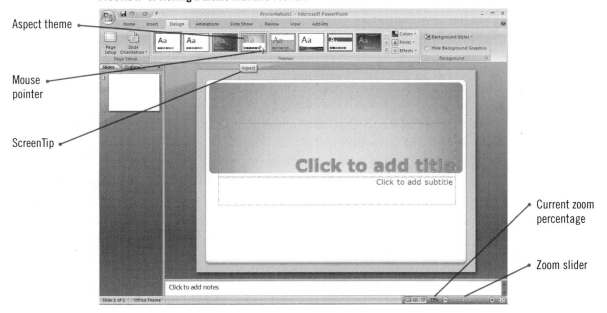

Mouse pointer

ScreenTip

Current zoom percentage

Zoom slider

Click to add title

Click to add subtitle

Click to add notes

Customizing the Quick Access toolbar

You can customize the Quick Access toolbar to display your favorite commands. To do so, click the Customize Quick Access Toolbar button ⏷ in the title bar, then click the command you want to add. If you don't see the command in the list, click More Commands to open the Customize tab of the Options dialog box. In the Options dialog box, use the Choose commands from list to choose a category, click the desired command in the list on the left, click Add to add it to the Quick Access toolbar, then click OK. To remove a button from the toolbar, click the name in the list on the right, then click Remove. To add a command to the Quick Access toolbar on

the fly, simply right-click the button on the Ribbon, then click Add to Quick Access Toolbar on the shortcut menu. You can also use the Customize Quick Access Toolbar button to move the toolbar below the ribbon, by clicking Show Below the Ribbon, or to minimize the Ribbon so it takes up less space onscreen. If you click Minimize the Ribbon, the Ribbon is minimized to display only the tabs. When you click a tab, the Ribbon opens so you can choose a command; once you choose a command, the Ribbon closes again, and only the tabs are visible.

Creating and Saving a File

When working in a program, one of the first things you need to do is to create and save a file. A **file** is a stored collection of data. Saving a file enables you to work on a project now, then put it away and work on it again later. In some Office programs, including Word, Excel, and PowerPoint, a new file is automatically created when you start the program, so all you have to do is enter some data and save it. In Access, you must expressly create a file before you enter any data. You should give your files meaningful names and save them in an appropriate location, so they're easy to find. ▄▄▄▄▄ Use Microsoft Word to familiarize yourself with the process of creating and saving a document. First you'll type some notes about a possible location for a corporate meeting, then you'll save the information for later use.

1. **Click Document1 – Microsoft Word on the taskbar**

2. **Type Locations for Corporate Meeting, then press [Enter] twice**

   The text appears in the document window, and a cursor blinks on a new blank line. The cursor indicates where the next typed text will appear.

3. **Type Las Vegas, NV, press [Enter], type Orlando, FL, press [Enter], type Chicago, IL, press [Enter] twice, then type your name**

   Compare your document to Figure A-7.

QUICK TIP

A filename can be up to 255 characters, including a file extension, and can include upper- or lowercase characters and spaces, but not ?, ", /, \, <, >, *, |, or :.

4. ▶ **Click the Save button 💾 on the Quick Access toolbar**

   Because this is the first time you are saving this document, the Save As dialog box opens, as shown in Figure A-8. The Save As dialog box includes options for assigning a filename and storage location. Once you save a file for the first time, clicking 💾 saves any changes to the file *without* opening the Save As dialog box, because no additional information is needed. In the Address bar, Office displays the default location for where to save the file, but you can change to any location. In the File name field, Office displays a suggested name for the document based on text in the file, but you can enter a different name.

QUICK TIP

You can create a desktop icon that you can double-click to both launch a program and open a document, by saving it to the desktop.

5. **Type Potential Corporate Meeting Locations**

   The text you type replaces the highlighted text.

6. ▶ **In the Save As dialog box, use the Address bar or Navigation pane to navigate to the drive and folder where you store your Data Files**

   Many students store files on a flash drive or Zip drive, but you can also store files on your computer, a network drive, or any storage device indicated by your instructor or technical support person.

QUICK TIP

To create a new blank file when a file is open, click the Office button, click New, then click Create.

7. ▶ **Click Save**

   The Save As dialog box closes, the new file is saved to the location you specified, then the name of the document appears in the title bar, as shown in Figure A-9. (You may or may not see a file extension.) See Table A-1 for a description of the different types of files you create in Office, and the file extensions associated with each. You can save a file in an earlier version of a program by choosing from the list of choices in the Save as type list arrow in the Save As dialog box.

TABLE A-1: Common filenames and default file extensions

File created in	is called a	and has the default extension
Excel	workbook	.xlsx
Word	document	.docx
Access	database	.accdb
PowerPoint	presentation	.pptx

FIGURE A-7: Creating a document in Word

Save button

Your name should appear here

Insertion point

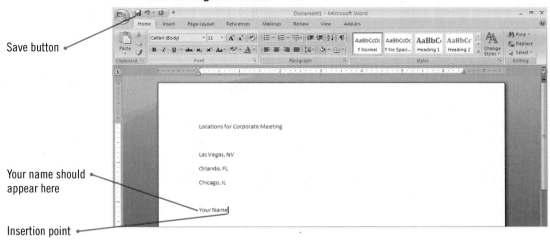

FIGURE A-8: Save As dialog box

Address bar

Navigation pane; your links and Folders setting may differ

File name field; your computer may not be set to display file extensions

Previous Locations list arrow

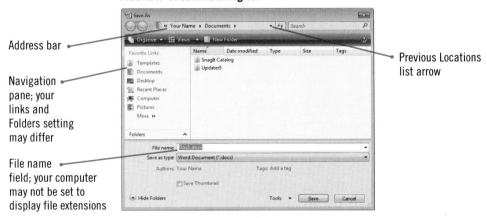

FIGURE A-9: Named Word document

Name appears in title bar

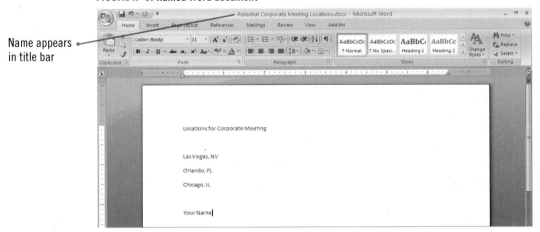

Using the Office Clipboard

You can use the Office Clipboard to cut and copy items from one Office program and paste them into others. The Clipboard can store a maximum of 24 items. To access it, open the Office Clipboard task pane by clicking the launcher in the Clipboard group in the Home tab. Each time you copy a selection, it is saved in the Office Clipboard. Each entry in the Office Clipboard includes an icon that tells you the program in which it was created. To paste an entry, click in the document where you want it to appear, then click the item in the Office Clipboard. To delete an item from the Office Clipboard, right-click the item, then click Delete.

Opening a File and Saving it with a New Name

In many cases as you work in Office, you start with a blank document, but often you need to use an existing file. It might be a file you or a co-worker created earlier as a work-in-progress, or it could be a complete document that you want to use as the basis for another. For example, you might want to create a budget for this year using the budget you created last year; you could type in all the categories and information from scratch, or you could open last year's budget, save it with a new name, and just make changes to update it for the current year. By opening the existing file and saving it with the Save As command, you create a duplicate that you can modify to your heart's content, while the original file remains intact.  Use Excel to open an existing workbook file, and save it with a new name so the original remains unchanged.

STEPS

QUICK TIP

If you point to a command on the Office menu that is followed by an arrow, a submenu opens displaying additional, related commands.

1. **Click Microsoft Excel – Book1 on the taskbar, click the Office button 🔘, then click Open**

   The Open dialog box opens, where you can navigate to any drive or folder location accessible to your computer to locate a file.

2. **In the Open dialog box, navigate to the drive and folder where you store your Data Files**

   The files available in the current folder are listed, as shown in Figure A-10. This folder contains one file.

3. **Click OFFICE A-1.xlsx, then click Open**

   The dialog box closes and the file opens in Excel. An Excel file is an electronic spreadsheet, so it looks different from a Word document or a PowerPoint slide.

QUICK TIP

The Recent Items list on the Office menu displays recently opened documents; you can click any file to open it.

4. **Click 🔘, then click Save As**

   The Save As dialog box opens, and the current filename is highlighted in the File name text box. Using the Save As command enables you to create a copy of the current, existing file with a new name. This action preserves the original file, and creates a new file that you can modify.

QUICK TIP

The Save As command works identically in all Office programs, except Access; in Access, this command lets you save a copy of the current database object, such as a table or form, with a new name, but not a copy of the entire database.

5. **Navigate to the drive and folder where your Data Files are stored if necessary, type Budget for Corporate Meeting in the File name text box, as shown in Figure A-11, then click Save**

   A copy of the existing document is created with the new name. The original file, Office A-1.xlsx, closes automatically.

6. **Click cell A19, type your name, then press [Enter], as shown in Figure A-12**

   In Excel, you enter data in cells, which are formed by the intersection of a row and a column. Cell A19 is at the intersection of column A and row 19. When you press [Enter], the cell pointer moves to cell A20.

7. **Click the Save button 🖫 on the Quick Access toolbar**

   Your name appears in the worksheet, and your changes to the file are saved.

Exploring File Open options

You might have noticed that the Open button on the Open dialog box includes an arrow. In a dialog box, if a button includes an arrow you can click the button to invoke the command, or you can click the arrow to choose from a list of related commands. The Open button list arrow includes several related commands, including Open Read-Only and Open as Copy. Clicking Open Read-Only opens a file that you can only save by saving it with a new name; you cannot save changes to the original file. Clicking Open as Copy creates a copy of the file already saved and named with the word "Copy" in the title. Like the Save As command, these commands provide additional ways to use copies of existing files while ensuring that original files do not get inadvertently changed.

FIGURE A-10: Open dialog box

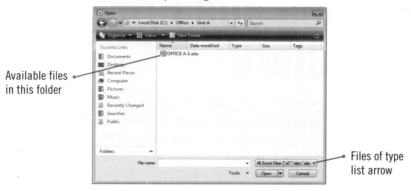

Available files in this folder

Files of type list arrow

FIGURE A-11: Save As dialog box

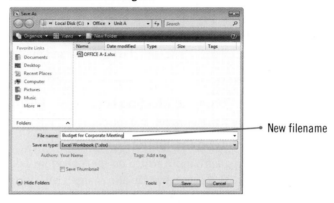

New filename

FIGURE A-12: Adding your name to the worksheet

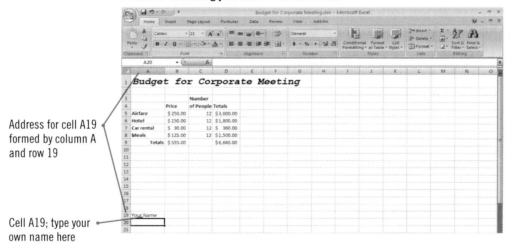

Address for cell A19 formed by column A and row 19

Cell A19; type your own name here

Working in Compatibility mode

Not everyone upgrades to the newest version of Office. As a general rule, new software versions are **backward-compatible**, meaning that documents saved by an older version can be read by newer software. The reverse is not always true, so Office 2007 includes a feature called Compatibility mode. When you open a file created in an earlier version of Office, "Compatibility Mode" appears in the title bar, letting you know the file was created in an earlier, but usable version of the program. If you are working with someone who may not be using the newest version of the software, you can avoid possible incompatibility problems by saving your file in another, earlier format. To do this, click the Office button, point to the Save As command, then click a choice on the Save As submenu. For example, if you're working in Excel, click Excel 97-2003 Workbook format. When the Save As dialog box opens, you'll notice that the Save as type box reads "Excel 97-2003 Workbook" instead of the default "Excel Workbook." To see more file format choices, such as Excel 97-2003 Template or Microsoft Excel 5.0/95 Workbook, click Other Formats on the Save As submenu. In the Save As dialog box, click the Save as type button, click the choice you think matches what your co-worker is using, then click Save.

Viewing and Printing Your Work

If your computer is connected to a printer or a print server, you can easily print any Office document. Printing can be as simple as clicking a button, or as involved as customizing the print job by printing only selected pages or making other choices, and/or **previewing** the document to see exactly what a document will look like when it is printed. (In order for printing and previewing to work, a printer must be installed.) In addition to using Print Preview, each Microsoft Office program lets you switch among various **views** of the document window, to show more or fewer details or a different combination of elements that make it easier to complete certain tasks, such as formatting or reading text. You can also increase or decrease your view of a document, so you can see more or less of it on the screen at once. Changing your view of a document does not affect the file in any way, it affects only the way it looks on screen.  Experiment with changing your view of a Word document, and then preview and print your work.

1. **Click** Potential Corporate Meeting Locations – Microsoft Word **on the taskbar**
    Word becomes the active program, and the document fills the screen.

2. **Click the** View tab **on the Ribbon**
    In most Office programs, the View tab on the Ribbon includes groups and commands for changing your view of the current document. You can also change views using the View buttons on the status bar.

3. **Click** Web Layout button **in the Document Views group on the View tab**
    The view changes to Web Layout view, as shown in Figure A-13. This view shows how the document will look if you save it as a Web page.

4. **Click the** Zoom in button ⊕ **on the status bar eight times until the zoom percentage reads** 180%
    Zooming in, or choosing a higher percentage, makes a document appear bigger on screen, but less of it fits on the screen at once; **zooming out**, or choosing a lower percentage, lets you see more of the document but at a reduced size.

5. **Drag the** Zoom slider ⬇ **on the status bar to the** center mark
    The Zoom slider lets you zoom in and out without opening a dialog box or clicking buttons.

6. **Click the** Print Layout button **on the View tab**
    You return to Print Layout view, the default view in Microsoft Word.

7. **Click the** Office button 🔘**, point to** Print**, then click** Print Preview
    The Print Preview presents the most accurate view of how your document will look when printed, displaying the entire page on screen at once. Compare your screen to Figure A-14. The Ribbon in Print Preview contains a single tab, also known as a **program** tab, with commands specific to Print Preview. The commands on this tab facilitate viewing and changing overall settings such as margins and page size.

8. **Click the** Print button **on the Ribbon**
    The Print dialog box opens, as shown in Figure A-15. You can use this dialog box to change which pages to print, the number of printed copies, and even the number of pages you print on each page. If you have multiple printers from which to choose, you can change from one installed printer by clicking the Name list arrow, then clicking the name of the installed printer you want to use.

9. **Click OK, then click the** Close Print Preview button **on the Ribbon**
    A copy of the document prints, and Print Preview closes.

FIGURE A-13: Web Layout view

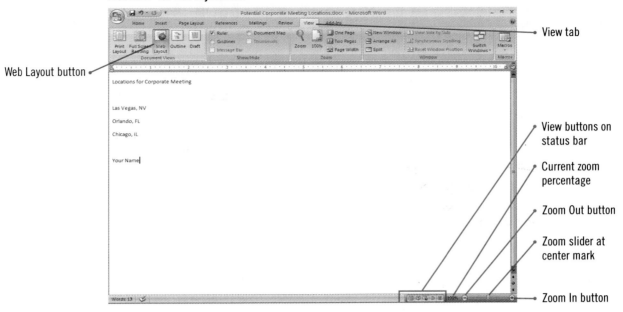

- Web Layout button
- View tab
- View buttons on status bar
- Current zoom percentage
- Zoom Out button
- Zoom slider at center mark
- Zoom In button

FIGURE A-14: Print Preview screen

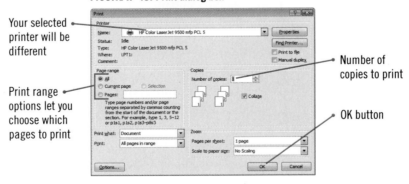

- Print button
- Orientation button
- Zoom button
- Close Print Preview button

FIGURE A-15: Print dialog box

- Your selected printer will be different
- Print range options let you choose which pages to print
- Number of copies to print
- OK button

Using the Print Screen feature to create a screen capture

At some point you may want to create a screen capture. A **screen capture** is a snapshot of your screen, as if you took a picture of it with a camera. You might want to take a screen capture if an error message occurs and you want Technical Support to see exactly what's on the screen. Or perhaps your instructor wants to see what your screen looks like when you create a particular document. To create a screen capture, press [PrtScn]. (Keyboards differ, but you may find the [PrtScn] button on the Insert key in or near your keyboard's function keys. You may have to press the [F Lock] key to enable the Function keys.) Pressing this key places a digital image of your screen in the Windows temporary storage area known as the **Clipboard**. Open the document where you want the screen capture to appear, click the Home tab on the Ribbon (if necessary), then click Paste on the Home tab. The screen capture is pasted into the document.

Getting Help and Closing a File

You can get comprehensive help at any time by pressing [F1] in an Office program. You can also get help in the form of a ScreenTip by pointing to almost any icon in the program window. When you're finished working in an Office document, you have a few choices regarding ending your work session. You can close a file or exit a program by using the Office button or by clicking a button on the title bar. Closing a file leaves a program running, while exiting a program closes all the open files in that program as well as the program itself. In all cases, Office reminds you if you try to close a file or exit a program and your document contains unsaved changes. ▓▓▓ Explore the Help system in Microsoft Office, and then close your documents and exit any open programs.

STEPS

1. **Point to the Zoom button on the View tab of the Ribbon**
   A ScreenTip appears that describes how the Zoom button works.

QUICK TIP
If you are not con-
nected to the
Internet, the Help
window displays
only the help con-
tent available on
your computer.

2. **Press [F1]**
   The Word Help window opens, as shown in Figure A-16, displaying the home page for help in Word. Each entry is a hyperlink you can click to open a list of related topics. This window also includes a toolbar of useful Help commands and a Search field. The connection status at the bottom of the Help window indicates that the connection to Office Online is active. Office Online supplements the help content available on your computer with a wide variety of up-to-date topics, templates, and training.

3. **Click the Getting help link in the Table of Contents pane**
   The icon next to Getting help changes and its list of subtopics expands.

QUICK TIP
You can also open
the Help window by
clicking the
Microsoft Office
Help button 🔘 to
the right of the tabs
on the Ribbon.

4. **Click the Work with the Help window link in the topics list in the left pane**
   The topic opens in the right pane, as shown in Figure A-17.

5. **Click the Hide Table of Contents button 🔲 on the Help toolbar**
   The left pane closes, as shown in Figure A-18.

QUICK TIP
You can print the
current topic by
clicking the Print
button 🖨 on the
Help toolbar to open
the Print dialog box.

6. **Click the Show Table of Contents button 📖 on the Help toolbar, scroll to the bottom of the left pane, click the Accessibility link in the Table of Contents pane, click the Use the keyboard to work with Ribbon programs link, read the information in the right pane, then click the Help window Close button**

7. **Click the Office button 🔘, then click Close; if a dialog box opens asking whether you want to save your changes, click Yes**
   The Potential Corporate Meeting Locations document closes, leaving the Word program open.

8. **Click 🔘, then click Exit Word**
   Microsoft Office Word closes, and the Excel program window is active.

9. **Click 🔘, click Exit Excel, click the PowerPoint button on the taskbar if necessary, click 🔘, then click Exit PowerPoint**
   Microsoft Office Excel and Microsoft Office PowerPoint both close.

FIGURE A-16: Word Help window

Help toolbar

Search field

Hide Table of
Contents
button

The colors
of your links
may differ

Connection status

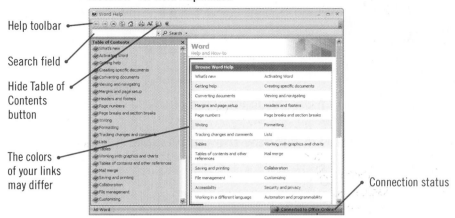

FIGURE A-17: Work with the Help window

Print button

Icon indicates
expanded topic

Work with
the Help
window link

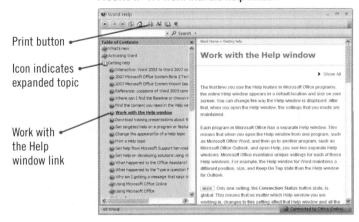

FIGURE A-18: Help window with Table of Contents closed

Show Table of
Contents button

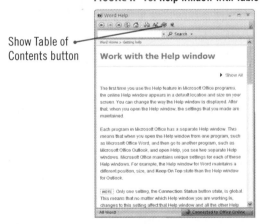

Recovering a document

Sometimes while you are using Office, you may experience a power failure or your computer may "freeze," making it impossible to continue working. If this type of interruption occurs, each Office program has a built-in recovery feature that allows you to open and save files that were open at the time of the interruption. When you restart the program(s) after an interruption, the Document Recovery task pane opens on the left side of your screen displaying both original and recovered versions of the files that were open. If you're not sure which file to open (original or recovered), it's usually better to open the recovered file because it will contain the latest information. You can, however, open and review all versions of the file that were recovered and save the best one. Each file listed in the Document Recovery task pane displays a list arrow with options that allow you to open the file, save it as is, delete it, or show repairs made to it during recovery.

Practice

If you have a SAM user profile, you may have access to hands-on instruction, practice, and assessment of the skills covered in this unit. Log in to your SAM account (http://sam2007.course.com/) to launch any assigned training activities or exams that relate to the skills covered in this unit.

▼ CONCEPTS REVIEW

Label the elements of the program window shown in Figure A-19.

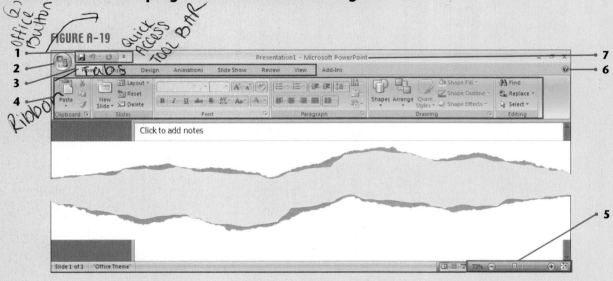

FIGURE A-19

(handwritten labels: Office Button (2), Quick Access Tool Bar, Ribbon)

Match each project with the program for which it is best suited.

8. Microsoft Office PowerPoint D
9. Microsoft Office Excel C A
10. Microsoft Office Word B
11. Microsoft Office Access A C

a. Corporate expansion budget with expense projections
b. Business résumé for a job application
c. Auto parts store inventory
d. Presentation for Board of Directors meeting

▼ INDEPENDENT CHALLENGE 1

You just accepted an administrative position with a local car dealership that's recently invested in computers and is now considering purchasing Microsoft Office. You are asked to propose ways Office might help the dealership. You produce your proposal in Microsoft Word.

a. Start Word, then save the document as **Microsoft Office Proposal** in the drive and folder where you store your Data Files.
b. Type **Microsoft Office Word**, press [Enter] twice, type **Microsoft Office Excel**, press [Enter] twice, type **Microsoft Office PowerPoint**, press [Enter] twice, type **Microsoft Office Access**, press [Enter] twice, then type your name.
c. Click the line beneath each program name, type at least two tasks suited to that program, then press [Enter].
d. Save your work, then print one copy of this document.

Advanced Challenge Exercise

■ Press the [PrtScn] button to create a screen capture, then press [Ctrl][V].
■ Save and print the document.

e. Exit Word.

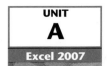

Getting Started with Excel 2007

Files You Will Need:

EX A-1.xlsx

EX A-2.xlsx

EX A-3.xlsx

EX A-4.xlsx

EX A-5.xlsx

In this unit, you will learn how spreadsheet software helps you analyze data and make business decisions, even if you aren't a math pro. You'll become familiar with the different elements of a spreadsheet and learn your way around the Excel program window. You will also work in an Excel worksheet and make simple calculations. You have been hired as an assistant at Quest Specialty Travel (QST), a company offering tours that immerse travelers in regional culture. You report to Grace Wong, the vice president of finance. As Grace's assistant, you create worksheets to analyze data from various divisions of the company, so you can help her make sound decisions on company expansion and investments.

OBJECTIVES

Understand spreadsheet software

Tour the Excel 2007 window

Understand formulas

Enter labels and values and use AutoSum

Edit cell entries

Enter and edit a simple formula

Switch worksheet views

Choose print options

Understanding Spreadsheet Software

Microsoft Excel is the electronic spreadsheet program within Microsoft Office. An **electronic spreadsheet** is an application you use to perform numeric calculations and to analyze and present numeric data. One advantage of spreadsheet programs over pencil and paper is that your calculations are updated automatically, so you can change entries without having to manually recalculate. Table A-1 shows some of the common business tasks people accomplish using Excel. In Excel, the electronic spreadsheet you work in is called a **worksheet**, and is contained in a file called a **workbook**, which has the file extension .xlsx. 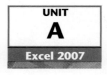 At Quest Specialty Travel, you use Excel extensively to track finances and manage corporate data.

When you use Excel, you have the ability to:

- **Enter data quickly and accurately**

    With Excel, you can enter information faster and more accurately than with pencil and paper. Figure A-1 shows a payroll worksheet created using pencil and paper. Figure A-2 shows the same worksheet created using Excel. Equations were added to calculate the hours and pay. You can copy the payroll deductions that don't change from quarter to quarter, then use Excel to calculate the gross and net payroll by supplying unique data and formulas for each quarter. You can also quickly create charts and other elements to help visualize how the payroll is distributed.

- **Recalculate data easily**

    Fixing typing errors or updating data is easy in Excel. In the payroll example, if you receive updated hours for an employee, you just enter the new hours and Excel recalculates the pay.

- **Perform what-if analysis**

    The ability to change data and quickly view the recalculated results gives you the power to make informed business decisions. For instance, if you're considering raising the hourly rate for an entry-level tour guide from $12.50 to $15.00, you can enter the new value in the worksheet and immediately see the impact on the overall payroll as well as on the individual employee. Any time you use a worksheet to ask the question "what if?" you are performing **what-if analysis**. Excel also includes a Scenario Manager where you can name and save different what-if versions of your worksheet.

- **Change the appearance of information**

    Excel provides powerful features for making information visually appealing and easier to understand. You can format text and numbers in different fonts, colors, and styles to make it stand out.

- **Create charts**

    Excel makes it easy to create charts based on worksheet information. Charts are updated automatically in Excel whenever data changes. The worksheet in Figure A-2 includes a 3-D pie chart.

- **Share information**

    It's easy for everyone at QST to collaborate in Excel, using the company intranet, the Internet, or a network storage device. For example, you can complete the weekly payroll that your boss, Grace Wong, started creating. You can also take advantage of collaboration tools such as shared workbooks, so that multiple people can edit a workbook simultaneously.

- **Build on previous work**

    Instead of creating a new worksheet for every project, it's easy to modify an existing Excel worksheet. When you are ready to create next week's payroll, you can open the file for last week's payroll, save it with a new filename, and modify the information as necessary. You can also use predesigned, formatted files called **templates** to create new worksheets quickly. Excel comes with many templates, that you can customize.

FIGURE A-1: Traditional paper worksheet

Quest Specialty Travel
Tour Guide Payroll Calculator

Name	Hours	O/T Hrs	Hrly Rate	Reg Pay	O/T Pay	Gross Pay
Brueghel, Pieter	40	4	15–	600–	120–	720–
Cortona, Livia	35	0	10–	350–	0–	350–
Klimt, Gustave	40	2	12^{50}	500–	50–	550–
Le Pen, Jean-Marie	29	0	15–	435–	0–	435–
Martinez, Juan	37	0	12^{50}	462.50	0–	462.50
Mioshi, Keiko	39	0	20–	780–	0–	780–
Sherwood, Burton	40	0	15–	600–	0–	600–
Strano, Riccardo	40	8	15–	600–	240–	840–
Wadsworth, Alicia	40	5	12^{50}	500–	125–	625–
Yamamoto, Johji	38	0	15–	570–	0–	570–

FIGURE A-2: Excel worksheet

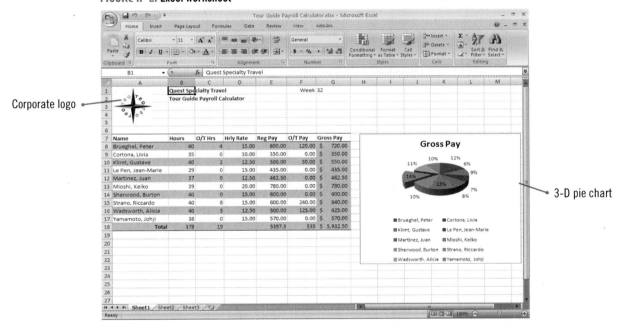

Corporate logo

3-D pie chart

TABLE A-1: Business tasks you can accomplish using Excel

you can use spreadsheets to	by
Perform calculations	Adding formulas and functions to worksheet data; for example, adding a list of sales results or calculating a car payment
Represent values graphically	Creating charts based on worksheet data; for example, creating a chart that displays expenses
Generate reports	Creating workbooks that combine information from multiple worksheets, such as summarized sales information from multiple stores
Organize data	Sorting data in ascending or descending order; for example, alphabetizing a list of products or customer names, or prioritizing orders by date
Analyze data	Creating data summaries and short lists using PivotTables or AutoFilters; for example, making a list of the top 10 customers based on spending habits
Create what-if data scenarios	Using variable values to investigate and sample different outcomes, such as changing the interest rate or payment schedule on a loan

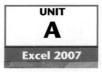

Touring the Excel 2007 Window

To start Excel, Microsoft Windows must be running. Similar to starting any program in Office, you can use the Start button on the Windows taskbar, or you may have a shortcut on your desktop you prefer to use. If you need additional assistance, ask your instructor or technical support person. ▟▟▓ You decide to start Excel and familiarize yourself with the worksheet window.

STEPS

QUICK TIP
For more information on starting a program or opening and saving a file, see the unit "Getting Started with Microsoft Office 2007."

TROUBLE
If you don't see the extension .xlsx on the filenames in the Open dialog box, don't worry; Windows can be set up to display or not to display the file extensions.

1. **Start Excel, click the Microsoft Office button ⊚, then click Open**

2. **In the Open dialog box, navigate to the drive and folder where you store your Data Files, click EX A-1.xlsx, then click Open**

3. **Click ⊚, then click Save As**

4. **In the Save As dialog box, navigate to the drive and folder where you store your Data Files if necessary, type Tour Guide Payroll Calculator in the File name text box, then click Save**

   Using Figure A-3 as a guide, identify the following items:
   - The **Name box** displays the active cell address. "A1" appears in the Name box.
   - The **formula bar** allows you to enter or edit data in the worksheet. The worksheet window contains a grid of columns and rows. Columns are labeled alphabetically and rows are labeled numerically. The worksheet window can contain a total of 1,048,576 rows and 16,384 columns.
   - The intersection of a column and a row is called a **cell**. Cells can contain text, numbers, formulas, or a combination of all three. Every cell has its own unique location or **cell address**, which is identified by the coordinates of the intersecting column and row.
   - The **cell pointer** is a dark rectangle that outlines the cell in which you are working. This cell is called the **active cell**. In Figure A-3, the cell pointer outlines cell A1, so A1 is the active cell. The column and row headings for the active cell are highlighted, making it easier to locate.
   - **Sheet tabs** below the worksheet grid let you switch from sheet to sheet in a workbook. By default, a workbook file contains three worksheets—but you can use just one, or have as many as 255, in a workbook. The Insert Worksheet button to the right of Sheet 3 allows you to add worksheets to a workbook. **Sheet tab scrolling buttons** let you navigate to additional sheet tabs when available.
   - You can use the **scroll bars** to move around in a document that is too large to fit on the screen at once.
   - The **status bar** is located at the bottom of the Excel window. It provides a brief description of the active command or task in progress. The **mode indicator** in the bottom-left corner of the status bar provides additional information about certain tasks.

5. **Click cell A4**

   Cell A4 becomes the active cell. To activate a different cell, you can click the cell or press the arrow keys on your keyboard to move to it.

6. **Click cell B5, press and hold the mouse button, drag ✛ to cell B14, then release the mouse button**

   You selected a group of cells and they are highlighted, as shown in Figure A-4. A selection of two or more cells such as B5:B14 is called a **range**; you select a range when you want to perform an action on a group of cells at once, such as moving them or formatting them. When you select a range, the status bar displays the average, count (or number of items selected), and sum of the selected cells as a quick reference.

FIGURE A-3: Open workbook

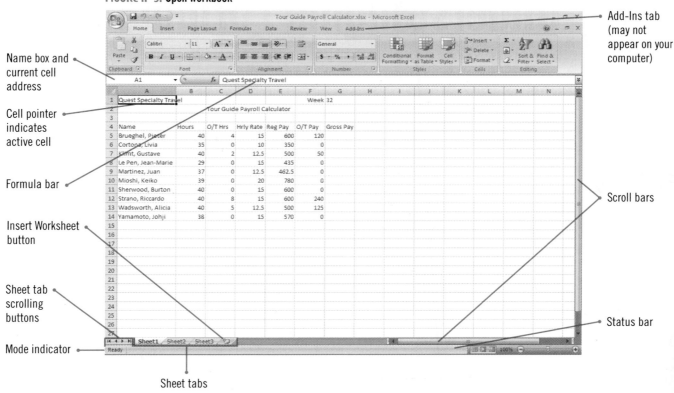

Name box and current cell address

Cell pointer indicates active cell

Formula bar

Insert Worksheet button

Sheet tab scrolling buttons

Mode indicator

Sheet tabs

Add-Ins tab (may not appear on your computer)

Scroll bars

Status bar

FIGURE A-4: Selecting a range

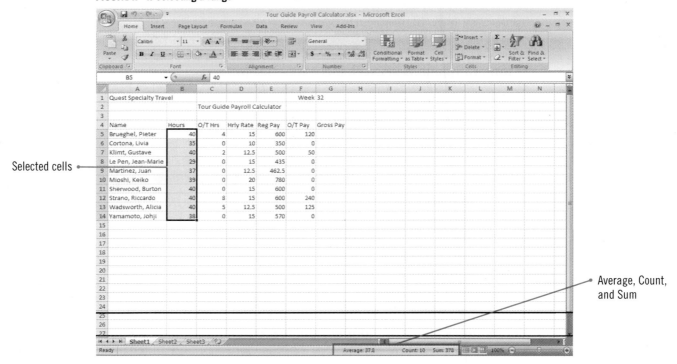

Selected cells

Average, Count, and Sum

Excel 2007

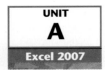

Understanding Formulas

Excel is a truly powerful program because users at every level of mathematical expertise can make calculations with accuracy. To do so, you use formulas. **Formulas** are equations in a worksheet. You use formulas to make calculations as simple as adding a column of numbers, or as complex as profit-and-loss projections for a global corporation. To tap into the power of Excel, you should understand how formulas work. Managers at QST use the Tour Guide Payroll Calculator workbook to keep track of employee hours prior to submitting them to the Payroll Department. You'll be using this workbook regularly, so you need to understand the formulas it contains and how Excel calculates the results.

STEPS

1. **Click cell E5**

   The active cell contains a formula, which appears on the formula bar. All Excel formulas begin with the equal sign (=). If you wanted a cell to show the result of adding 4 plus 2, the formula in the cell would look like this: =4+2. If you wanted a cell to show the result of multiplying two values in your worksheet, such as the values in cells B5 and D5, the formula would look like this: =B5*D5, as shown in Figure A-5.

2. **Click cell F5**

   While you're entering a formula in a cell, the cell references and arithmetic operators appear on the formula bar. See Table A-2 for a list of common Excel arithmetic operators. When you're finished entering the formula, you can either click the Enter button on the formula bar, or press [Enter]. An example of a more complex formula is the calculation of overtime pay. At QST, overtime pay is calculated at twice the regular hourly rate times the number of overtime hours. The formula used to calculate overtime pay for the employee in row 5 is:

   O/T Hrs times (2 times Hrly Rate)

   In a worksheet cell, you would enter: =C5*(2*D5), as shown in Figure A-6.

   The use of parentheses creates groups within the formula and indicates which calculations to complete first—an important consideration in complex formulas. In this formula, the hourly rate is doubled, and that value is multiplied by the number of overtime hours. Because overtime is calculated at twice the hourly rate, managers are aware that they need to closely watch this expense.

DETAILS

In creating calculations in Excel, it is important to:

- **Know where the formulas should be**

  Excel formulas are created in the cell where they are viewed. This means that the formula calculating Gross Pay for the employee in row 5 will be entered in cell G5.

- **Know exactly what cells and arithmetic operations are needed**

  Don't guess; make sure you know exactly what cells are involved before creating a formula.

- **Create formulas with care**

  Make sure you know exactly what you want a formula to accomplish before it is created. An inaccurate formula may have far-reaching effects if the formula or its results are referenced by other formulas.

- **Use cell references rather than values**

  The beauty of Excel is that whenever you change a value in a cell, any formula containing a reference to that cell is automatically updated. For this reason, it's important that you use cell references in formulas, rather than actual values whenever possible.

- **Determine what calculations will be needed**

  Sometimes it's difficult to predict what data will be needed within a worksheet, but you should try to anticipate what statistical information may be required. For example, if there are columns of numbers, chances are good that both column and row totals should be present.

FIGURE A-5: Viewing a formula

Formula appears in formula bar

Result of formula appears in cell

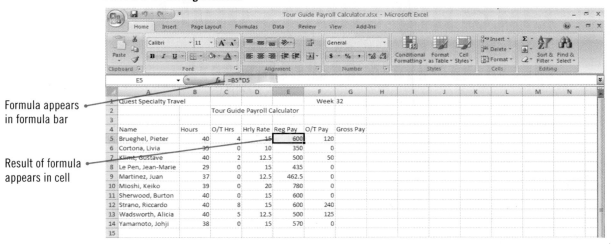

FIGURE A-6: Formula with multiple operators

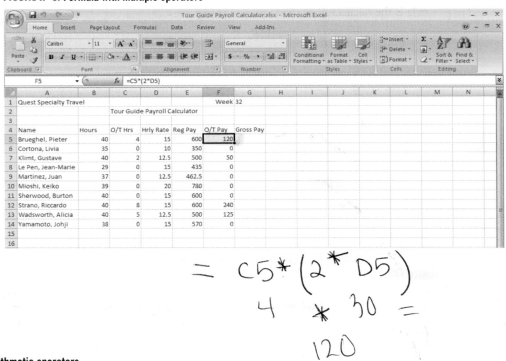

$$= C5 * (2 * D5)$$
$$4 * 30 =$$
$$120$$

TABLE A-2: Excel arithmetic operators

operator	purpose	example
+	Addition	=A5+A7
-	Subtraction or negation	=A5-10
*	Multiplication	=A5*A7
/	Division	=A5/A7
%	Percent	=35%
^ (caret)	Exponent	=6^2 (same as 6^2)

Entering Labels and Values and Using AutoSum

(handwritten margin note, left side, rotated): a) use labels (text) 14

To enter content in a cell, you can type on the formula bar or directly in the cell itself. When entering content in a worksheet, you should start by entering all the labels first. **Labels** are entries that contain text and numerical information not used in calculations, such as "2009 Sales" or "Travel Expenses." Labels help you identify data in worksheet rows and columns, making your worksheet easier to understand. **Values** are numbers, formulas, and functions that can be used in calculations. To enter a calculation, you type an equal sign (=) plus the formula for the calculation; some examples of an Excel calculation are "=2+2" and "=C5+C6." Functions are Excel's built-in formulas; you learn more about them in the next unit. You want to enter some information in the Tour Guide Payroll Calculator workbook, and use a very simple function to total a range of cells.

STEPS

(handwritten margin note, left side): function - built in Formula nec. to calculate the answer

1. **Click cell A15, then click in the formula bar**

   Notice that the **mode indicator** on the status bar now reads "Edit," indicating you are in Edit mode. You are in Edit mode any time you are entering or changing the contents of a cell.

2. **Type Totals, then click the Enter button ✓ on the formula bar**

   Clicking the Enter button accepts the entry. The new text is left-aligned. Labels are left-aligned by default, and values are right-aligned by default. Excel recognizes an entry as a value if it is a number or it begins with one of these symbols: +, -, =, @, #, or $. When a cell contains both text and numbers, Excel recognizes it as a label.

3. **Click cell B15**

   You want this cell to total the hours worked by all the tour guides. You might think you need to create a formula that looks like this: =B5+B6+B7+B8+B9+B10+B11+B12+B13+B14. However, there's an easier way to achieve this result.

4. **Click the AutoSum button Σ in the Editing group on the Home tab of the Ribbon**

   The SUM function is inserted in your formula, and a suggested range appears in parentheses, as shown in Figure A-7. A **function** is a built-in formula; it includes the **arguments** (the information necessary to calculate an answer), as well as cell references and other unique information. Clicking the AutoSum button sums the adjacent range (that is, the cells next to the active cell) above or to the left, though you can adjust the range if necessary. Using the SUM function is quicker than entering a formula, and using the range B5:B14 is more efficient than entering individual cell references.

5. **Click ✓**

   Excel calculates the total contained in cells B5:B14 and displays the result, 378, in cell B15. The cell actually contains the formula =SUM(B5:B14), and the result is displayed.

6. **Click cell C13, type 6, then press [Enter]**

   The number 6 is right-aligned, the cell pointer moves to cell C14 and the value in cell F13 changes.

7. **Click cell C18, type Average Gross Pay, then press [Enter]**

   The new label is entered in cell C18. The contents appear to spill into the empty cells to the right.

8. **Click and hold cell B15, drag the mouse pointer to cell G15, click the Fill button ▣▾ in the Editing group, then click Right in the Fill menu**

   Calculated values appear in the selected range, as shown in Figure A-8. Each filled cell contains a formula that sums the range of cells above. The Fill button fills cells based on the first number sequence in the range.

9. **Save your work**

FIGURE A-7: Creating a formula using the AutoSum button

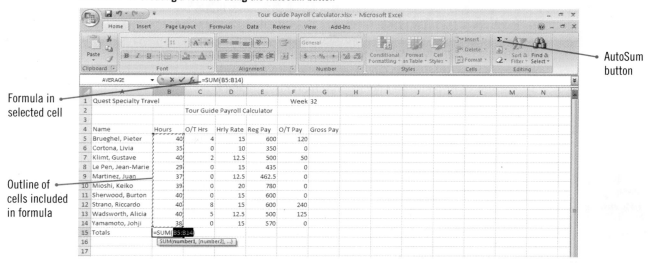

AutoSum button

Formula in selected cell

Outline of cells included in formula

FIGURE A-8: Calculated values

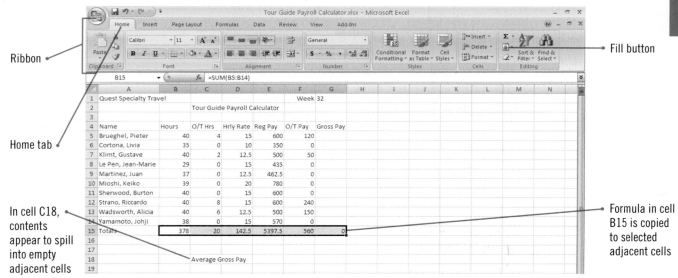

Ribbon

Home tab

In cell C18, contents appear to spill into empty adjacent cells

Fill button

Formula in cell B15 is copied to selected adjacent cells

Navigating a worksheet

With over a million cells available in a worksheet, it is important to know how to move around in, or **navigate**, a worksheet. You can use the arrow keys on the keyboard [↑], [↓], [←], or [→] to move a cell at a time, or press [Page Up] or [Page Down] to move a screen at a time. To move a screen to the left press [Alt][Page Up]; to move a screen to the right press [Alt][Page Down]. You can also use the mouse pointer to click the desired cell. If the desired cell is not visible in the worksheet window, use the scroll bars or the Go To command by clicking the Find & Select button in the Editing group on the Home tab of the Ribbon. To quickly jump to the first cell in a worksheet press [Ctrl][Home]; to jump to the last cell, press [Ctrl][End].

Editing Cell Entries

You can change, or **edit**, the contents of an active cell at any time. To do so, double-click the cell, click in the formula bar, or just start typing. Excel switches to Edit mode when you are making cell entries. Different pointers, shown in Table A-3, guide you through the editing process. You noticed some errors in the worksheet and want to make corrections. The first error is in cell A5, which contains a misspelled name.

STEPS

QUICK TIP
Pressing [Enter] also accepts the cell entry, but moves the cell pointer down one cell.

1. **Click cell A5, then click to the right of P in the formula bar**

    As soon as you click in the formula bar, a blinking vertical line called the **insertion point** appears on the formula bar at the location where new text will be inserted. See Figure A-9. The mouse pointer changes to I when you point anywhere in the formula bar.

2. **Press [Delete], then click the Enter button ✓ on the formula bar**

    Clicking the Enter button accepts the edit, and the spelling of the employee's first name is corrected. You can also press [Enter] or [Tab] to accept an edit.

QUICK TIP
On some keyboards, you might need to press an "F Lock" key to enable the function keys.

3. **Click cell B6, then press [F2]**

    Excel switches to Edit mode, and the insertion point blinks in the cell. Pressing [F2] activates the cell for editing directly in the cell instead of the formula bar. Some people prefer editing right in the cell instead of using the formula bar, but it's simply a matter of preference; the results in the worksheet are the same.

QUICK TIP
The Undo button allows you to reverse up to 100 previous actions, one at a time.

4. **Press [Backspace], type 8, then press [Enter]**

    The value in the cell changes from 35 to 38, and cell B7 becomes the active cell. Did you notice that the calculations in cells B15 and E15 also changed? That's because those cells contain formulas that include cell B6 in their calculations. If you make a mistake when editing, you can click the Cancel button ✕ on the formula bar *before* pressing [Enter] to confirm the cell entry. The Enter and Cancel buttons appear only when you're in Edit mode. If you notice the mistake *after* you have confirmed the cell entry, click the Undo button ↺ on the Quick Access toolbar.

5. **Click cell A9, press [F2], press and hold [Shift], press [Home], then release [Shift]**

    Pressing and holding [Shift] lets you select text using the keyboard. Pressing [Home] moves the cursor to the beginning of the cell; pressing [End] would move the cursor to the end or the cell.

6. **Type Maez, Javier, then press [Enter]**

    When text is selected, typing deletes it and replaces it with the new text.

7. **Double-click cell C12, press [Delete], type 4, then click ✓**

    Double-clicking a cell activates it for editing directly in the cell. Compare your screen to Figure A-10.

8. **Save your work**

    Your changes to the workbook are saved.

Recovering a lost workbook file

Sometimes while you are using Excel, you may experience a power failure or your computer may "freeze," making it impossible to continue working. If this type of interruption occurs, Excel has a built-in recovery feature that allows you to open and save files that were open at the time of the interruption. When you restart Excel after an interruption, File Recovery mode automatically starts and tries to make any necessary repairs. If you need to use a corrupted workbook, you can try and repair it manually by clicking the Office button, then clicking Open. Select the workbook file you want to repair, click the Open list arrow, then click Open and Repair.

FIGURE A-9: Worksheet in Edit mode

Enter button

Active cell

Insertion point

Mode indicator

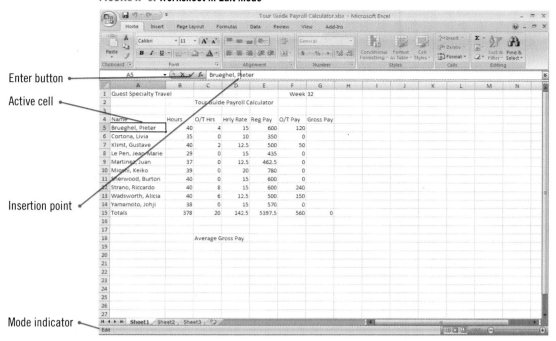

FIGURE A-10: Edited worksheet

Edited label

Edited value

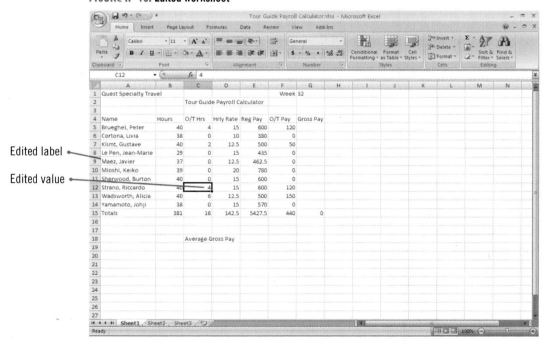

TABLE A-3: Common pointers in Excel

name	pointer	use to
Normal	✛	Select a cell or range; indicates Ready mode
Copy	⬚⁺	Create a duplicate of the selected cell(s)
Fill handle	✚	Create an alphanumeric series in a range
I-beam	I	Edit contents of formula bar
Move	✢	Change the location of the selected cell(s)

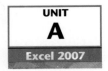

Entering and Editing a Simple Formula

You use formulas in Excel to perform calculations such as adding, multiplying, and averaging. Formulas in an Excel worksheet start with the equal sign (=), also called the **formula prefix**, followed by cell addresses, range names, and values, along with calculation operators. **Calculation operators** indicate what type of calculation you want to perform on the cells, ranges or values. They can include **arithmetic operators**, which perform mathematical calculations such as adding and subtracting, **comparison operators**, which compare values for the purpose of true/false results, **text concatenation operators**, which join strings of text in different cells, and **reference operators**, which enable you to use ranges in calculations. You want to create a formula in the worksheet that calculates gross pay for each employee.

(handwritten note in left margin: Formula Prefix)

STEPS

1. **Click cell G5**

   This is the first cell where you want to insert the formula. To calculate gross pay, you need to add regular pay and overtime pay. For employee Peter Brueghel, regular pay appears in cell E5 and overtime pay appears in cell F5.

2. **Type =, click cell E5, type +, then click cell F5**

   Compare your formula bar to Figure A-11. The blue and green cell references in cell G5 correspond to the colored cell outlines. When entering a formula, it's a good idea to use cell references instead of values whenever you can. That way, if you later change a value in a cell (if, for example, Peter's regular pay changes to 615), any formula that includes this information reflects accurate, up-to-date results.

   QUICK TIP
   You can reference a cell in a formula either by typing the cell reference or clicking the cell in the worksheet; when you click a cell to add a reference, the Mode indicator changes to "Point."

3. **Click the Enter button ✓ on the formula bar**

   The results of the formula =E5+F5, 720, appear in cell G5. This same value appears in cell G15 because cell G15 contains a formula that totals the values in cells G5:G14, and there are no other values now.

4. **Click cell F5**

   The formula in this cell calculates overtime pay by multiplying overtime hours (C5) times twice the regular hourly rate (2*D5). You want to edit this formula to reflect a new overtime pay rate.

5. **Click to the right of 2 in the formula bar, then type .5 as shown in Figure A-12**

   The formula that calculates overtime pay has been edited.

6. **Click ✓ on the formula bar**

   Compare your screen to Figure A-13. Notice that the calculated values in cells G5, F15, and G15 have all changed to reflect your edits to cell F5.

7. **Save your work**

Understanding named ranges

It can be difficult to remember the cell locations of critical information in a worksheet, but using cell names can make this task much easier. You can name a single cell or range of contiguous, or touching, cells. For example, you might name a cell that contains data on average gross pay "AVG_GP" instead of trying to remember the cell address C18. A named range must begin with a letter or an underscore. It cannot contain any spaces or be the same as a built-in name, such as a function or another object (such as a different named range) in the workbook. To name a range, select the cell(s) you want to name, click the name box in the formula bar, type the name you want to use, then press [Enter]. You can also name a range by clicking the Formulas tab, clicking the Define Name list arrow in the Defined Names group, then clicking Define Name. Type the new range name in the Name text box of the New Name dialog box, verify the selected range, then click OK. When you use a named range in a formula, the named range appears, rather than the cell address. You can also create a named range using the contents of a cell already in the range. Select the range containing the text you want to use as a name, then click Create from Selection button in the Defined Names group. The Create Names from Selection dialog box opens. Choose the location of the name you want to use, then click OK.

FIGURE A-11: Simple formula in a worksheet

Cell outline color
corresponds to
cell reference

Referenced cells
are inserted in
formula

Mode indicator
changes to Point

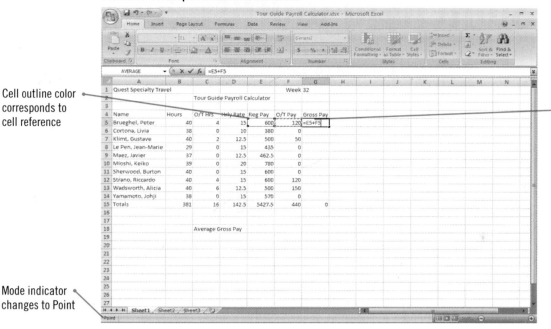

FIGURE A-12: Edited formula in a worksheet

Edited value

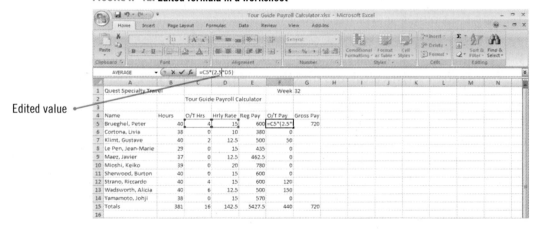

FIGURE A-13: Edited formula with changes

Edited formula
results in
changes to
these other cells

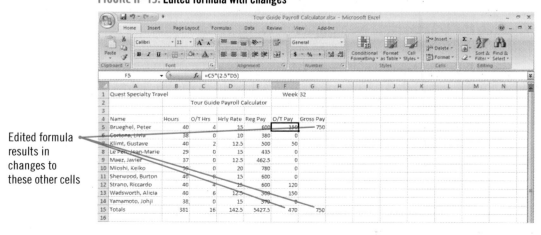

Switching Worksheet Views

You can change your view of the worksheet window at any time, using either the View tab on the Ribbon or the View buttons on the status bar. Changing your view does not affect the contents of a worksheet; it just makes it easier for you to focus on different tasks, such as entering content or preparing a worksheet for printing. The View tab includes a variety of viewing options, such as View buttons, zoom controls, and the ability to show or hide worksheet elements such as gridlines. The status bar offers fewer View options, but can be more convenient to use. You want to make some final adjustments to your worksheet, including adding a header so the document looks more polished.

STEPS

QUICK TIP
Although a worksheet can contain more than a million rows and columns, the current document contains only as many pages as necessary for the current project.

1. **Click the View tab on the Ribbon, then click the Page Layout View button in the Workbook Views group**

   The view switches from the default view, Normal, to Page Layout view. **Normal view** shows the worksheet without including certain details like headers and footers or tools like rulers and a page number indicator; it's great for creating and editing a worksheet, but may not be detailed enough when you want to put the finishing touches on a document. **Page Layout View** provides a more accurate view of how a worksheet will look when printed, as shown in Figure A-14. The margins of the page are displayed, along with a text box for the header. A footer text box appears at the bottom of the page, but your screen may not be large enough to view it without scrolling. Above and to the left of the page are rulers. Part of an additional page appears to the right of this page, but it is dimmed, indicating that it does not contain any data. A page number indicator on the status bar tells you the current page and the total number of pages in this worksheet.

2. **Drag the pointer over the header without clicking**

   The header is made up of three text boxes: left, center, and right.

QUICK TIP
You can change header and footer information using the Header & Footer Tools Design tab that opens when a header or footer is active. For example, you can insert the date by clicking the Current Date button in the Header & Footer Elements group, or the time by clicking the Current Time button.

3. **Click the left header text box, type Quest Specialty Travel, click the center text box, type Tour Guide Payroll Calculator, click the right header text box, then type Week 32**

   The new text appears in the text boxes, as shown in Figure A-15.

4. **Select the range A1:G2, then press [Delete]**

   The duplicate information you just entered in the header is deleted from cells in the worksheet.

5. **Click the Ruler checkbox in the Show/Hide group on the View tab, then click the Gridlines checkbox**

   The rulers and the gridlines are hidden. By default, gridlines in a worksheet do not print, so hiding them gives you a more accurate image of your final document.

6. **Click the Page Break Preview button on the status bar, then click OK in the Welcome to Page Break Preview dialog box, if necessary**

   Your view changes to **Page Break Preview**, which displays a reduced view of each page of your worksheet, along with page break indicators that you can drag to include more or less information on a page.

7. **Drag the bottom page break indicator to the bottom of row 21**

   See Figure A-16. When you're working on a large worksheet with multiple pages, sometimes you need to adjust where pages break; in this worksheet, however, the information all fits comfortably on one page.

QUICK TIP
Once you view a worksheet in Page Break Preview, the page break indicators appear as dotted lines after you switch back to Normal view.

8. **Click the View tab if necessary, click Page Layout in the Workbook Views group, click the Ruler checkbox in the Show/Hide group in the View tab, then click the Gridlines checkbox**

   The rulers and gridlines are no longer hidden. You can show or hide View tab items in any view.

9. **Save your work**

FIGURE A-14: Page Layout View

Ruler checkbox

Gridlines checkbox

Workbook Views group

Header text box

Vertical ruler

Current page and total number of pages

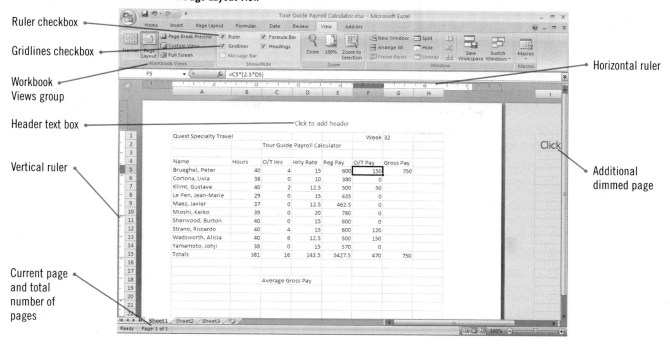

Horizontal ruler

Additional dimmed page

FIGURE A-15: Header boxes

Header areas

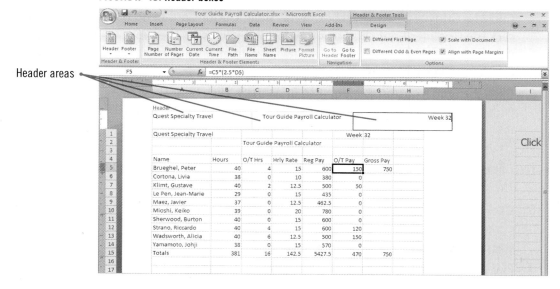

Click

FIGURE A-16: Page Break Preview

Blue outline indicates print area

Bottom page break indicator

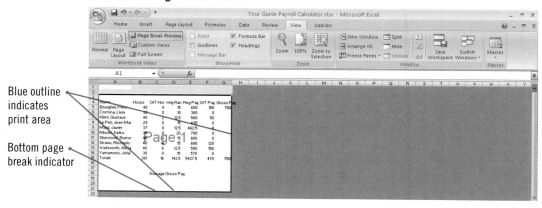

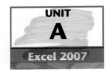
Choosing Print Options

Before printing a document, you may want to review it using the Page Layout tab and Print Preview to fine-tune your printed output. You should also review your settings in the Print dialog box, to make sure you are printing the desired number of copies and using the correct printer. Tools on the Page Layout tab include a Page Setup group, where you can adjust print orientation (the direction in which the content prints across the page), paper size, and page breaks. The Scale to Fit group makes it possible to fit a large amount of data on a single page without making changes to individual margins. In the Sheet Options group, you can turn on and off gridlines and column/row headings. Reviewing your final worksheet in Print Preview shows you exactly how the worksheet will look when printed. You are ready to prepare your worksheet for printing.

STEPS

1. **Click cell A21, type your name, then press [Enter]**

2. **Click the Page Layout tab on the Ribbon**
   Compare your screen to Figure A-17. The dotted line indicates the **print area**, the area to be printed.

> **QUICK TIP**
> You can use the Zoom slider at any time to enlarge your view of specific areas of your worksheet.

3. **Click the Orientation button in the Page Setup group, then click Landscape**
   The paper orientation changes to **landscape**, so the contents will print across the length of the page instead of across the width.

4. **Click the Orientation button in the Page Setup group, then click Portrait**
   The orientation returns to **portrait**, so the contents will print across the width of the page.

5. **Click the Gridlines View checkbox in the Sheet Options group on the Page Layout tab, click the Gridlines Print checkbox to select it if necessary, then save your work**
   Printing gridlines makes the data easier to read, but the gridlines will not print unless the Gridlines Print checkbox is checked.

> **QUICK TIP**
> You can print your worksheet using the default settings by clicking the Office button, pointing to Print, then clicking Quick Print.

6. **Click the Office button, point to Print, then click Print Preview**
   Print Preview shows exactly how your printed copy will look. You can print from this view by clicking the Print button on the Ribbon, or close Print Preview without printing by clicking the Close Print Preview button.

7. **Click the Zoom button in the Zoom group on the Print Preview tab**
   The image of your worksheet is enlarged. Compare your screen to Figure A-18.

> **QUICK TIP**
> To change the active printer, click the Name list arrow, then choose a different printer.

8. **Click the Print button in the Print group, compare your settings to Figure A-19, then click OK**
   One copy of the worksheet prints.

9. **Exit Excel**

Printing worksheet formulas

Sometimes you need to keep a record of all the formulas in a worksheet. You might want to do this to see exactly how you came up with a complex calculation, so you can explain it to others. You can do this by printing out the formulas in a worksheet rather than the results of those calculations. To do so, open the workbook containing the formulas you want to print. Click the Office button, then click Excel Options. Click Advanced in the left pane, scroll to the Display options for this worksheet section, click the list arrow and select the entire workbook or the sheet in which you want the formulas displayed, click the Show formulas in cells instead of their calculated results checkbox, then click OK.

FIGURE A-17: Worksheet with Portrait orientation

Page Layout tab

Scale field

Dotted line surrounds print area

Your name appears here

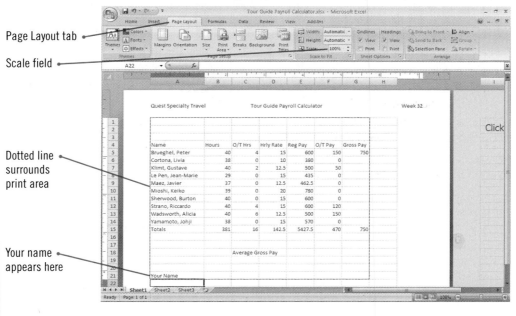

FIGURE A-18: Worksheet in Print Preview

Print button

Zoom button

Close Print Preview button

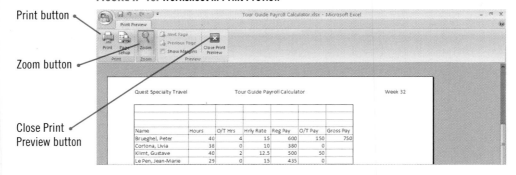

FIGURE A-19: Print dialog box

Active printer: yours will be different

Choose which pages to print

Number of copies field

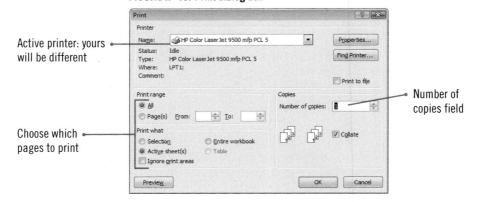

Scaling to fit

If you have a large amount of data that you want to fit to a single sheet of paper, but you don't want to spend a lot of time trying to adjust the margins and other settings, use the Fit to option in the Page Setup dialog box. Open this dialog box by clicking the launcher in the Scale to Fit group in the Page Layout tab. Make sure the Page tab is selected, then click the Fit to option button. Select the number of pages you want the worksheet to fit on, then click OK. If you're ready to print, click Print and the Print dialog box will open. Select the pages you want to print and the number of copies you want, then click OK.

Practice

▼ CONCEPTS REVIEW

Label the elements of the Excel worksheet window shown in Figure A-20.

FIGURE A-20

1. Normal View
2. Formula Bar
3.
4. Ruler
5. Insert W.S. Button
6. Mode Indicator

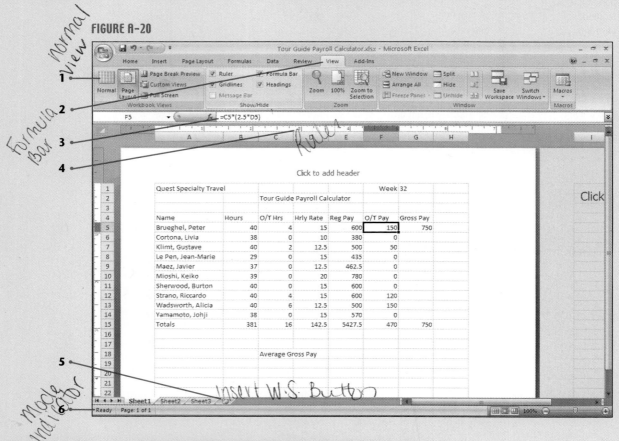

Match each term with the statement that best describes it.

7. Cell *F*
8. Normal View *d*
9. Workbook *(c)*
10. Name Box *(e)*
11. Formula prefix *(B)*
12. Orientation *(a)*

a. Direction in which contents of page will print
b. Equal sign preceding a formula
c. File consisting of one or more worksheets
d. Default view in Excel
e. Part of the Excel program window that displays the active cell address
f. Intersection of a column and a row

Select the best answer from the list of choices.

13. In Excel, order of precedence determines:
   a. The order in which worksheets are printed.
   b. The colors used to distinguish cell references.
   c. The order in which calculations are performed. *(circled)*
   d. How values are multiplied.

14. The maximum number of worksheets you can include in a workbook is:
   a. 3.
   b. 250.
   c. 255. *(circled)*
   d. Unlimited.

15. A selection of multiple cells is called a:
   a. Group.
   b. Range. *(circled)*
   c. Reference.
   d. Package.

16. Using a cell address in a formula is known as:
   a. Formularizing.
   b. Prefixing.
   c. Cell referencing. *(circled)* — column letter + row #
   d. Cell mathematics.

17. Which worksheet view shows how your worksheet will look when printed?
   a. Page Layout *(circled)*
   b. Data
   c. Review
   d. View

18. Which button should you click if you want to print formulas in a worksheet?
   a. Save button
   b. Fill button
   c. Any button on the Quick Access Toolbar
   d. Office button *(circled)*

19. Clicking the launcher in the Scale to Fit group on the Page Layout tab opens which dialog box?
   a. Print
   b. Scale to Fit
   c. Width/Height
   d. Page Setup *(circled)*

20. In which view can you see the header and footer areas of a worksheet?
   a. Normal View *(circled)*
   b. Page Layout View
   c. Page Break Preview
   d. Header/Footer View *(circled)*

21. Which key can you press to switch to Edit mode?
   a. [F1]
   b. [F2] *(circled)*
   c. [F4]
   d. [F6]

▼ SKILLS REVIEW

1. Understand spreadsheet software.
   a. What is the difference between a workbook and a worksheet?
   b. Identify five common business uses for electronic spreadsheets. *Resumes, payroll*
   c. What is 'what-if' analysis?

2. Tour the Excel 2007 window.
   a. Start Excel.
   b. Open the file EX A-2.xlsx from the drive and folder where you store your Data Files, then save it as **Weather Statistics**.
   c. Locate the formula bar, the Sheet tabs, the mode indicator, and the cell pointer.

3. Understand formulas.
   a. What is the average high temperature of the listed cities? (*Hint*: Select the range B5:G5 and use the status bar.)
   b. What formula would you create to calculate the difference in altitude between Chicago and Phoenix? *436*

4. Enter labels and values and use AutoSum.
   a. Click cell H7, then use the AutoSum button to calculate the total rainfall.
   b. Click cell H8, then use the AutoSum button to calculate the total snowfall.
   c. Save your changes to the file.

5. Edit cell entries.
   a. Use the [F2] key to correct the spelling of Sante Fe in a worksheet cell (the correct spelling is Santa Fe).
   b. Click cell A12, then type your name.
   c. Save your changes.

▼ SKILLS REVIEW (CONTINUED)

6. Enter and edit a simple formula.

   a. Change the value 41 in cell B8 to **52**.

   b. Change the value 35 in cell C7 to **35.4**.

   c. Select the range B10:G10, then use the Fill button in the Editing group on the Home tab to fill the formula to the remaining cells in the selection. (*Hint*: If you see a warning icon, click it, then click Ignore Error.)

   d. Save your changes.

7. Switch worksheet views.

   a. Click the View tab on the Ribbon, then switch to Page Layout view.

   b. Add the header **Average Annual Weather Statistics** to the center header box.

   c. Add your name to the right header box.

   d. Delete the contents of cell A1.

   e. Delete the contents of cell A12.

   f. Save your changes.

8. Choose Print options.

   a. Use the Page Layout tab to change the orientation to Portrait.

   b. Turn off gridlines by deselecting both the Gridlines View and Gridlines Print checkboxes in the Sheet Options group.

   c. View the worksheet in Print Preview, then zoom in to enlarge the preview. Compare your screen to Figure A-21.

   d. Open the Print dialog box, then print one copy of the worksheet.

   e. Save your changes, then close the workbook.

FIGURE A-21

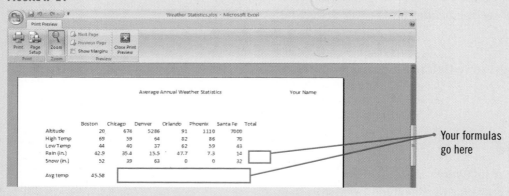

▼ INDEPENDENT CHALLENGE 1

A local real estate office has hired you to help them make the transition to using Excel in their office. They would like to list their properties in a worksheet. You've started a worksheet for this project that contains labels but no data.

   a. Open the file EX A-3.xlsx from where you store your Data Files, then save it as **Real Estate Listings**.

   b. Enter the data shown in Table A-4 in columns A, C, D, and E (the property address information should spill into column B).

TABLE A-4

Property Address	Price	Bedrooms	Bathrooms
1507 Cactus Lane	350000	3	2.5
32 California Lane	325000	3	4
60 Pottery Lane	475500	2	2
902 Fortunata Drive	295000	4	3
Total			

▼ INDEPENDENT CHALLENGE 1 (CONTINUED)

c. Use Page Layout View to create a header with the following components: a title in the center and your name on the right.

d. Create formulas for totals in cells C6:E6.

e. Save your changes, then preview your work and compare it to Figure A-22.

f. Print the worksheet.

g. Close the worksheet and exit Excel.

FIGURE A-22

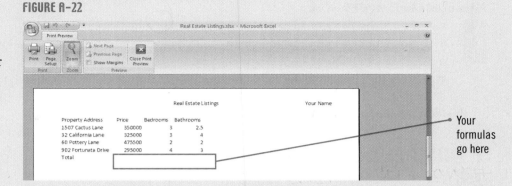

▼ INDEPENDENT CHALLENGE 2

FIGURE A-23

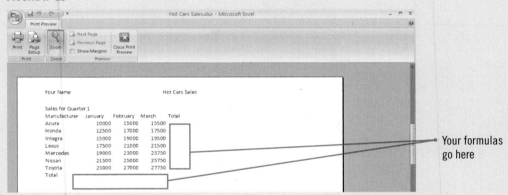

You are the General Manager for Hot Cars, a small auto parts supplier. Although the company is just three years old, it is expanding rapidly, and you are continually looking for ways to save time. You recently began using Excel to manage and maintain data on inventory and sales, which has greatly helped you to track information accurately and efficiently.

a. Start Excel.

b. Save a new workbook as **Hot Cars Sales** in the drive and folder where you store your Data Files.

c. Switch to an appropriate view, then add a header that contains your name in the left header text box and a title in the center header text box.

d. Using Figure A-23 as a guide, create labels for at least seven car manufacturers and sales for three months. Include other labels as appropriate. The car manufacturers should be in column A, and the months in columns B, C, and D. A Total row should be beneath the data, and a Total column should be in column E.

e. Enter values of your choice for the monthly sales for each manufacturer.

f. Add a formula in the Total column to calculate total monthly sales for each manufacturer. Add formulas at the bottom of each column of values to calculate the total for that column. Remember that you can use the SUM function to save time.

g. Save your changes, preview the worksheet, then print it.

▼ INDEPENDENT CHALLENGE 2 (CONTINUED)

Advanced Challenge Exercise

- Create a label two rows beneath the data in column A that says 15% increase.
- Create a formula in the row containing the 15% increase label that calculates a 15% increase in total monthly sales.
- Save the workbook.
- Display the formulas in the worksheet, then print a copy of the worksheet with formulas displayed.

h. Close the workbook(s) and exit Excel.

▼ INDEPENDENT CHALLENGE 3

FIGURE A-24

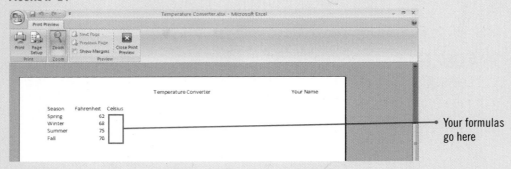

This Independent Challenge requires an Internet connection. Your office is starting a branch in Paris and you think it would be helpful to create a worksheet that can be used to convert Fahrenheit temperatures to Celsius, to help employees who are unfamiliar with this type of temperature measurement.

a. Start Excel, then save a blank workbook as **Temperature Converter** in the drive and folder where you store your Data Files.

b. Create column and row titles using Figure A-24 as a guide.

c. Create labels for each of the seasons.

d. In the appropriate cells, enter what you determine to be an ideal indoor temperature for each season.

e. Use your Web browser to find out the conversion rate for Fahrenheit to Celsius. (*Hint*: Use your favorite search engine to search on a term such as "temperature conversion.")

f. In the appropriate cells, create an equation that calculates the conversion of the Fahrenheit temperature you entered into a Celsius temperature.

g. Preview the worksheet in Page Layout View, adding your name to the header, as well as a meaningful title.

h. Save your work, then print the worksheet.

i. Close the file, then exit Excel.

▼ REAL LIFE INDEPENDENT CHALLENGE

FIGURE A-25

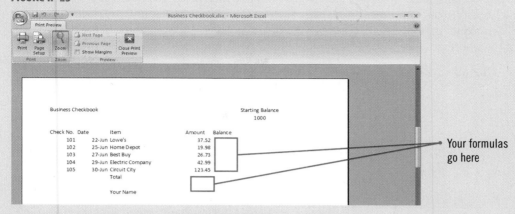

You've decided to quit your day job and turn your favorite hobby into a business. You've set up a small business selling the product or service of your choice. You want to use Excel to keep track of your many start-up costs.

   a. Start Excel, open the file EX A-4.xlsx from the drive and folder where you store your Data Files, then save it as **Business Checkbook**.

   b. Type check numbers (using your choice of a starting number) in cells A5 through A9.

   c. Create sample data for the date, item, and amount in cells B5 through D9.

   d. Save your work.

Advanced Challenge Exercise

   ■ Use Help to find out about creating a series of numbers.

   ■ Delete the contents of cells A5:A9.

   ■ Create a series of numbers in cells A5:A9.

   ■ In cell C15, type a brief description of how you created the series.

   ■ Save the workbook.

   e. Create formulas in cells E5:E9 that calculate a running balance. (*Hint*: For the first check, the running balance equals the starting balance minus a check; for the following checks, the running balance equals the previous balance value minus each check value.)

   f. Create a formula in cell D10 that totals the amount of the checks.

   g. Enter your name in cell C12, then compare your screen to Figure A-25.

   h. Save your changes to the file, preview and print the worksheet, then exit Excel.

▼ VISUAL WORKSHOP

Open the file EX A-5.xlsx from the drive and folder where you store your Data Files, then save it as **Inventory Items**. Using the skills you learned in this unit, modify your worksheet so it matches Figure A-26. Enter formulas in cells D4 through D13 and in cells B14 and C14. Use the AutoSum button to make entering your formulas easier. Add your name in the left header text box, then print one copy of the worksheet once with the formulas not displayed, and one copy with the formulas displayed.

FIGURE A-26

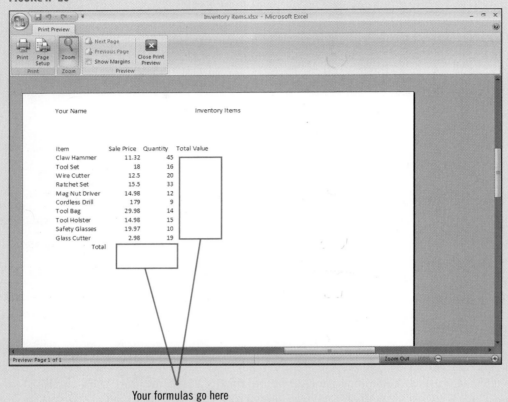

Your formulas go here

Working with Formulas and Functions

Using your knowledge of Excel basics, you can expand your worksheets to include more complex formulas and functions. To work more efficiently, you can copy and move existing formulas into other cells instead of manually retyping the same information. When copying or moving, you can also control how cell references are handled, so that your formulas always reference the intended cells. Grace Wong, vice president of finance at Quest Specialty Travel, needs to analyze tour revenue for the current year. She has asked you to prepare a worksheet that summarizes this revenue data and includes some statistical analysis. She would also like you to perform some what-if analysis, to see what quarterly revenues would look like with various projected increases.

OBJECTIVES

Create a complex formula

Insert a function

Type a function

Copy and move cell entries

Understand relative and absolute cell references

Copy formulas with relative cell references

Copy formulas with absolute cell references

Round a value with a function

Creating a Complex Formula

A **complex formula** is one that uses more than one arithmetic operator. You might, for example, need to create a formula that uses addition and multiplication. You can use arithmetic operators to separate tasks within a complex equation. In formulas containing more than one arithmetic operator, Excel uses the standard order of precedence rules to determine which operation to perform first. You can change the order of precedence in a formula by using parentheses around the part you want to calculate first. For example, the formula =4+2*5 equals 14, because the order of precedence dictates that multiplication is performed before addition. However, the formula =(4+2)*5 equals 30, because the parentheses cause 4+2 to be calculated first. ▰▰▰ You want to create a formula that calculates a 20% increase in tour revenue.

STEPS

1. **Start Excel, open the file EX B-1.xlsx from the drive and folder where you store your Data Files, then save it as** Tour Revenue Analysis

2. **Click cell B14, type =, click cell B12, then type +**
   In this first part of the formula, you are creating references to the total for Quarter 1.

QUICK TIP

When you click a cell reference, the mode indicator on the status bar reads "Point," indicating that you can click additional cell references to add them to the formula.

3. **Click cell B12, then type *.2**
   The second part of this formula adds a 20% increase (B12*.2) to the original value of the cell. Compare your worksheet to Figure B-1.

4. **Click the Enter button ✔ on the formula bar**
   The result, 386122.344, appears in cell B14.

5. **Press [Tab], type =, click cell C12, type +, click cell C12, type *.2, then click ✔**
   The result, 410969.712, appears in cell C14.

6. **Drag the ✛ pointer from cell C14 to cell E14, click the Fill button 🔲▾ in the Editing group on the Home tab of the Ribbon, then click Right**
   The calculated values appear in the selected range, as shown in Figure B-2.

7. **Save your work** ✓

Reviewing the order of precedence

When you work with formulas that contain more than one operator, the order of precedence is very important because it affects the final value. For example, you might think the formula 4+2*5 equals 30, but because the order of precedence dictates that multiplication is performed before addition, the actual result is 14. If a formula contains two or more operators, such as 4+.55/4000*25, Excel performs the calculations in a particular sequence based on the following rules: Operations inside parentheses are calculated before any other operations. Reference operators (such as ranges) are calculated first. Exponents are calculated next, then any multiplication and division—progressing from left to right. Finally, addition and subtraction are calculated from left to right. In the example 4+.55/4000*25, Excel performs the arithmetic operations by first dividing 4000 into .55, then multiplying the result by 25, then adding 4. You can change the order of calculations by using parentheses. For example, in the formula (4+.55)/4000*25, Excel would first add 4 and .55, then divide that amount by 4000, then finally multiply by 25.

FIGURE B-1: Formula containing multiple arithmetic operators

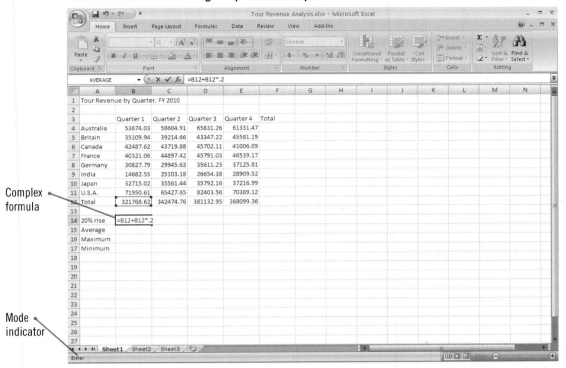

Complex formula

Mode indicator

FIGURE B-2: Complex formulas in worksheet

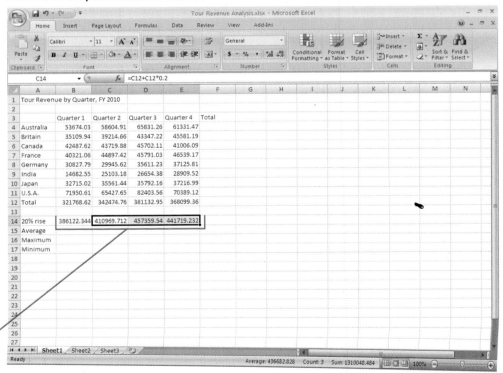

Formula in cell C14 copied to cells D14 and E14

Inserting a Function

Functions are predefined worksheet formulas that enable you to perform complex calculations easily. You can use the Insert Function button on the formula bar to choose a function from a dialog box. In addition to using the AutoSum button on the Ribbon to quickly insert the SUM function, you can click the AutoSum button list arrow to enter other frequently used functions, such as Average. Functions are organized into categories, such as Financial, Date & Time, and Statistical, based on their purpose. You can insert a function on its own, or as part of another formula. For example, you have used the SUM function on its own to add a range of cells. You could also use the SUM function within a formula that adds a range of cells and then multiplies the total by a decimal. If you use a function alone, it always begins with the formula prefix = (the equal sign). ▓▓▓▓ You need to calculate the average sales for the first quarter of the year, and decide to use a function to do so.

STEPS

QUICK TIP

When using the Insert Function button or the AutoSum button list arrow, it is not necessary to type the equal sign (=); Excel adds it as necessary.

1. **Click cell B15**

   This is the cell where you want to enter the calculation that averages revenue for the first quarter. You want to use the Insert Function dialog box to enter this function.

2. **Click the Insert Function button f_x on the formula bar**

   An equal sign (=) is inserted in the active cell and in the formula bar, and the Insert Function dialog box opens, as shown in Figure B-3. In this dialog box, you specify the function you want to add by clicking it in the Select a function list. The Select a function list initially displays recently used functions. If you don't see the function you want, you can click the Or select a category list arrow to choose the desired category or, if you're not sure what category to choose, you can type the function name or a description in the Search for a function field. The AVERAGE function is a statistical function, but you don't need to open the Statistical category because this function appears in the Most Recently Used list.

QUICK TIP

To learn about a function, click it in the Select a function list. Read the arguments and format required for the function.

3. **Click AVERAGE, if necessary, read the information that appears under the list, then click OK**

   The Function Arguments dialog box opens, where you define the range of cells you want to average.

QUICK TIP

When selecting a range, remember to select all the cells between and including the two references in the range.

4. **Click the Collapse button ▦ in the Number1 field of the Function Arguments dialog box, drag the ✛ pointer to select the range B4:B11, release the mouse button, then click the Expand button ▦**

   Clicking the Collapse button minimizes the dialog box so you can select cells in the worksheet. When you click the Expand button, the dialog box is restored, as shown in Figure B-4. You can also begin dragging in the worksheet to automatically minimize the dialog box; after you select the desired range, the dialog box is restored.

5. **Click OK**

   The Function Arguments dialog box closes and the calculated value displays in cell C15. The average revenue per country for Quarter 1 is 40221.0775.

6. **Click cell C15, click the AutoSum button list arrow Σ ▾ in the Editing group on the Home tab, then click Average**

   A ScreenTip beneath cell C15 displays the arguments needed to complete the function. The text number1 is shown in boldface type, telling you that the next step is to supply the first cell in the group you want to average. You want to average a range of cells.

7. **Drag ✛ to select the range C4:C11, then click the Enter button ✓ on the formula bar**

   The average revenue per country for the second quarter appears in cell C15.

8. **Select the range C15:E15, click the Fill button ▣▾ in the Editing group, then click Right**

   The formula in cell C15 is copied to the rest of the selected range, as shown in Figure B-5.

9. **Save your work**

FIGURE B-3: Insert Function dialog box

Search for a function field →

Your list of recently used functions may differ →

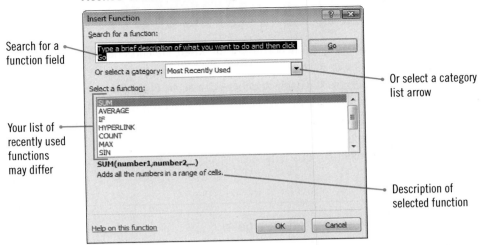

← Or select a category list arrow

← Description of selected function

FIGURE B-4: Expanded Function Arguments dialog box

Function in formula bar →

Insert Function button →

Argument →

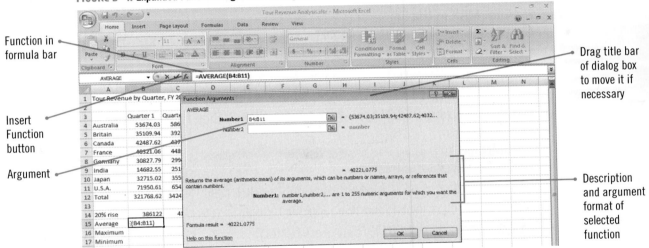

Drag title bar of dialog box to move it if necessary →

Description and argument format of selected function →

FIGURE B-5: Average function in worksheet

Completed function appears in formula bar →

Formula in cell C15 copied to cells D15 and E15 →

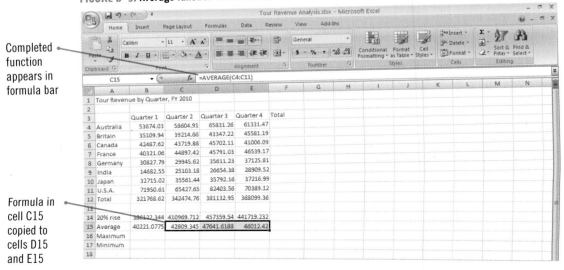

Working with Formulas and Functions

Excel 29

Typing a Function

In addition to entering a function using the Insert Function dialog box or the AutoSum button on the Ribbon, you can manually type the function into a cell and complete the arguments needed. This method requires that you know the name and initial characters of the function, but can be faster than opening several dialog boxes. Experienced Excel users often prefer this method, but it is only an alternative, not better or more correct than any other method. The AutoComplete feature makes it easier to enter function names because it suggests functions depending on the first letters you type. ▓▓▓▓▓ You want to calculate the maximum and minimum quarterly sales in your worksheet, and decide to manually enter these statistical functions.

STEPS

1. **Click cell B16, type =, then type m**

   Since you are manually typing this function, it is necessary to begin with the equal sign (=). The AutoComplete feature displays a list of function names beginning with M. Once you type an equal sign in a cell, each letter you type acts as a trigger to activate the AutoComplete feature. This feature minimizes the amount of typing you need to do to enter a function, and reduces typing and syntax errors.

QUICK TIP
You can single-click any function in the AutoComplete list to open a Screentip describing the selected function.

2. **Click MAX in the list**

   A Screentip appears, describing the function.

3. **Double-click MAX**

   The function is added to the cell and a Screentip appears beneath the cell to help you complete the formula. See Figure B-6.

4. **Select the range B4:B11, as shown in Figure B-7, then click the Enter button ✔ on the formula bar**

   The result, 71950.61, appears in cell B16. When you completed the entry, the closing parenthesis was automatically added to the formula.

5. **Click cell B17, type =, type m, then double-click MIN**

   The argument for the MIN function appears in the cell.

6. **Select the range B4:B11, then press [Enter]**

   The result, 14682.55, appears in cell B17.

7. **Select the range B16:E17, click the Fill button list arrow ▣▾ in the Editing group, then click Right**

   The maximum and minimum values for all of the quarters display in the selected range, as shown in Figure B-8.

8. **Save your work**

Using the COUNT and COUNTA functions

When you select a range, a count of cells in the range that are not blank appears in the status bar. For example, if you select the range A1:A5 and only cells A1 and A2 contain data, the status bar displays "Count: 2." To count nonblank cells more precisely, or to incorporate these calculations in a worksheet, you can use the COUNT and COUNTA functions. COUNT returns the number of cells that contain numeric data, including numbers, dates, and formulas. COUNTA returns the number of cells that contain any data at all, even text or a blank space. For example, the formula =COUNT(A1:A5) returns the number of cells in the range that contain numeric data, and the formula =COUNTA(A1:A5) returns the number of cells in the range that are not blank.

FIGURE B-6: MAX function in progress

13					
14	20% rise	386122.344	410969.712	457359.54	441719.232
15	Average	40221.0775	42809.345	47641.6188	46012.42
16	Maximum	=MAX(			
17	Minimum	MAX(number1, [number2], ...)			
18					

FIGURE B-7: Completing the MAX function

Closing parenthesis will be added automatically when you accept entry

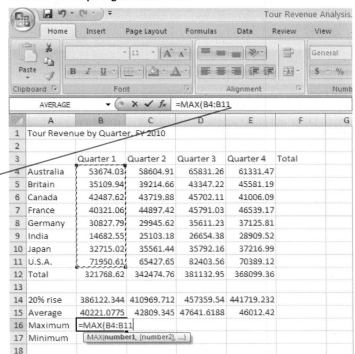

FIGURE B-8: Completed MAX and MIN functions

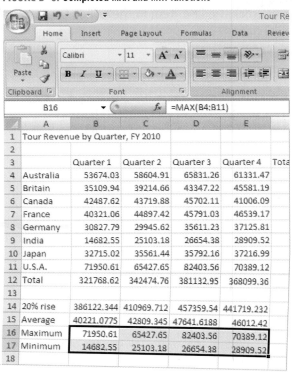

Excel 2007

Copying and Moving Cell Entries

You can copy or move cells and ranges (or the contents within them) from one location to another using the Cut, Copy, and Paste buttons; the fill handle in the lower-right corner of the active cell; or the drag-and-drop feature. When you copy cells, the original data remains in the original location; when you cut or move it, the original data is deleted. You can also cut, copy, and paste cells or ranges from one worksheet to another. ▰▰▰ In addition to the 20% rise in tour revenue, you also want to show a 30% rise. Rather than retype this information, you copy and move the labels in these cells.

STEPS

QUICK TIP

To cut or copy selected contents within a cell, activate the cell and then select the characters within the cell that you want to cut or copy.

1. **Select the range B3:E3, then click the Copy button 🖹 in the Clipboard group**

    The selected range (B3:E3) is copied to the **Office Clipboard**, a temporary storage area that holds the selections you copy or cut. A moving border surrounds the selected range until you press [Esc] or copy an additional item to the Clipboard. Notice that the information you copied remains in the selected range; if you had cut instead of copied, the information would have been deleted once it was pasted.

QUICK TIP

The Clipboard can hold up to 24 items. Once the clipboard is full, the oldest existing item is automatically deleted each time you add an item.

2. **Click the launcher 🖽 in the Clipboard group, click cell B19, then click the Paste button in the Clipboard group**

    The Office Clipboard pane opens, as shown in Figure B-9. Your Clipboard may contain additional items. When pasting an item from the Clipboard into the worksheet, you only need to specify the upper-left cell of the range where you want to paste the selection.

3. **Press [Delete]**

    The selected cells are empty. You have decided to paste the cells in a different row. You can repeatedly paste an item from the Office Clipboard as many times as you like, as long as the item remains in the Clipboard.

QUICK TIP

You can also close the Clipboard pane by clicking the launcher in the Clipboard group.

4. **Click cell B20 , click the first item in the Office Clipboard, then click the Close button on the Clipboard pane**

    Cells B20:E20 contain the copied labels.

5. **Click cell A14 , press and hold [Ctrl], point to any edge of the cell until the pointer changes to ⬄, drag ⬄ to cell A21, then release [Ctrl]**

    As you drag, the pointer changes to ⬄, as shown in Figure B-10.

6. **Click to the right of 2 in the formula bar, press [Backspace] , type 3, then press [Enter]**

7. **Click cell B21, type =, click cell B12 , type *1.3, then click ✓ on the formula bar**

    This new formula calculates a 30% increase of the revenue for Quarter 1, though using a different method from what you used previously. Anything you multiply by 1.3 returns an amount that's 130% of the original amount, or a 30% increase. Compare your screen to Figure B-11.

8. **Save your work**

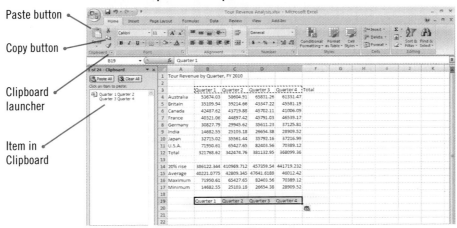

FIGURE B-9: Copied data in Clipboard

Paste button

Copy button

Clipboard launcher

Item in Clipboard

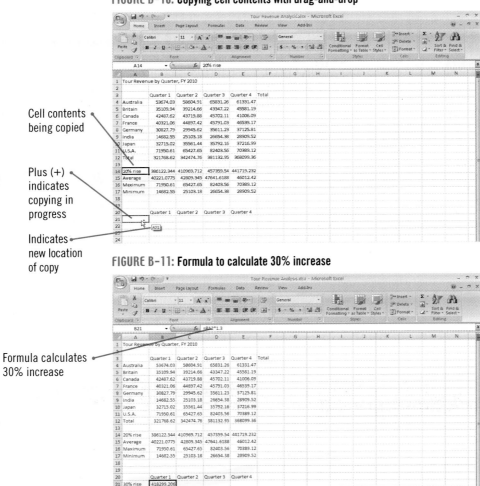

FIGURE B-10: Copying cell contents with drag-and-drop

Cell contents being copied

Plus (+) indicates copying in progress

Indicates new location of copy

FIGURE B-11: Formula to calculate 30% increase

Formula calculates 30% increase

Inserting and deleting selected cells

As you add formulas to your workbook, you may need to insert or delete cells. When you do this, Excel automatically adjusts cell references to reflect their new locations. To insert cells, click the Insert button list arrow in the Cells group on the Home tab, then click Insert Cells. The Insert dialog box opens, asking if you want to insert a cell and move the selected cell down or to the right of the new one. To delete one or more selected cells, click the Delete button list arrow in the Cells group, click Delete Cells, and in the Delete dialog box, indicate which way you want to move the adjacent cells. When using this option, be careful not to disturb row or column alignment that may be necessary to maintain the accuracy of cell references in the worksheet. Click the Insert or Delete button to add/delete a single cell.

Understanding Relative and Absolute Cell References

As you work in Excel, you may want to reuse formulas in different parts of a worksheet to reduce the amount of data you have to retype. For example, you might want to include a what-if analysis in one part of a worksheet showing a set of sales projections if sales increase by 10%, and another analysis in another part of the worksheet showing projections if sales increase by 50%; you can copy the formulas from one section to another and just change the "1" to a "5". But when you copy formulas, it is important to make sure that they refer to the correct cells. To do this, you need to understand the difference between relative and absolute cell references. ▰▰▰▰▰ You plan to reuse formulas in different parts of your worksheets, so you want to understand relative and absolute cell references.

- **Use relative references when you want to preserve the relationship to the formula location**

  When you create a formula that references other cells, Excel normally does not "record" the exact cell address. Instead, it looks at the relationship that cell has to the cell containing the formula. For example, in Figure B-12, cell F5 contains the formula: =SUM(B5:E5). When Excel retrieves values to calculate the formula in cell F5, it actually looks for "the cell four columns to the left of the formula," which in this case is cell B5. This way, if you copy the cell to a new location, such as cell F6, the results will reflect the new formula location, and will automatically retrieve the values in cells B6, C6, D6, and E6. These are **relative cell references**, because Excel is recording the input cells *in relation to* or *relative to* the formula cell.

  In most cases, you want to use relative cell references when copying or moving, so this is the Excel default. In Figure B-12, the formulas in F5:F12 and in B13:F13 contain relative cell references. They total the "four cells to the left of" or the "eight cells above" the formulas.

- **Use absolute cell references when you want to preserve the exact cell address in a formula**

  There are times when you want Excel to retrieve formula information from a specific cell, and you don't want the cell address in the formula to change when you copy it to a new location. For example, you might have a price in a specific cell that you want to use in all formulas, regardless of their location. If you used relative cell referencing, the formula results would be incorrect, because Excel would use a different cell every time you copied the formula. Therefore you need to use an **absolute cell reference**, a reference that does not change when you copy the formula.

  You create an absolute cell reference by placing a $ (dollar sign) in front of both the column letter and the row number of the cell address. You can either type the dollar sign when typing the cell address in a formula (for example, "=C12*$B$16"), or you can select a cell address on the formula bar and then press [F4] and the dollar signs are added automatically. Figure B-13 show formulas containing both absolute and relative references. The formulas in cells B19 to E26 use absolute cell references to refer to a potential sales increase of 50%, shown in cell B16.

FIGURE B-12: Formulas containing relative references

Formula containing relative references

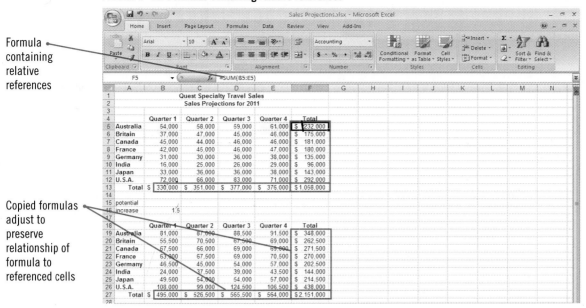

Copied formulas adjust to preserve relationship of formula to referenced cells

FIGURE B-13: Formulas containing absolute and relative references

Cell referenced in absolute formulas

Relative references in copied formulas adjust

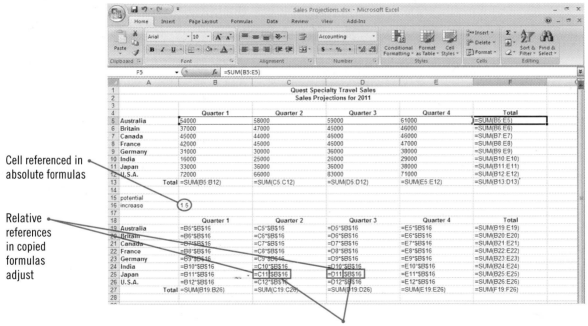

Absolute references in copied formulas do not adjust

Using a mixed reference

Sometimes when you copy a formula, you want to change the row reference, but keep the column reference the same. This type of cell referencing combines elements of both absolute and relative referencing and is called a **mixed reference**. For example, when copied, a formula containing the mixed reference C$14 would change the column letter relative to its new location, but not the row number.

In the mixed reference $C14, the column letter would not change, but the row number would be updated relative to its location. Like the absolute reference, a mixed reference can be created using the [F4] function key. With each press of the [F4] key, you cycle through all the possible combinations of relative, absolute, and mixed references ($C$14, C$14, $C14, C14).

Copying Formulas with Relative Cell References

Copying and moving a cell allows you to reuse a formula you've already created. Copying cells is usually faster than retyping the formulas in them, and helps to prevent typing errors. You can use the Copy and Paste commands or the fill handle to copy formulas. The Fill button list arrow can also be used to fill cells containing formulas going left, right, up, down, and in series. If the cells you are copying contain relative cell references and you want to maintain the relative referencing, you don't need to make any changes to the cells before copying them. ▰▰▰ You want to copy the formula in cell B21, which calculates the 30% increase in quarterly sales for quarter 1, to cells C21 through E21. You also want to create formulas to calculate total sales for each tour country.

STEPS

1. **Click cell B21, if necessary, then click the Copy button 📋 in the Clipboard group**

   The formula for calculating the 30% sales increase during Quarter 1 is copied to the Clipboard. Notice that the formula =B12*1.3 appears in the formula bar and a moving border surrounds the active cell.

2. **Click cell C21, then click the Paste button in the Clipboard group**

   The formula from cell B21 is copied into cell C21, where the new result of 445217.188 appears. Notice in the formula bar that the cell references have changed, so that cell C12 is referenced in the formula. This formula contains a relative cell reference, which tells Excel to substitute new cell references within the copied formulas as necessary. This maintains the same relationship between the new cells containing the formula and the cells within the formula. In this case, Excel adjusted the formula so that cell C12—the cell reference nine rows above C21—replaced cell B12, the cell reference nine rows above B21. You can drag the fill handle in a cell to copy cells or to continue a series of data (such as Quarter 1, Quarter 2, etc.) based on previous cells. This option is called **Auto Fill**.

3. **Point to the fill handle in cell C21 until the pointer changes to ➕, press and hold the left mouse button, drag ➕ to select the range C21:E21, then release the mouse button**

   See Figure B-14. A formula similar to the one in cell C21 now appears in the range D21:E21. After you release the mouse button, the **Auto Fill Options button** appears, so you can fill the cells with only specific elements of the copied cell if you wish.

4. **Click cell F4, click the AutoSum button Σ in the Editing group, then click the Enter button ✓ on the formula bar**

5. **Click 📋 in the Clipboard group, select the range F5:F6, then click Paste**

   See Figure B-15. After you release the mouse button, the **Paste Options button** appears, so you can paste only specific elements of the copied selection if you wish. The formula for calculating quarterly revenue for tours in Britain appears in the formula bar. You would like totals to appear in cells F7:F11. The Fill command in the Editing group can be used to copy the formula into the remaining cells.

6. **Select the range F6:F11**

7. **Click the Fill button list arrow 📥▾ in the Editing group, then click Down**

   The formulas are copied to each cell. Compare your worksheet to Figure B-16.

8. **Save your work**

FIGURE B-14: Copying a formula with the fill handle

Paste button list arrow

Fill handle

Auto Fill Options button

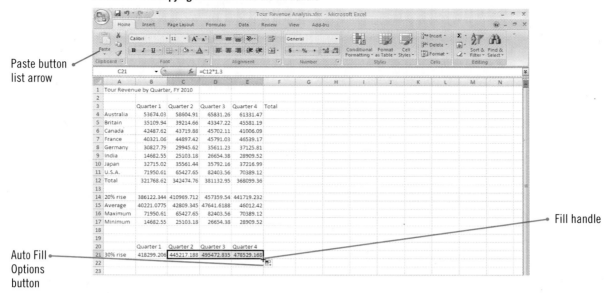

FIGURE B-15: The results of using the Paste button

Paste Options button

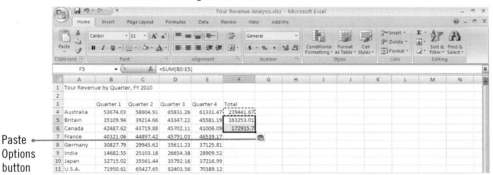

FIGURE B-16: Copying cells using Fill Down

Fill button list arrow

Filled cells

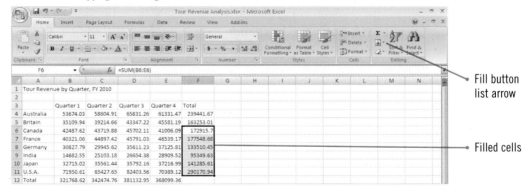

Using Auto Fill options

When you use the fill handle to copy cells, the Auto Fill Options button appears. Auto Fill options differ depending on what you are copying. If you had selected cells containing a series (such as "Monday" and "Tuesday") and then used the fill handle, you would see options for continuing the series (such as "Wednesday" and "Thursday") or for simply pasting the copied cells. Clicking the Auto Fill Options button opens a list that lets you choose from the following options: Copy Cells, Fill Series (if applicable), Fill Formatting

Only, or Fill Without Formatting. Choosing Copy Cells means that the cell and its formatting will be copied. The Fill Formatting Only option copies only the formatting attributes, but not the formula and its cell references. The Fill Without Formatting option copies the formula and its cell references, but no formatting attributes. Copy Cells is the default option when using the fill handle to copy a formula, so if you want to copy the cell, its references and formatting, you can ignore this button.

Copying Formulas with Absolute Cell References

When copying formulas, you might want one or more cell references in the formula to remain unchanged in relation to the formula. In such an instance, you need to apply an absolute cell reference before copying the formula, to preserve the specific cell address when the formula is copied. You create an absolute reference by placing a dollar sign ($) before the row letter and column number of the address (for example $A$1). You need to do some what-if analysis to see how various sales percentage increases might affect total revenues. You decide to add a column that calculates a possible increase in the total tour revenue, and then change the percentage to see various potential results.

STEPS

1. **Click cell H1, type Change, then press [→]**

2. **Type 1.1, then press [Enter]**

   You store the increase factor that will be used in the what-if analysis in this cell. The value 1.1 can be used to calculate a 10% increase; anything you multiply by 1.1 returns an amount that's 110% of the original amount, or a 10% increase.

3. **Click cell H3, type What if?, then press [Enter]**

4. **In cell H4, type =, click F4, type *, click cell I1, then click the Enter button ✓ on the formula bar**

   The result, 263385.8, appears in cell H4. This value represents the total annual revenue for Australia if there is a 10% increase. You want to perform a what-if analysis for all the tour countries.

5. **Drag the fill handle of cell H4 to extend the selection to cell H11**

   The resulting values in the range H5:H11 are all zeros, which is not the result you wanted. See Figure B-17. Because you used relative cell addressing in cell H4, the copied formula adjusted so that the formula in cell H5 is =F5*I2. Because there is no value in cell I2, the result is 0, an error. You need to use an absolute reference in the formula to keep the formula from adjusting itself. That way, it will always reference cell I1.

6. **Click cell H4, press [F2] to change to Edit mode, then press [F4]**

   When you press [F2], the range finder outlines the arguments of the equation in blue and green. When you press [F4], dollar signs are inserted in the cell address, changing the I1 cell reference to an absolute reference.

7. **Click ✓, then drag ✛ to extend the selection to range H4:H11**

   The formula correctly contains an absolute cell reference, and the value of H4 remains unchanged. The correct values for a 10% increase appear in cells H4:H11. You now want to see a 20% increase in sales.

8. **Click cell I1, type 1.2, then click ✓**

   The values in the range H4:H11 change to reflect the 20% increase. Compare your worksheet to Figure B-18.

9. **Save your work**

FIGURE B-17: Creating an absolute reference in formula

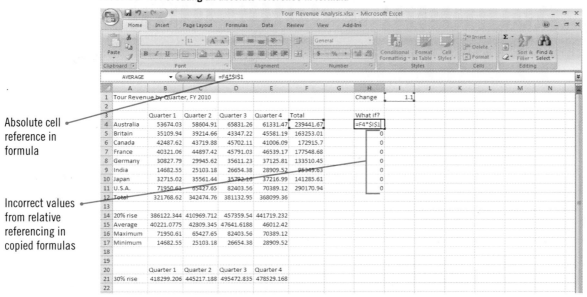

Absolute cell reference in formula

Incorrect values from relative referencing in copied formulas

FIGURE B-18: What-if analysis with modified change factor

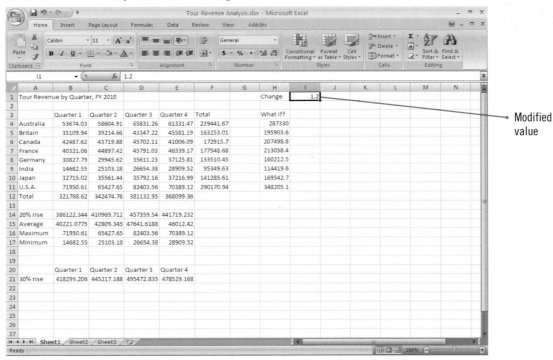

Modified value

Using the fill handle for sequential text or values

Often, you need to fill cells with sequential text: months of the year, days of the week, years, or text plus a number (Quarter 1, Quarter 2,...). For example, you might want to create a worksheet that calculates data for every month of the year. Using the fill handle, you can quickly and easily create labels for the months of the year just by typing January in a cell. Drag the fill handle from the cell containing January until you have all the monthly labels you need. You can easily fill cells using sequences by dragging the fill handle. As you drag the fill handle, Excel automatically extends the existing sequence. (The content of the last filled cell appears in the ScreenTip.) Use the Fill button list arrow in the Editing group, then click Series to examine all the fill series options for the current selection.

Rounding a Value with a Function

The more you explore features and tools in Excel, the more ways you'll find to simplify your work and convey information more efficiently. For example, cells containing financial data are often easier to read if they contain fewer decimals than those that appear by default. You can achieve this result by using the ROUND function, to round down your results. ▄▄▓▓▓ In your worksheet, you'd like to round the cells showing the 20% rise in sales to show fewer digits; after all, it's not important to show cents in the projections, only whole dollars. You want Excel to round the calculated value to the nearest integer. You decide to edit cell B14 so it includes the ROUND function, and then copy the edited formula into the other formulas in this row.

STEPS

1. **Click cell B14, then click to the right of = on the formula bar**

   You want to position the function at the beginning of the formula, before any values or arguments.

2. **Type RO**

   AutoComplete displays a list of functions beginning with RO.

3. **Double-click ROUND in the AutoComplete list**

   The new function and an opening parenthesis are added to the formula, as shown in Figure B-19. A few additional modifications are needed to complete your edit of the formula. You need to indicate the number of digits to which the function should round numbers down, and you also need to add a closing parenthesis around the set of arguments that come after the ROUND function.

4. **Press [END], type ,0), then click the Enter button ☑ on the formula bar**

   The comma separates the arguments within the formula, and 0 indicates that you don't want any decimals to appear in the calculated value. When you complete the edit, the parenthesis at either end of the formula briefly become bold, indicating that the formula has the correct number of open and closed parentheses and is balanced.

5. **Click the fill handle of cell B14, then drag the ✚ pointer to cell E14**

   When you release the mouse button, the formula in cell B14 is copied to the selected range. All the values are rounded to display no decimals. Compare your worksheet to Figure B-20.

6. **Click cell A25, type your name, then click ☑ on the formula bar**

7. **Save your work, preview and print the worksheet, then exit Excel**

FIGURE B-19: Adding a function to an existing formula

ROUND function
and opening
parenthesis
inserted in
formula

ScreenTip indicates
what information
is needed

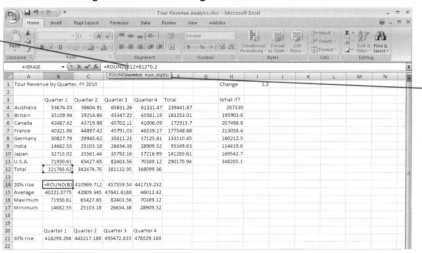

FIGURE B-20: Function added to formula

Function
surrounds
existing
formula

Calculated
values with
no decimals

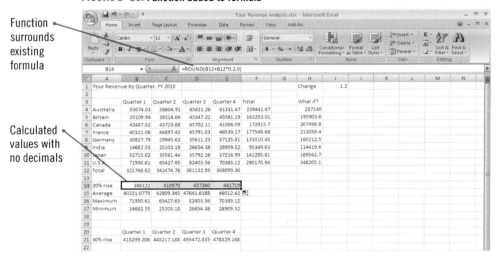

Creating a new workbook using a template

Excel **templates** are predesigned workbook files intended to save time when you create common documents such as balance sheets, expense statements, loan amortizations, sales invoices, or timecards. They contain labels, values, formulas, and formatting, so when you use a template all you have to do is customize it with your own information. Excel comes with many templates, and you can also create your own or find additional templates on the Web. Unlike a typical workbook, which has the file extension .xlsx, a template has the extension .xltx. To create a workbook using a template, click the Office button, then click New. The New Workbook dialog box opens. The Blank Workbook template is selected by default, because this is the template used to create a blank workbook with no content or special formatting. The left pane lists templates installed on your computer as well as many categories of templates available through Microsoft Office Online. Click a category, find the template you want, as shown in Figure B-21, click Download, then click Continue. A new workbook is created based on the template, so when you save the new file in the default format, it will have the

regular .xlsx extension. To save a workbook of your own as a template, open the Save As dialog box, then click the Save as type list arrow and change the file type to Excel Template.

FIGURE B-21: New Workbook dialog box

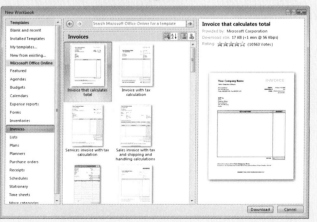

Practice

▼ CONCEPTS REVIEW

Label each element of the Excel worksheet window shown in Figure B-22.

FIGURE B-22

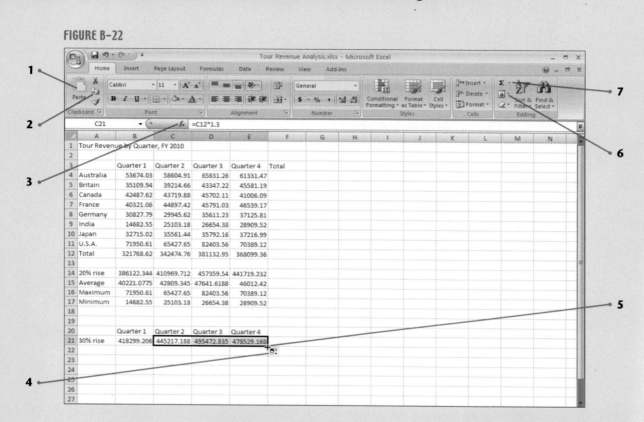

Match each term or button with the statement that best describes it.

8. **Launcher**

9. **Formula AutoComplete**

10. **Drag-and-drop**

11. **Fill handle**

12. **[Delete]**

a. Clears the contents of selected cells

b. Item on the Ribbon that opens a dialog box or task pane

c. Lets you move data from one cell to another without using the Clipboard

d. Displays an alphabetical list of functions from which you can choose

e. Lets you copy cell contents or continue a series of data into a range of selected cells

Select the best answer from the list of choices.

13. **What type of cell reference changes when it is copied?**
    a. Circular
    b. Absolute
    c. Relative
    d. Specified

14. **What type of cell reference is C$19?**
    a. Relative
    b. Absolute
    c. Mixed
    d. Certain

15. **Which key do you press to convert a relative cell reference to an absolute cell reference?**
    a. [F2]
    b. [F4]
    c. [F5]
    d. [F6]

16. **You can use any of the following features to enter a function *except*:**
    a. Insert Function button.
    b. Formula AutoComplete.
    c. AutoSum button list arrow.
    d. Clipboard.

17. **Which key do you press to copy while dragging-and-dropping selected cells?**
    a. [Alt]
    b. [Ctrl]
    c. [F2]
    d. [Tab]

▼ SKILLS REVIEW

1. Create a complex formula.

a. Open the file EX B-2.xlsx from the drive and folder where you store your Data Files, then save it as **Candy Supply Company Inventory**.

b. In cell B11, create a complex formula that calculates a 30% decrease in the total number of cases of Snickers bars.

c. Use the Fill button to copy this formula into cell C11 through cell E11, as shown in Figure B-23.

d. Save your work.

FIGURE B-23

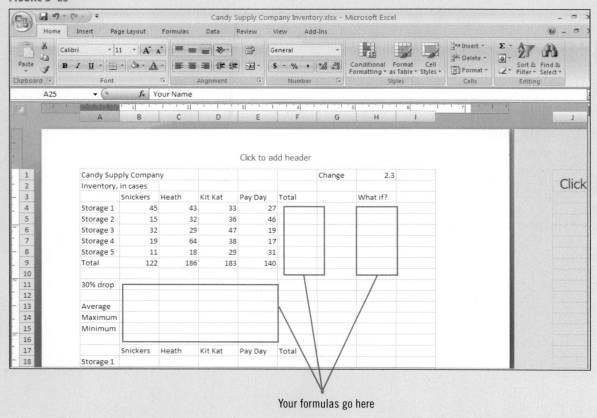

Your formulas go here

2. Insert a function.

a. Use the AutoSum button to create a formula in cell B13 that averages the number of cases of Snickers bars in each storage area. (*Hint*: Click the AutoSum button list arrow to open a list of available functions.)

b. Use the Insert Function button to create a formula in cell B14 that calculates the most cases of Snickers bars in a storage area.

c. Use the AutoSum button to create a formula in cell B15 that calculates the minimum number of cases of Snickers bars in a storage area.

d. Save your work.

3. Type a function.

a. In cell C13, type a formula that includes a function to average the number of cases of Heath bars. (*Hint*: Use AutoComplete to enter the function.)

b. In cell C14, type a formula that includes a function to calculate the maximum number of cases of Heath bars in a storage area.

c. In cell C15, type a formula that includes a function to calculate the minimum number of cases of Heath bars in a storage area.

d. Save your work.

4. **Copy and move cell entries.**
   a. Select the range B3:F3.
   b. Copy the selection into the Clipboard.
   c. Open the Clipboard task pane, then paste the selection into cell B17.
   d. Select the range A4:A9.
   e. Use the drag-and-drop method to copy the selection to cell A18. (*Hint*: The results should fill the range A18:A23.)
   f. Select the range H1:I1.
   g. Move the selection using the drag-and-drop method to cell G1.
   h. Save your work.

5. **Understand relative and absolute cell referencess.**
   a. Write a brief description of the difference between relative and absolute references.
   b. List at least three situations in which you think a business might use an absolute reference in its calculations. Examples can include calculations for different types of worksheets, such as timecards, invoices, and budgets.

6. **Copy formulas with relative cell references.**
   a. Select the range C13:C15.
   b. Use the fill handle to copy these cells to the range D13:E15.
   c. Calculate the total in cell F4.
   d. Use the Fill button to copy the formula in cell F4 down to cells F5:F9.
   e. Use the fill handle to copy the formula in cell E11 to cell F11.
   f. Save your work.

7. **Copy formulas with absolute cell references.**
   a. In cell H1, enter the value **1.575**.
   b. In cell H4, create a formula that multiplies F4 and an absolute reference to cell H1.
   c. Use the fill handle to copy the formula in cell H4 to cells H5 and H6.
   d. Use the Copy and Paste buttons to copy the formula in cell H4 to cells H7 and H8.
   e. Change the amount in cell H1 to **2.3**.
   f. Save your work.

8. **Round a value with a function.**
   a. Click cell H4.
   b. Edit this formula to include the ROUND function showing one digit.
   c. Use the fill handle to copy the formula in cell H4 to the range H5:H8.
   d. Enter your name in cell A25, then compare your work to Figure B-23.
   e. Save, preview, print, and close the workbook, then exit Excel.

▼ INDEPENDENT CHALLENGE 1

You are thinking of starting a small breakfast and lunch diner. Before you begin, you need to evaluate what you think your monthly expenses will be. You've started a workbook, but need to complete the entries and add formulas.

a. Open the file EX B-3.xlsx from the drive and folder where you store your Data Files, then save it as **Estimated Diner Expenses**.

b. Make up your own expense data and enter it in cells B4:B10. (Monthly sales are included in the worksheet.)

c. Create a formula in cell C4 that calculates the annual rent.

d. Copy the formula in cell C4 to the range C5:C10.

e. Move the label in cell A15 to cell A14.

f. Create a formula in cells B11 and C11 that totals the expenses.

g. Create a formula in cell C13 that calculates annual sales.

h. Create a formula in cell B14 that determines whether you will make a profit or loss, then copy the formula into cell C14.

i. Copy the labels in cells B3:C3 to cells E3:F3.

j. Type **Projection increase** in cell G1, then type **.2** in cell I1.

k. Create a formula in cell E4 that calculates an increase in the monthly rent by the amount in cell I1. You will be copying this formula to other cells, so you'll need to use an absolute reference.

l. Create a formula in cell F4 that calculates an annual increase based on the calculation in cell E4.

m. Create formulas in cells E13 and E14 and cells F13 and F14 that calculates monthly and annual sales and profit/loss based on the increase in cell E4.

n. Copy the formulas in cells E4:F4 in the remaining monthly and annual expenses.

o. Change the projection increase to **.15**, then compare your work to the sample in Figure B-24.

p. Enter your name in a cell in the worksheet.

q. Save your work, preview and print the worksheets, then close the workbook and exit Excel.

FIGURE B-24

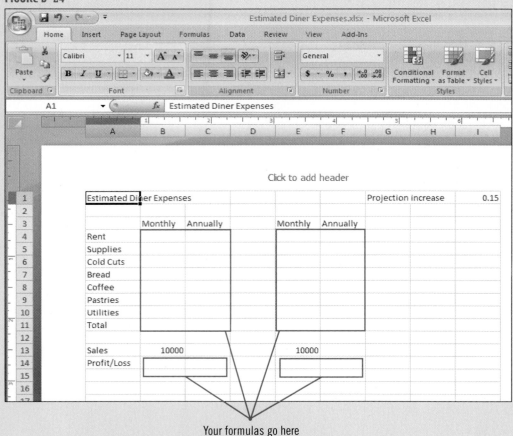

▼ INDEPENDENT CHALLENGE 2

The Pamper Yourself Salon & Day Spa is a small, growing spa that has hired you to organize its accounting records using Excel. The owners want you to track the company's expenses. Before you were hired, one of the bookkeepers began entering last year's expenses in a workbook, but the analysis was never completed.

a. Start Excel, open the file EX B-4.xlsx from the drive and folder where you store your Data Files, then save it as **Pamper Yourself Finances**. The worksheet includes labels for functions such as the Average, Maximum, and Minimum amounts of each of the expenses in the worksheet.

b. Think about what information would be important for the bookkeeping staff to know.

c. Create formulas in the Total column and row using the Sum function.

d. Create formulas in the Average, Maximum, and Minimum columns and rows using the method of your choice.

e. Save your work, then compare your worksheet to the sample shown in Figure B-25.

Advanced Challenge Exercise

- Create the label **Expense categories** in cell B19.
- In cell A19, create a formula using the COUNT function that determines the total number of expense categories listed per quarter.
- Save the workbook.

f. Enter your name in cell A25.

g. Preview the worksheet, then print it.

h. Save your work, then close the workbook and exit Excel.

FIGURE B-25

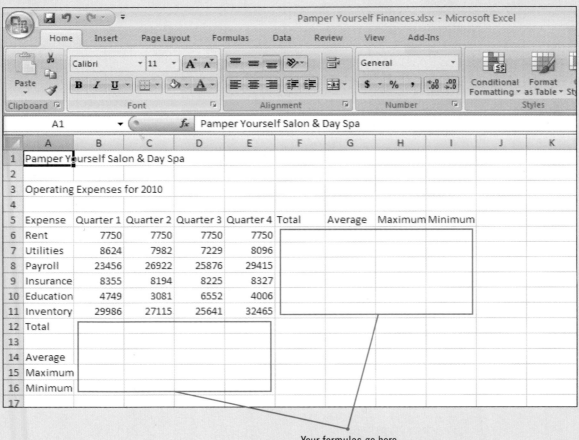

Your formulas go here

▼ INDEPENDENT CHALLENGE 3

As the accounting manager of a locally-owned clothing store, it is your responsibility to calculate and submit accrued sales tax payments on a monthly basis to the state government. You've decided to use an Excel workbook to make these calculations.

a. Start Excel, then save a new, blank workbook to the drive and folder where you store your Data Files as **Sales Tax Calculations**.

b. Decide on the layout for all columns and rows. The worksheet will contain data for four stores, which you can name by store number, neighborhood, or another method of your choice. For each store, you will calculate total sales tax based on the local sales tax rate. You'll also calculate total tax owed for all four stores.

c. Make up sales data for at least four stores.

d. Enter the rate to be used to calculate the sales tax, using your own local rate.

e. Create formulas to calculate the sales tax owed for each store. If you don't know the local tax rate, use **6.5%**.

f. Create a formula to total all the owed sales tax, then compare your work to the sample shown in Figure B-26.

Advanced Challenge Exercise

- Use the ROUND function to eliminate any decimals in the sales tax figures for each store and the total due.
- Save the workbook.

g. Add your name to the header.

h. Save your work, preview and print each worksheet, then close the workbook and exit Excel.

FIGURE B-26

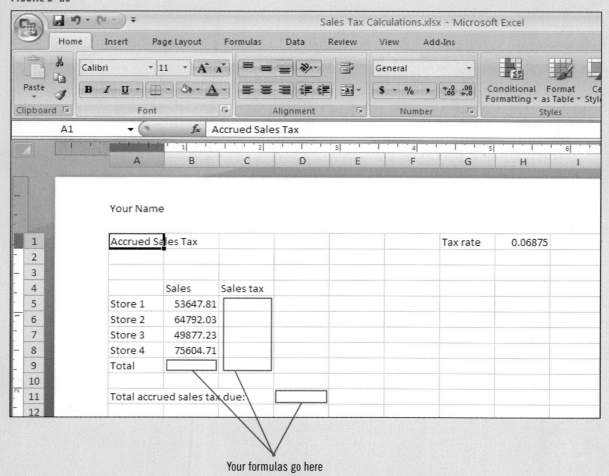

▼ REAL LIFE INDEPENDENT CHALLENGE

Many of your friends are purchasing homes, and you are thinking about taking the plunge yourself. As you begin the round of open houses and realtors' listings, you notice that there are many fees associated with buying a home. Some fees are based on a percentage of the purchase price and others are a flat fee; overall, they seem to represent a substantial amount above the purchase prices you see listed. You've seen three houses so far that interest you; one is moderately priced, one is more expensive, and the third is still more expensive. You decide to create an Excel workbook to figure out the real cost of buying each one.

a. Find out the typical cost or percentage rate of at least three fees that are usually charged when buying a home and taking out a mortgage. (*Hint*: If you have access to the Internet you can research the topic of home-buying on the Web, or you can ask friends about standard rates or percentages for items such as title insurance, credit reports, and inspection fees.)

b. Start Excel, then save a new, blank workbook to the drive and folder where you store your Data Files as **Home Purchase Fees**.

c. Create labels and enter data for three homes. If you enter this information across the columns in your worksheet, you should have one column for each house, with the purchase price in the cell below each label. Be sure to enter a different purchase price for each house.

FIGURE B-27

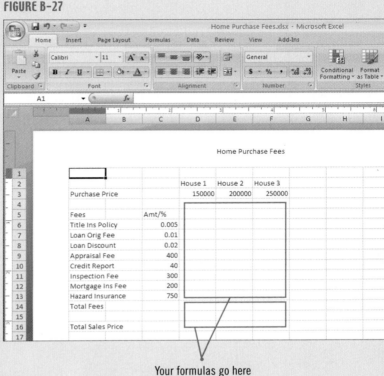

Your formulas go here

d. Create labels for the Fees column and for an Amount or Rate column. Enter the information on the three fees you have researched.

e. In each house column, enter formulas that calculate the fee for each item. The formulas (and use of absolute or relative referencing) will vary depending on whether the charges are a flat fee or based on a percentage of the purchase price.

f. Total the fees for each house, create formulas that add the total fees to the purchase price, then compare your work to the sample in Figure B-27.

g. Enter a title for the worksheet in the header.

h. Enter your name in the header, preview the worksheet, then print it.

i. Save your work, then close the file and exit Excel.

▼ VISUAL WORKSHOP

Create the worksheet shown in Figure B-28 using the skills you learned in this unit. Save the workbook as **Sales Analysis** to the drive and folder where you store your Data Files. Enter your name in the header as shown, then preview and print one copy of the worksheet. Print a second copy of the worksheet with the formulas showing.

FIGURE B-28

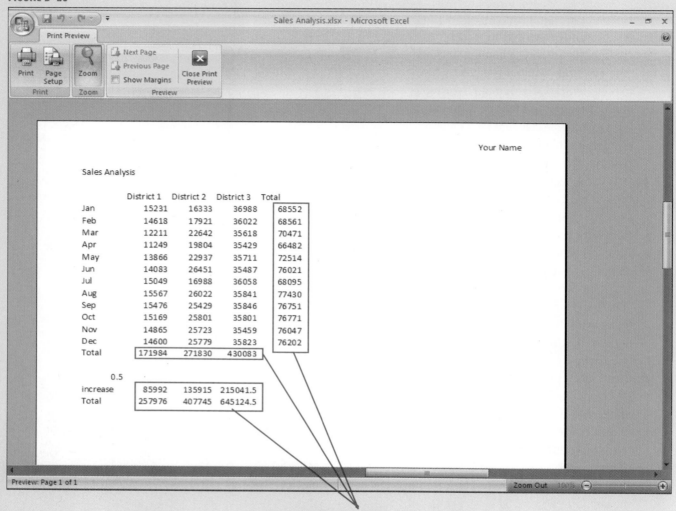

Enter formulas and not values in these cells

Working with Formulas and Functions

Start

Formatting a Worksheet

You can use formatting features to make a worksheet more attractive or easier to read, and to emphasize key data. You can apply different formatting attributes such as colors, font styles, and font sizes to the cell contents, you can adjust column width and row height, and you can insert or delete columns and rows. You can also apply conditional formatting so that cells meeting certain criteria are formatted differently. This makes it easy to emphasize selected information, such as sales that exceed or fall below a certain threshold. The marketing managers at QST have requested information on advertising expenses for all QST locations during the past four quarters. Grace Wong has created a worksheet listing this information. She asks you to format the worksheet to make it easier to read and to call attention to important data.

OBJECTIVES

Format values

Change font and font size

Change attributes and alignment

Adjust column width

Insert and delete rows and columns

Apply colors, patterns, and borders

Apply conditional formatting

Name and move a sheet

Check spelling

Formatting Values

The **format** of a cell determines how the labels and values look—for example, whether the contents appear boldfaced, italicized, or with dollar signs and commas. Formatting changes only the appearance of a value or label; it does not alter the actual data in any way. To format a cell or range, first you select it, then you apply the formatting using the Ribbon or a keyboard shortcut. You can apply formatting before or after you enter data in a cell or range. ▰▰▰▰▰ Grace has provided you with a worksheet that lists individual advertising expenses, and you're ready to improve its appearance and readability. You decide to start by formatting some of the values so they display as currency, percentages, and dates.

STEPS

1. **Start Excel, open the file EX C-1.xlsx from the drive and folder where you store your Data Files, save it as QST Advertising Expenses, click the View tab on the Ribbon, then click the Page Layout button**

   This worksheet is difficult to interpret because all the information looks the same. In some columns, the contents appear cut off because there is too much data to fit given the current column width. You decide not to widen the columns yet, because the other changes you plan to make might affect column width and row height. The first thing you want to do is format the data showing the cost of each ad.

2. **Select the range E4:E32, then click the Accounting Number Format button $ in the Number group on the Home tab**

   The default Accounting Number format adds dollar signs and two decimal places to the data, as shown in Figure C-1. Formatting this data in accounting format makes it easier to recognize. Excel automatically resizes the column to display the new formatting. The Accounting and Currency formats are both used for monetary values, but the Accounting format aligns currency symbols and decimal points of numbers in a column.

3. **Select the range G4:I32, then click the Comma Style button ⁹ in the Number group**

   The values in columns G, H, and I display the Comma Style format, which does not include a dollar sign but can be useful for some types of accounting data.

4. **Select the range J4:J32, click the Number Format list arrow, click Percentage, then click the Increase Decimal button ⁺⁰̟₀₀ in the Number group**

   The data in the % of Total column is now formatted with a percent sign (%) and three decimal places. The Format list arrow lets you choose from popular number formats and shows an example of what the selected cell or cells would look like in each format (when multiple cells are selected, the example is based on the first cell in the range). Each time you click the Increase Decimal button, you add one decimal place; clicking the button twice would add two decimal places.

5. **Click the Decrease Decimal button ˙⁰⁰ in the Number group twice**

   Two decimal places are removed.

6. **Select the range B4:B31, click the launcher ⬚ in the Number group**

   The Format Cells dialog box opens with the Date category already selected on the Number tab.

7. **Select the first 14-Mar-01 format in the Type list box as shown in Figure C-2, then click OK**

   The dates in column B appear in the 14-Mar-01 format. The second 14-Mar-01 format in the list displays all days in two digits (it adds a leading zero if the day is only a single-digit number), while the one you chose displays single-digit days without a leading zero. You can also open the Format Cells dialog box by right-clicking a selected range.

8. **Select the range C4:C31, right-click the range, click Format Cells on the shortcut menu, click 14-Mar in the Type list box in the Format Cells dialog box, then click OK**

   Compare your worksheet to Figure C-3.

9. **Press [Ctrl][Home], then save your work**

Formatting a Worksheet

FIGURE C-1: Advertising expense worksheet

Number Format
list arrow

Accounting
Number Format
button

Commands in Number
group change the
appearance of numbers

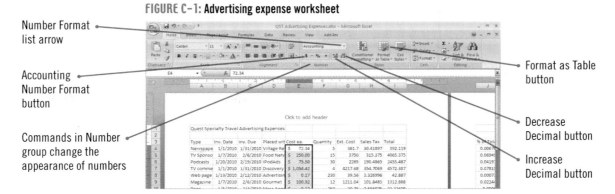

Format as Table
button

Decrease
Decimal button

Increase
Decimal button

FIGURE C-2: Format Cells dialog box

Number
format
categories

Date formats

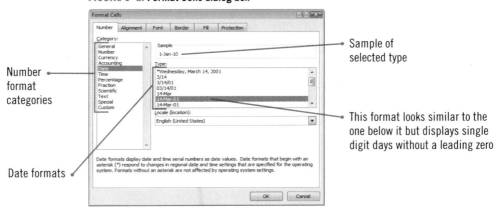

Sample of
selected type

This format looks similar to the
one below it but displays single
digit days without a leading zero

FIGURE C-3: Worksheet with formatted values

New format
displays in
the format box

Date formats
appear with-
out year

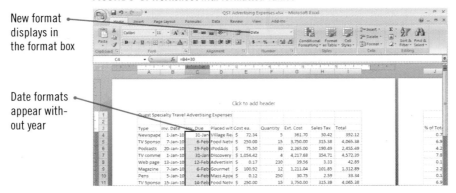

Formatting as a table

Excel includes 60 predefined table styles to make it easy to format selected worksheet cells as a table. You can apply table styles to any range of cells that you want to format quickly, or even to an entire worksheet, but they're especially useful for those ranges with labels in the left column and top rows, and totals in the bottom row or right column. To apply a table style, select the data to be formatted or click anywhere within the intended range (Excel can automatically detect a range of cells), click the Format as Table button in the Styles group on the Home tab, then click a style in the gallery, as shown in Figure C-4. Table styles are organized in three categories (Light, Medium, and Dark). Once you click a style, Excel confirms the range selection, then applies the style. Once you have formatted a range as a table, you can use Live Preview to preview with different choices by pointing to any style in the Table Styles gallery.

FIGURE C-4: Table Styles gallery

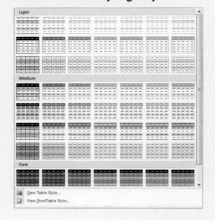

Changing Font and Font Size

A **font** is the name for a collection of characters (letters, numerals, symbols, and punctuation marks) with a similar, specific design. The **font size** is the physical size of the text, measured in units called points. A **point** is equal to 1/72 of an inch. The default font in Excel is 11-point Calibri. Table C-1 shows several fonts in different sizes. You can change the font and font size of any cell or range using the Ribbon, the Format Cells dialog box, or the Mini toolbar. You can open the Format Cells dialog box by clicking the launcher in the Font, Alignment, or Number group on the Home tab, or by right-clicking a selection, then clicking Format Cells in the shortcut menu. The Mini toolbar opens when you right-click a cell or range. You want to change the font and size of the labels and the worksheet title so that they stand out more from the data.

STEPS

QUICK TIP

To preview font and font size changes directly in selected cells, use the Font group on the Home tab; Live Preview shows font, font size, font color, and fill color when you hover the mouse pointer over selections in these lists and palettes.

1. **Right-click cell A1, click Format Cells on the shortcut menu, then click the Font tab in the Format Cells dialog box if necessary**
   See Figure C-5.

2. **Scroll down in the Font list to see an alphabetical listing of the fonts available on your computer, click Times New Roman in the Font list box, click 20 in the Size list box, preview the results in the Preview area, then click OK**
   The title appears in 20-point Times New Roman, and the Font group on the Home tab displays the new font and size information.

3. **Click the Increase Font Size button A˄ in the Font group twice**
   The size of the title increases to 24-point.

QUICK TIP

You can also format an entire row by clicking the row indicator button (or an entire column by clicking the column indicator button).

4. **Select the range A3:J3, right-click, then click the Font list arrow on the Mini toolbar**
   The Mini toolbar includes the most commonly used formatting tools, so it's great for making quick formatting changes. Notice that the font names on this font list are displayed in the font they represent.

QUICK TIP

Once you click the Font list arrow, you can quickly move to a font in the list by typing the first few characters of its name.

5. **Click Times New Roman, click the Font Size list arrow, then click 14**
   The Mini toolbar closes when you move the pointer away from the selection. Compare your worksheet to Figure C-6. Notice that some of the column headings are now too wide to appear fully in the column. Excel does not automatically adjust column widths to accommodate cell formatting; you have to adjust column widths manually. You'll learn to do this in a later lesson.

6. **Save your work**

TABLE C-1: Examples of fonts and font sizes

font	12 point	24 point
Calibri	Excel	Excel
Playbill	Excel	Excel
Comic Sans MS	Excel	Excel
Times New Roman	Excel	Excel

FIGURE C-5: Font tab in the Format Cells dialog box

Currently selected font

Available fonts might differ on your computer

Effects options

Type a custom font size or select from the list

Font style options

Preview area shows sample of selected formatting

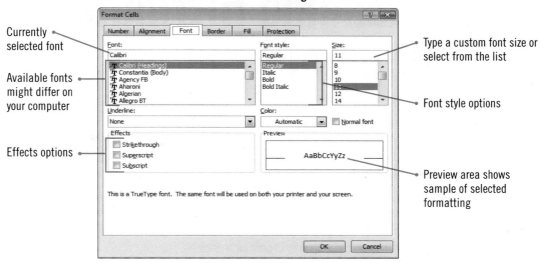

FIGURE C-6: Worksheet with formatted title and labels

Font and size of active cell or range

Title appears in 24-point Times New Roman

Column headings now 14-point Times New Roman

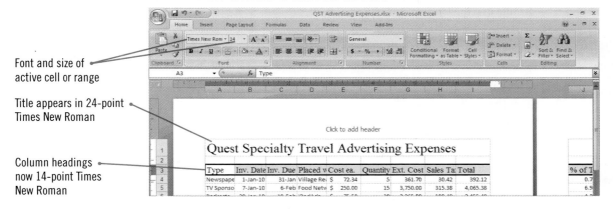

Inserting and adjusting clip art and other images

You can illustrate your worksheets using clip art and other images. A **clip** is an individual media file, such as art, sound, animation, or a movie. **Clip art** refers to images such as a corporate logo, a picture, or a photo. Microsoft Office comes with many clips available for your use. To add a clip to a worksheet, click Clip Art in the Illustrations group on the Insert tab. The Clip Art task pane opens. Here you can search for clips by typing one or more keywords (words related to your subject) in the Search for text box, then click Go. Clips that relate to your keywords appear in the Clip Art task pane, as shown in Figure C-7. (If you have a standard Office installation and an active Internet connection, you will see many clips available through Microsoft Office Online in addition to those on your computer.) Click the image you want, and it is inserted at the location of the active cell. You can also add your own images to a worksheet by clicking the Insert tab on the Ribbon, then clicking the Picture button. Navigate to the file you want, then click Insert Picture from File. To resize an image, drag any corner sizing handle. To move an image, point inside the clip until the pointer changes to ⊹, then drag it to a new location.

FIGURE C-7: Results of Clip Art search

Type keyword(s) here

Click to begin search

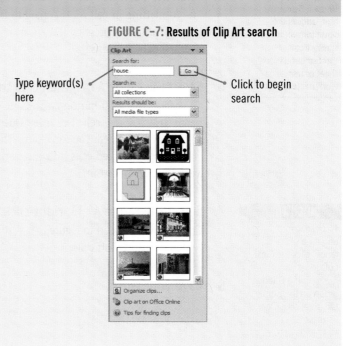

Changing Attributes and Alignment

Attributes are styling formats such as bold, italic, and underlining that you can apply to affect the way text and numbers look in a worksheet. You can "paint" or copy a cell's format into other cells by using the Format Painter button in the Clipboard group on the Home tab of the Ribbon. This is similar to using copy and paste, but instead of copying cell contents, it copies only the cell's formatting. You can also change the **alignment** of labels and values in cells to be left, right, or center. You can apply attributes and alignment options using the Home tab, the Format Cells dialog box, or the Mini toolbar. See Table C-2 for a description of common attribute and alignment buttons that are available on the Home tab of the Ribbon and the Mini toolbar. You want to further enhance the worksheet's appearance by adding bold and underline formatting and centering some of the labels.

STEPS

1. **Press [Ctrl][Home], then click the Bold button B in the Font group**
   The title in cell A1 appears in bold.

QUICK TIP
You can use the following keyboard shortcuts to format a selected range: [Ctrl][B] to bold, [Ctrl][I] to italicize, and [Ctrl][U] to underline.

2. **Click cell A3, then click the Underline button U in the Font group**
   The column heading is now underlined, though this may be difficult to see with the cell selected.

3. **Click the Italic button I in the Font group, then click B**
   The heading now appears in boldface, underlined, italic type. Notice that the Bold, Italic, and Underline buttons in the Font group are all selected.

QUICK TIP
Overuse of any attribute or random formatting can make a workbook difficult to read. Be consistent, adding the same formatting to similar items throughout a worksheet or related worksheets.

4. **Click I**
   The italic attribute is removed from cell A3, but the bold and underline attributes remain.

5. **Click the Format Painter button in the Clipboard group, then select the range B3:J3**
   The formatting in cell A3 is copied to the rest of the labels in the column headings. You can turn off the Format Painter by pressing [Esc] or by clicking. You decide the title would look better if it were centered over the data columns.

6. **Select the range A1:J1, then click the Merge & Center button in the Alignment group**
   The Merge & Center button creates one cell out of the 10 cells across the row, then centers the text in that newly created large cell. The title "Quest Specialty Travel Advertising Expenses" is centered across the 10 columns you selected. You can change the alignment within individual cells using buttons on the Home tab; you can split merged cells into their original components by selecting the merged cells, then clicking the Merge & Center button.

QUICK TIP
To clear all formatting for a selected range, click the Clear button list arrow in the Editing group on the Home tab, then click Clear Formats.

7. **Select the range A3:J3, right-click, then click the Center button on the Mini toolbar**
   Compare your screen to Figure C-8. Although they may be difficult to read, notice that all the headings are centered within their cells.

8. **Save your work**

FIGURE C-8: Worksheet with formatting attributes applied

Formatting buttons selected

Merge & Center button

Title centered across columns

Center button

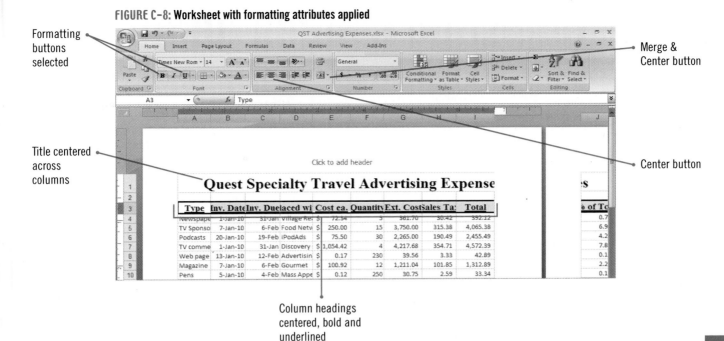

Column headings centered, bold and underlined

Rotating and indenting cell entries

In addition to applying fonts and formatting attributes, you can rotate or indent data within a cell to further change its appearance. You can rotate text within a cell by altering its alignment. To change alignment, select the cells you want to modify, then click the launcher ⬚ in the Alignment group to open the Alignment tab of the Format Cells dialog box. Click a position in the Orientation box or type a number in the Degrees text box to change from the default horizontal alignment, then click OK. You can indent cell contents using the Increase Indent button ⬚ on the Alignment group on the Home tab on the Ribbon, which moves cell contents to the right one space, or the Decrease Indent button ⬚, which moves cell contents to the left one space.

TABLE C-2: Common attribute and alignment buttons

button	description	button	description
B	Bolds text	▤	Aligns text at the left edge of the cell
I	Italicizes text	▤	Centers text horizontally within the cell
U	Underlines text	▤	Aligns text at the right edge of the cell
⬚	Adds lines or borders	▤	Centers text across columns, and combines two or more selected, adjacent cells into one cell

Adjusting Column Width

As you format a worksheet, you might need to adjust the width of one or more columns to accommodate text or larger font size or style. The default column width is 8.43 characters wide, a little less than one inch. With Excel, you can adjust the width of one or more columns by using the mouse, the Ribbon, or the shortcut menu. Using the mouse, you can drag or double-click the right edge of a column heading. The Ribbon and shortcut menu include commands for making more detailed width adjustments. Table C-3 describes common column adjustment commands. ▓▓▓▓ You notice that some of the labels in column A don't fit in the cells. You want to adjust the widths of the columns so that the labels appear in their entirety.

STEPS

1. **Position the mouse pointer on the line between the column A and column B headings until it changes to ↔**

   See Figure C-9. The **column heading** is the box at the top of each column containing a letter. Before you can adjust column width using the mouse, you need to position the pointer on the right edge of the column you want to adjust. The entries for TV commercials are the widest in the column.

2. **Click and drag the ↔ to the right until the column displays the TV commercials entries fully**

3. **Position the pointer on the column line between columns B and C until it changes to ↔, then double-click**

   Column B automatically widens to fit the widest entry, in this case, the column label. Double-clicking activates the **AutoFit** feature, which automatically resizes a column so it accommodates the widest entry in a cell.

4. **Use AutoFit to resize columns C, D, and J**

5. **Select the range F5:I5**

   You can change the width of multiple columns at once, by first selecting either the column headings or at least one cell in each column.

6. **Click the Format button in the Cells group, then click Column Width**

   The Column Width dialog box opens. Column width measurement is based on the number of characters that will fit in the column when formatted in the Normal font and font size (in this case, 11 pt Calibri).

7. **Drag the dialog box by its title bar if its placement obscures your view of the worksheet, type .91" in the Column width text box, then click OK**

   The widths of columns F, G, H, and I change to reflect the new setting. See Figure C-10.

8. **Save your work**

QUICK TIP

To reset columns to the default width, click the column headings to select the columns, click the Format button in the Cells group, click Default Width, then click OK in the Standard Width dialog box.

QUICK TIP

If a column heading is selected, you can change the width of the column by right-clicking, then clicking Column Width in the shortcut menu.

QUICK TIP

If "#######" appears after you adjust a column of values, the column is too narrow to display the contents; increase the column width until the values appear.

Changing row height

Changing row height is as easy as changing column width. Row height is calculated in points, the same units of measure used for fonts. The row height must exceed the size of the font you are using. Normally, you don't need to adjust row heights manually, because row height adjusts automatically to accommodate other formatting changes. If you format something in a row to be a larger point size, Excel adjusts the row to fit the largest point size in the row. However, you have just as many options for changing row height as you do column width. Using the mouse, you can place the ↕ pointer on the line dividing the row heading from the heading below, and dragging to the desired height; double-clicking the line autofits the row height where necessary. You can also select one or more rows, then use the Row Height command on the shortcut menu, or the Row Height or AutoFit Row Height command on the Format button in the Cells group on the Home tab.

FIGURE C-9: Preparing to change the column width

Click to change column or row formatting

Resize pointer

Row 2 heading

Column D heading

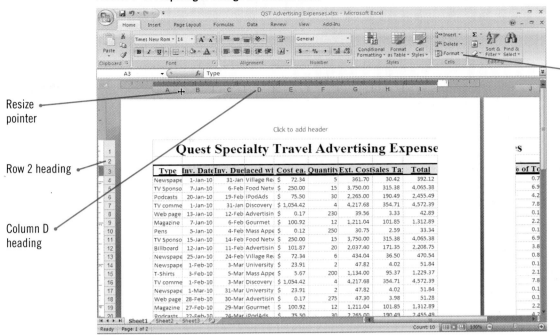

FIGURE C-10: Worksheet with column widths adjusted

Columns widened to display text

Columns widened to same width

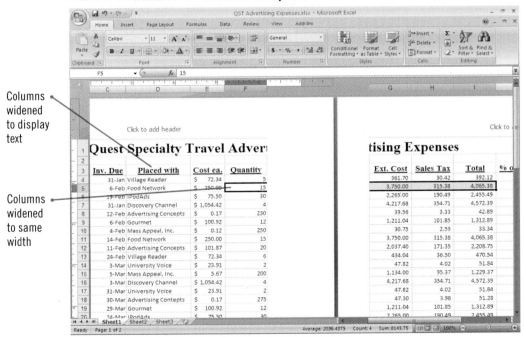

TABLE C-3: Common column formatting commands

command	description	available using
Column Width	Sets the width to a specific number of characters	Format button, shortcut menu
AutoFit Column Width	Fits to the widest entry in a column	Format button, mouse
Hide & Unhide	Hides or displays hidden column(s)	Format button, shortcut menu
Default Width	Changes the default column width for current worksheet	Format button

Inserting and Deleting Rows and Columns

As you modify a worksheet, you might find it necessary to insert or delete rows and columns to keep your worksheet current. For example, you might need to insert rows to accommodate new inventory products or remove a column of yearly totals that are no longer necessary. When you insert a new row, the contents of the worksheet shift down from the newly inserted row. When you insert a new column, the contents of the worksheet shift to the right from the point of the new column. Excel inserts rows above the cell pointer and inserts columns to the left of the cell pointer. To insert multiple rows, drag across row headings to select the same number of rows as you want to insert. You want to improve the overall appearance of the worksheet by inserting a row between the last row of data and the totals. Also, you have learned that row 27 and column J need to be deleted from the worksheet.

STEPS

1. **Right-click cell A32, then click Insert on the shortcut menu**
   The Insert dialog box opens. See Figure C-11. You can choose to insert a column or a row, or you can shift the data in the cells in the active column right or in the active row down. An additional row between the last row of data and the totals will visually separate the totals.

QUICK TIP
To insert a single row or column, you can also right-click the row heading immediately below where you want the new row or the column heading to the right of where you want the new column, then click Insert in the shortcut menu.

2. **Click the Entire row option button, then click OK**
   A blank row appears between the Billboard data and the totals, and the formula result in cell E33 has not changed. The Insert Options button ✎ appears beside cell A33. Pointing to the button displays a list arrow, which you can click and then choose from the following options: Format Same As Above, Format Same As Below, or Clear Formatting. You want the default formatting, Same as Above.

3. **Click the row 27 heading**
   All of row 27 is selected, as shown in Figure C-12.

QUICK TIP
If you inadvertently click the Delete list arrow instead of the button itself, click Delete Sheet Rows in the menu that opens.

4. **Click the Delete button in the Cells group; *do not click the button arrow***
   Excel deletes row 27, and all rows below this shift up one row. You must use the Delete button or the Delete command on the shortcut menu to delete a row or column; pressing [Delete] on the keyboard removes only the *contents* of a selected row or column.

5. **Click the column J heading**
   The percentage information is calculated elsewhere and is no longer necessary in this worksheet.

QUICK TIP
After inserting or deleting rows or columns in a worksheet, be sure to proof formulas that contain relative cell references.

6. **Click the Delete button in the Cells group**
   Excel deletes column J. The remaining columns to the right shift left one column.

7. **Save your work**

Hiding and unhiding columns and rows

When you don't want data in a column or row to be visible, but you don't want to delete it, you can hide the column or row. To hide a selected column, click the Format button in the Cells group, point to Hide & Unhide, then click Hide Columns. A hidden column is indicated by a dark black vertical line in its original position. This black line disappears when you click elsewhere in the worksheet. You can display a hidden column by selecting the columns on either side of the hidden column, clicking the Format button in the Cells group, pointing to Hide & Unhide, and then clicking Unhide Columns. (To hide or unhide one or more rows, substitute Hide Rows and Unhide Rows for the Hide Columns and Unhide Columns commands.)

FIGURE C-11: Insert dialog box

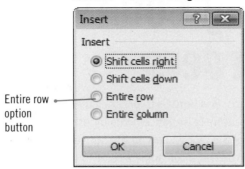

Entire row option button

FIGURE C-12: Worksheet with row 27 selected

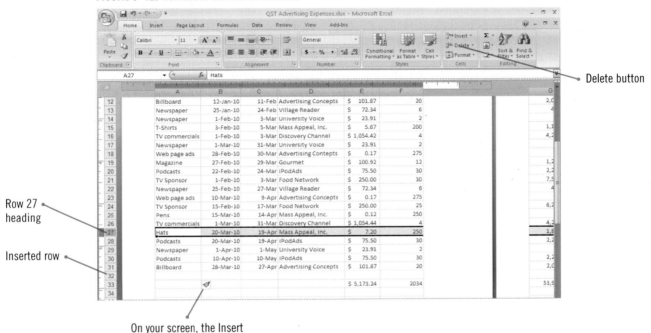

Delete button

Row 27 heading

Inserted row

On your screen, the Insert Options button might appear in a different location

Adding and editing comments

Much of your work in Excel may be in collaboration with teammates with whom you share worksheets. You can share ideas with other worksheet users by adding comments within selected cells. To include a comment in a worksheet, click the cell where you want to place the comment, click the Review tab on the Ribbon, then click the New Comment button in the Comments group. A resizable text box containing the computer user's name opens in which you can type your comments. A small, red triangle appears in the upper-right corner of a cell containing a comment. If comments are not already displayed in a workbook, other users can point to the trian-gle to display the comment. To see all worksheet comments, as shown in Figure C-13, click the Show All Comments button in the Comments group. To edit a comment, click the cell containing the comment, then click the Edit Comment button in the Comments group. To delete a comment, click the cell containing the comment, then click the Delete button in the Comments group.

FIGURE C-13: Comments in worksheet

18	Web page abs	28-Feb-10	30-Mar	Advertising Contepts	$ 0.17
19	Magazine	27-Feb-10	29-Mar	Gourmet	$ 100.92
20	Podcasts	22-Feb-10	24-Mar	iPodAds	$ 75.50
21	TV Sponsor	1-Feb-10	3-Mar	Food Networ	
22	Newspaper	25-Feb-10	27-Mar	Village Reade	
23	Web page ads	10-Mar-10	9-Apr	Advertising C	
24	TV Sponsor	15-Feb-10	17-Mar	Food Networ	
25	Pens	15-Mar-10	14-Apr	Mass Appeal, Inc.	$ 0.12
26	TV commercials	1-Mar-10	31-Mar	Discovery Channel	
27	Podcasts	20-Mar-10	19-Apr	iPodAds	
28	Newspaper	1-Apr-10	1-May	University Vo	
29	Podcasts	10-Apr-10	10-May	iPodAds	
30	Billboard	28-Mar-10	27-Apr	Advertising Concepts	$ 101.87
31					
32					$5,166.04
33					

Grace Wong: Should we continue with this market, or expand to other publications?

Grace Wong: I think this will turn out to be a very good decision.

Excel 2007

Applying Colors, Patterns, and Borders

You can use colors, patterns, and borders to enhance the overall appearance of a worksheet and to make it easier to read. You can add these enhancements by using the Border and Fill Color buttons in the Font group on the Home tab of the Ribbon and on the Mini toolbar, or by using the Fill tab and the Border tab in the Format Cells dialog box. You can apply a color to the background of a cell or a range, or to cell contents, and you can apply a pattern to a cell or range. You can apply borders to all the cells in a worksheet or only to selected cells to call attention to selected information. To save time, you can also apply **cell styles**, predesigned combinations of formatting attributes. ▰▰▰ You want to add a pattern, a border, and color to the title of the worksheet to give the worksheet a more professional appearance.

STEPS

1. **Select cell A1, click the Fill Color list arrow button** ⬇ **in the Font group, then hover the pointer over the Turquoise, Accent 2 color (first row, sixth column from the left)**
   See Figure C-14. Live Preview shows you how the color will look *before* you apply it.

2. **Click the Turquoise, Accent 2 color (first row, sixth column from the left)**
   The color is applied to the background or fill of this cell. (Remember that cell A1 spans columns A through I because the Merge and Center command was applied.)

3. **Right-click cell A1, then click Format Cells on the shortcut menu**
   The Format Cells dialog box opens. Adding a pattern to cells can add to the visual interest of your worksheet. To format an entire row or column at once, click the row heading or column heading button.

4. **Click the Fill tab, click the Pattern Style list arrow, click the 6.25% Gray style (first row, sixth column from the left), then click OK**

5. **Click the Borders list arrow** ⊞ **in the Font group, then click Thick Bottom Border**
   Unlike underlining, which is a text-formatting tool, borders extend to the width of the cell, and can appear at the bottom of the cell, at the top, or on either side. It can be difficult to see a border when the cell is selected.

6. **Select the range A3:I3, click the Font Color list arrow** ▲ **in the Font group, then click the Blue, Accent 1 color (first Theme color row, fifth column from the left) on the palette**
   The new color is applied to the selected range.

7. **Select the range J1:K1, click the Cell Styles button in the Styles group, then click the Neutral button (first row, fourth column from the left) on the palette**
   The font and color change in the range, as shown in Figure C-15.

8. **Save your work**

FIGURE C-14: Viewing fill color using Live Preview

Font color list arrow

Cell A1 with light blue background

Click to apply styles to selected cells

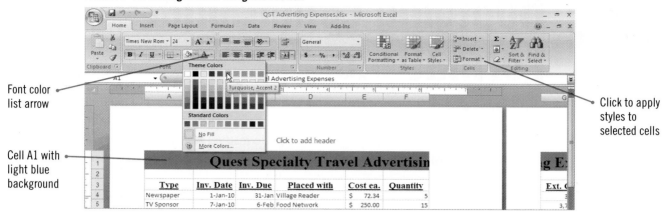

FIGURE C-15: Worksheet with color, patterns, border, and style applied

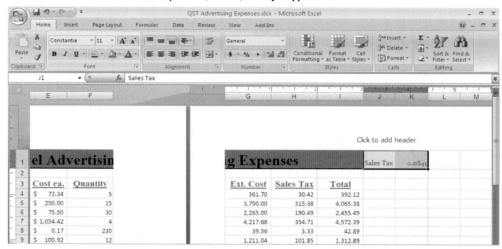

Saving time with themes and cell styles

You can save yourself time by formatting with themes and cell styles. A **theme** is a predefined set of attributes that gives your Excel worksheet a professional look. Formatting choices included in a theme are colors, fonts, and line and fill effects. A theme can be applied using the Themes button in the Themes group on the Page Layout tab on the Ribbon, as shown in Figure C-16. **Cell styles** are sets of attributes based on themes, so they are automatically updated if you change a theme. For example, if you apply the 20% - Accent1 cell style to cell A1 in a worksheet that has no theme applied, the fill color changes to light blue and the font changes to Constantia. If you change the theme of the worksheet to Metro, cell A1's fill color changes to light green and the font changes to Corbel, because these are the attributes that coordinate with the selected theme. Using themes and cell styles makes it easier to ensure that your worksheets are consistent and saves you from a lot of reformatting every time you make a change.

FIGURE C-16: Themes gallery

Formatting a Worksheet

Applying Conditional Formatting

So far, you've used formatting to change the appearance of different types of data, such as dates, dollar amounts, worksheet titles, and column labels. But you can also use formatting to highlight important aspects of the data itself. For example, you can apply formatting that automatically changes the font color to red for any cells where ad costs exceed $100 and to green where ad costs are below $50. This type of formatting is called **conditional formatting** because Excel automatically applies different formats depending on conditions you specify. If the data meets your conditions, Excel applies the formats you specify. The formatting is updated if you change data in the worksheet. Data bars are a type of conditional formatting that visually illustrate differences among values. ▰▰▰▰▰ Grace is concerned about advertising costs exceeding yearly budget. You decide to use conditional formatting to highlight certain trends and patterns in the data, so it's easy to spot the most expensive expenditures.

STEPS

1. **Select the range I4:I30, click the Conditional Formatting button in the Styles group, point to Data Bars, then point to the Light Blue Data Bar (second row, second from left)**
   Live Preview shows how this formatting will appear in the worksheet, as shown in Figure C-17. Notice that the length of the bar in each cell reflects its value relative to other cells in the selection.

2. **Preview the Green Data Bar (first row, second from left), then click it**

QUICK TIP
You can apply an Icon Set to a selected range by clicking the Conditional Formatting button in the Styles group, then pointing to Icon Sets; icons appear within the cells to illustrate differences in values.

3. **Select the range G4:G30, click the Conditional Formatting button in the Styles group, then point to Highlight Cells Rules**
   The Conditional Formatting menu displays choices for creating different types of formatting rules. For example, you can create a rule for values that are greater than a certain amount, less than a certain amount, or between two amounts.

4. **Click Between**
   The Between dialog box opens. Depending on the choice you made in the Highlight Cells Rules menu (such as "Greater Than" or "Less Than"), this dialog box displays different input boxes. You can define multiple different conditions and then assign formatting attributes to each one. You define the condition first. The default setting for the first condition is "Cell Value Is" "between." The value can be a constant, formula, cell reference, or date. The formatting default format is exactly what you want: Light Red Fill with Dark Red Text.

QUICK TIP
You can copy conditional formats the same way you copy other formats.

5. **Type 2000 in the first text box, type 4000 in the second text box, compare your settings to Figure C-18, then click OK**
   All cells with values between 2000 and 4000 in column G appear with a light red fill and dark red text.

6. **Click cell G7, type 3975.55, then press [Enter]**
   When the value in cell G7 changes, the formatting also changes, because the new value meets the condition to apply the format. Compare your results to Figure C-19.

7. **Press [Ctrl][Home] to select cell A1, then save your work**

Managing conditional formatting rules

If you create a conditional formatting rule and then want to change the conditions to reflect a different value or format, you don't need to create a new rule; instead, you can modify the rule using the Rule Manager. Select the cell(s) containing conditional formatting, click the Conditional Formatting button in the Styles group, then click

Manage Rules. The Conditional Formatting Rules Manager dialog box opens. Select the rules you want to edit or delete, click Edit Rule, modify the settings in the Edit the Rule Description area, click OK, then click OK again to close the dialog box. The rule is modified, and the new conditions are applied to the selected cells.

FIGURE C-17: Previewing a Data Bar

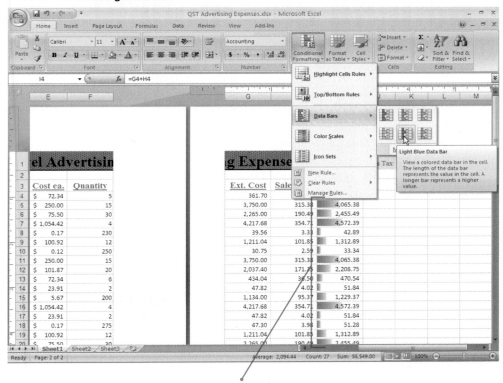

Data bars displayed
in sheet

FIGURE C-18: Setting conditions in Between dialog box

FIGURE C-19: Results of Conditional Formatting

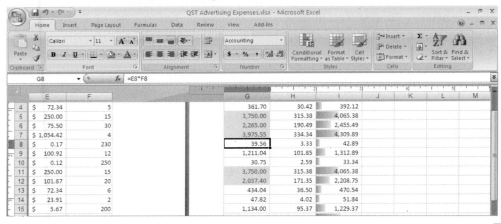

Naming and Moving a Sheet

By default, an Excel workbook initially contains three worksheets, named Sheet1, Sheet2, and Sheet3. The sheet name appears on the sheet tab at the bottom of the worksheet. When you open a workbook, the first worksheet is the active sheet. To move from sheet to sheet, you can click any sheet tab at the bottom of the worksheet window. The sheet tab scrolling buttons, located to the left of the sheet tabs, are useful when a workbook contains too many sheet tabs to display at once. To make it easier to identify the sheets in a workbook, you can rename each sheet and add color to the tabs. You can also organize them in a logical way. For instance, to better track performance goals, you could name each workbook sheet for an individual salesperson, and you could move the sheets so they appeared in alphabetical order. ▰▰▰▰ In the current worksheet, Sheet1 contains information on advertising expenses. Sheet2 contains an advertising budget, and Sheet3 contains no data. You want to name the two sheets in the workbook to reflect their contents, add color to a sheet tab to easily distinguish one from the other, and change their order.

STEPS

1. **Click the Sheet2 tab**

   Sheet2 becomes active, appearing in front of the Sheet1 tab; this is the worksheet that contains the budgeted expenses. See Figure C-20.

QUICK TIP

You can also rename a sheet by right-clicking the tab, clicking Rename on the shortcut menu, typing the new name, then pressing [Enter].

2. **Click the Sheet1 tab**

   Sheet1, which contains the actual expenses, becomes active again.

▶ 3. **Double-click the Sheet2 tab, type Budget, then press [Enter]**

   The new name for Sheet2 automatically replaces the default name on the tab. Worksheet names can have up to 31 characters, including spaces and punctuation.

QUICK TIP

To delete a work-sheet, select the worksheet you want to delete, click the Delete button list arrow in the Cells group, then click Delete Sheet. To insert a worksheet, click the Insert Worksheet button 🗗 to the right of the sheet tabs.

▶ 4. **Right-click the Budget tab, point to Tab Color on the shortcut menu, then click the Bright Green, Accent 4, Lighter 80% color (second row, third column from the right) as shown in Figure C-21**

   The tab color changes to a bright green gradient.

5. **Double-click the Sheet1 tab, type Actual, then press [Enter]**

   Notice that the color of the Budget tab changes depending on whether it is the active tab; when the Actual tab is active, the color of the Budget tab changes to solid bright green. You decide to rearrange the order of the sheets, so that the Budget tab is to the left of the Actual tab.

6. **Click the Budget sheet tab, hold down the mouse button, drag it to the left of the Actual sheet tab, as shown in Figure C-22, then release the mouse button**

   As you drag, the pointer changes to ▧, the sheet relocation pointer, and a small, black triangle shows its position. The first sheet in the workbook is now the Budget sheet. See Figure C-23. To see hidden sheets, click the far left tab scrolling button to display the first sheet tab; click the far right navigation button to display the last sheet tab. The left and right buttons move one sheet in their respective directions.

7. **Click the Actual sheet tab, then enter your name in the left-side header box**

8. **Click the Page Layout tab on the Ribbon, click the Orientation button in the Page Setup group, then click Landscape**

9. **Press [Ctrl][Home], then save your work**

FIGURE C-20: Sheet tabs in workbook

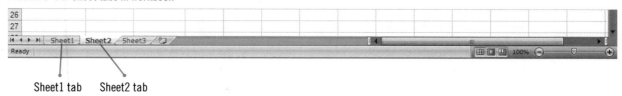

Sheet1 tab   Sheet2 tab

FIGURE C-21: Tab Color palette

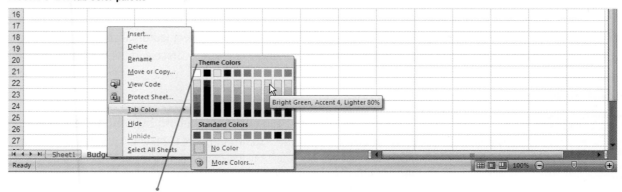

Available colors

FIGURE C-22: Sheet during move

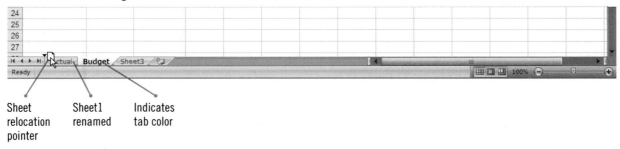

Sheet relocation pointer

Sheet1 renamed

Indicates tab color

FIGURE C-23: Reordered sheets

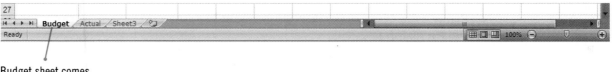

Budget sheet comes before Actual sheet

Copying worksheets

There are times when you may want to copy a worksheet. For example, a workbook might contain a sheet with Quarter 1 expenses, and you want to use that sheet as the basis for a sheet containing Quarter 2 expenses. To copy a sheet within the same workbook, press and hold [Ctrl], drag the sheet tab to the desired tab location, release the mouse button, then release [Ctrl]. A duplicate sheet appears with the same name as the copied sheet followed by "(2)" indicating it is a copy. You can then rename the sheet to a more meaningful name. To copy a sheet to a different workbook, both the source and destination workbooks must be open. Select the sheet to copy or move, right-click the sheet tab, then click Move or Copy in the shortcut menu. Complete the information in the Move or Copy dialog box. Be sure to click the Create a copy check box if you are copying rather than moving the worksheet. Carefully check your calculation results whenever you move or copy a worksheet.

Checking Spelling

Excel includes a spelling checker to help you ensure that the words in your worksheet are spelled correctly. The spelling checker scans your worksheet, displays words it doesn't find in its built-in dictionary, and suggests replacements when they are available. To check other sheets in a multiple-sheet workbook, you need to display each sheet and run the spelling checker again. Because the built-in dictionary cannot possibly include all the words that anyone needs, you can add words to the dictionary, such as your company name, an acronym, or an unusual technical term. Once you add a word or term, the spelling checker will no longer consider that word misspelled. Any words you've added to the dictionary using Word, Access, or PowerPoint are also available in Excel. Another feature, AutoCorrect, automatically corrects some spelling errors as you type. ▨▨▨ Before you distribute this workbook to Grace and the marketing managers, you check its spelling.

STEPS

QUICK TIP

The Spelling dialog box lists the name of the language currently being used in its title bar.

1. **Click the Review tab on the Ribbon, then click the Spelling button in the Proofing group**

   The Spelling: English (U.S.) dialog box opens, as shown in Figure C-24, with "iPodAds" selected as the first misspelled word in the worksheet. For any word, you have the option to Ignore this case of the flagged word, Ignore All cases of the flagged word, or Add the word to the dictionary.

2. **Click Ignore All**

   Next, the spelling checker finds the word "Contepts" and suggests "Concepts" as an alternative.

QUICK TIP

To customize AutoCorrect to add or remove automatic corrections, click the Office button, click Excel Options, click Proofing, click AutoCorrect Options, choose options in the AutoCorrect dialog box for how you want this feature to work, then click OK.

3. **Verify that the word Concepts is selected in the Suggestions list, then click Change**

   When no more incorrect words are found, Excel displays a message indicating that all the words on the worksheet have been checked.

4. **Click OK**

5. **Click the Home tab, click Find & Select in the Editing group, then click Replace**

   The Find and Replace dialog box opens. You can use this dialog box to replace a word or phrase. It might be a misspelling that the Spelling Checker didn't recognize as wrong, such as a word that wasn't corrected with the spelling checker, or simply something you want to change. Grace has just told you that each instance of 'Billboard' in the worksheet should be changed to 'Sign'.

6. **Type Billboard in the Find what text box, press [Tab], then type Sign in the Replace with text box**

   Compare your dialog box to Figure C-25.

7. **Click Replace All, click OK to close the warning box, then click Close to close the Find and Replace dialog box**

   Excel has made two replacements.

QUICK TIP

The Fit to option button is on the Page tab of the Page Setup dialog box.

8. **Save your work, view the Actual sheet in Print Preview, click the Page Setup button on the Ribbon, fit the worksheet to one page, then return to Print Preview**

   Compare your worksheet to Figure C-26.

9. **Print one copy of the worksheet, close it, then exit Excel**

E-mailing a workbook

You can send an entire workbook from within Excel using your installed email program, such as Microsoft Office Outlook or Outlook Express. To send a workbook as an e-mail message attachment, open the workbook, click the Office button 📋, point to Send, then click E-mail. An email message opens with the workbook automatically attached; the filename appears in the Attached field. Complete the To and optional Cc fields, include a message if you wish, then click Send.

FIGURE C-24: Spelling: English dialog box

Misspelled word

Suggested replacements for misspelled word

Click to ignore all occurrences of misspelled word

Click to add word to dictionary

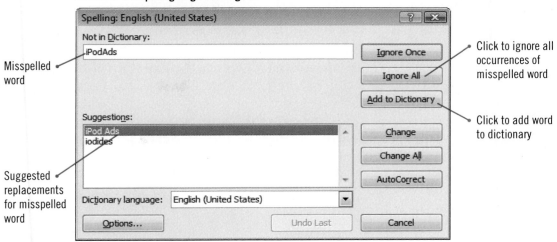

FIGURE C-25: Find and Replace dialog box

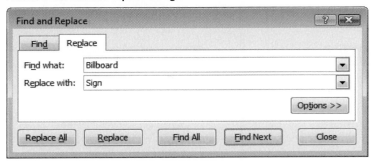

FIGURE C-26: Viewing worksheet in Print Preview

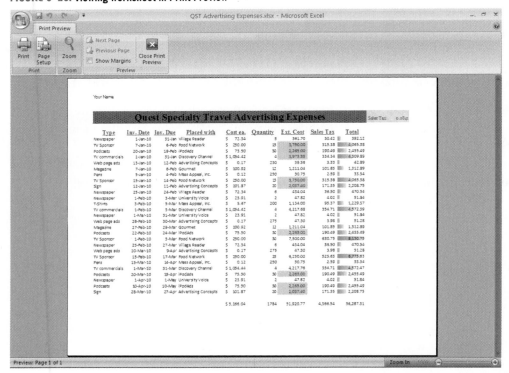

Practice

▼ CONCEPTS REVIEW

Label each element of the Excel worksheet window shown in Figure C-27.

FIGURE C-27

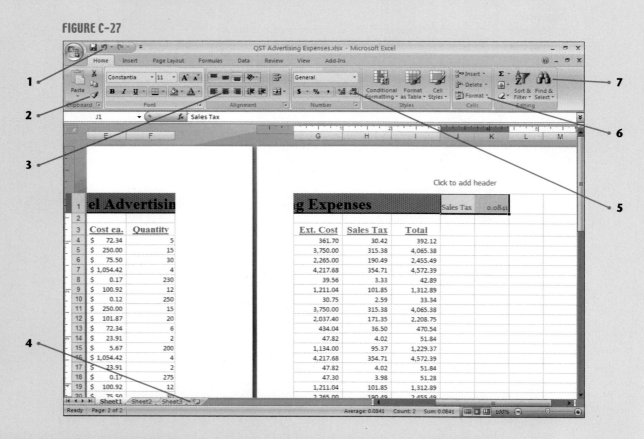

Match each command or button with the statement that best describes it.

8. **Spelling & Grammar button**
9. [image]
10. [image]
11. **[Ctrl][Home]**
12. **Conditional Formatting**
13. **[Delete]**

a. Erases the contents of a cell
b. Changes formatting of a cell based on cell contents
c. Moves cell pointer to cell A1
d. Checks for apparent misspellings in a worksheet
e. Displays options for erasing the contents of a cell
f. Centers cell contents over multiple cells

Select the best answer from the list of choices.

14. **Which of the following is an example of an accounting number format?**
    a. 5555
    b. $5,555.55
    c. 55.55%
    d. 5,555.55

15. **What feature is used to delete a conditional formatting rule?**
    a. Rule Reminder
    b. Conditional Rule Manager
    c. Rule Manager
    d. Format Manager

16. **Which button removes boldface formatting from selected cells?**
    a. *I*
    b. **B**
    c. (decimal button)
    d. **B**

17. **Which button opens the Format Cells dialog box?**
    a. (dialog launcher)
    b. (format painter)
    c. **B**
    d. (undo)

18. **What is the name of the feature used to resize a column to accommodate its widest entry?**
    a. AutoFormat
    b. AutoFit
    c. AutoResize
    d. AutoRefit

19. **Which button increases the number of decimal places in selected cells?**
    a. (indent button)
    b. (decrease decimal)
    c. (increase decimal)
    d. (indent button)

20. **Which button applies multiple formatting styles to selected cells?**
    a. (undo)
    b. (format painter)
    c. (cell styles)
    d. (paste)

▼ SKILLS REVIEW

1. **Format values.**
   a. Start Excel, open the file EX C-2.xlsx from the drive and folder where you store your Data Files, then save it as **Health Insurance Premiums**.
   b. Enter a formula in cell B10 that totals the number of employees.
   c. Create a formula in cell C5 that calculates the monthly insurance premium for the accounting department. (*Hint*: Make sure you use the correct type of cell reference in the formula. To calculate the monthly premium, multiply the number of employees by the monthly premium.)
   d. Copy the formula in cell C5 to the range C6:C10.
   e. Format the range C5:C10 using the Accounting Number Format.
   f. Change the format of the range C6:C9 to the Comma Style.
   g. Reduce the number of decimals to 0 in cell B14, using a button in the Number group.
   h. Save your work.

2. **Change fonts and font sizes.**
   a. Select the range of cells containing the column labels (in row 4).
   b. Change the font of the selection to Times New Roman.
   c. Increase the font size of the selection to 12 points.
   d. Increase the font size of the label in cell A1 to 14 points.
   e. Save your changes.

3. **Change attributes and alignment.**
   a. Apply the bold and italic attributes to the worksheet title **QST Corporate Office**.
   b. Use the Merge & Center button to center the Health Insurance Premiums label over columns A through C.
   c. Apply the italic attribute to the Health Insurance Premiums label.
   d. Add the bold attribute to the labels in row 4.
   e. Use the Format Painter to copy the format in cell A4 to the range A5:A10.
   f. Apply the format in cell C10 to cell B14.

g. Change the alignment of cell A10 to Align Right.

h. Select the range of cells containing the column titles, then center them.

i. Remove the italic attribute from the Health Insurance Premiums label, then increase the font size to 14.

j. Move the Health Insurance Premiums label to cell A3, then add the bold and underline attributes.

k. Add a bottom double border to the cell in the last cell in the Total column, above the calculated total value.

l. Save your changes.

4. **Adjust column width.**

a. Resize column C to a width of 10.71.

b. Use the AutoFit feature to resize columns A and B.

c. Clear the contents of cell A13 (do not delete the cell).

d. Change the text in cell A14 to **Monthly Insurance Premium**, then change the width of the column to **25**.

e. Resize any remaining columns as needed to view all the data.

f. Save your changes.

5. **Insert and delete rows and columns.**

a. Insert a new row between rows 5 and 6.

b. Add a new department—**Humanitarian Aid**—in the newly inserted row. Enter **5** for the Employees.

c. Copy the formula in cell C5 to C6.

d. Add the following comment to cell A6: **New department**. Display the comment, then drag to move it out of the way, if necessary.

e. Add a new column between the Department and Employees columns with the title **Family Coverage**, then resize the column using AutoFit.

f. Delete the Legal row.

g. Move the value in cell C14 to B14.

h. Save your changes.

6. **Apply colors, patterns, and borders.**

a. Add an outside border around the range A4:D10.

b. Apply the Aqua, Accent 5, Lighter 80% fill color to the labels in the Department column (do not include the Total label).

c. Apply the Orange, Accent 6, Lighter 60% fill color to the range A4:D4.

d. Change the color of the font in the range A4:D4 to Red, Accent 2, Darker 25%.

e. Add a 12.5% Gray pattern style to cell A1.

f. Format the range A14:B14 with a pattern style of Thin Diagonal Stripes, a fill color of Dark Blue, Text 2, Lighter 40%, then apply the bold attribute.

g. Save your changes.

7. **Apply conditional formatting.**

a. Select the range D5:D9, then create a conditional format that changes cell contents to green fill with dark green text if the value is between 4000 and 7000.

b. Select the range C5:C9, then create a conditional format that changes cell contents to red text if the number of employees exceeds 10.

c. Select the range C5:C9, then create a blue data bar.

d. Use the Rule Manager to modify the conditional format in cell C5 to display the cell contents in bold red text.

e. Copy the format in cell C5 to the range in C6:C9.

f. Merge and center the title over columns A-D.

8. **Name and move a sheet.**

a. Name the Sheet 1 tab **Insurance Data**.

b. Name the Sheet 3 tab **Employee Data**.

c. Change the Insurance Data tab color to Red, Accent 2, Lighter 40%.

d. Change the Employee Data tab color to Aqua, Accent 5, Lighter 40%.

▼ SKILLS REVIEW (CONTINUED)

   e. Move the Employee Data sheet so it comes after (to the right of) the Insurance Data sheet.

   f. Make the Insurance Data sheet active, enter your name in cell A20, then save your work.

9. Check spelling.

   a. Move the cell pointer to cell A1.

   b. Use the Find & Select feature to replace the Accounting label in cell A5 with Accounting/Legal.

   c. Check the spelling in the worksheet using the spelling checker, and correct any spelling errors.

   d. Save your changes.

   e. Preview and print the Insurance Data sheet, compare your work to Figure C-28, then close the workbook and exit Excel.

FIGURE C-28

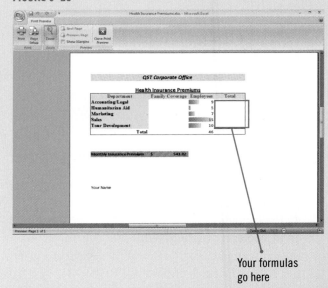

Your formulas go here

▼ INDEPENDENT CHALLENGE 1

You run a freelance accounting business, and one of your newest clients is Lovely Locks, a small beauty salon. Now that you've converted the salon's accounting records to Excel, the manager would like you to work on an analysis of the inventory. Although more items will be added later, the worksheet has enough items for you to begin your modifications.

   a. Start Excel, open the file EX C-3.xlsx from the drive and folder where you store your Data Files, then save it as **Lovely Locks Inventory**.

   b. Create a formula in cell E4 that calculates the value of the on-hand inventory, based on the price paid for the item, in cell B4. Format the cell in the Comma Style.

   c. Use an absolute reference to calculate the sale price of the item in cell F4, using the markup value shown in cell I1.

   d. Copy the formulas created above into the range E5:F14; first convert any necessary cell references to absolute so that the formulas work correctly.

   e. Add the bold attribute to the column headings, and italicize the items in column A.

   f. Make sure all columns are wide enough to display the data and headings.

   g. Format the Sale Price column so it displays the Accounting Number Format with two decimal places.

   h. Change the Price Paid column so it displays the Comma style with two decimal places.

   i. Add a row under #2 Curlers for **Nail files**, price paid **$0.31**, sold individually **(each)**, with **56** on hand.

   j. Verify that all the formulas in the worksheet are correct. Adjust any items as needed, and check the spelling.

   k. Use conditional formatting to call attention to items with a quantity of less than 20 on hand. Use yellow fill with dark yellow text.

   l. Create an icon set for the range D4:D15 using the symbols of your choosing.

   m. Add an outside border around the data in the Item column.

   n. Delete the row containing the Pins item.

   o. Enter your name in an empty cell below the data, then save the file.

   p. Preview and print the worksheet, compare your work to the sample of page 1 shown in Figure C-29, close the workbook, then exit Excel.

FIGURE C-29

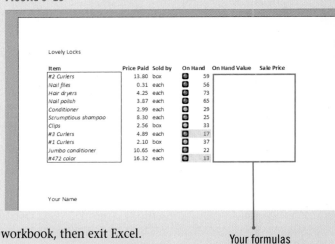

Your formulas go here

▼ INDEPENDENT CHALLENGE 2

You volunteer several hours each week with the Assistance League of South Bend, and are in charge of maintaining the membership list. You're currently planning a mailing campaign to members in certain regions of the city. You also want to create renewal letters for members whose membership expires soon. You decide to format the list to enhance the appearance of the worksheet and make your upcoming tasks easier to plan.

a. Start Excel, open the file EX C-4.xlsx from the drive and folder where you store your Data Files, then save it as **South Bend Assistance League**.

b. Remove any blank columns.

c. Create a conditional format in the Zip Code column so that entries greater than 46649 appear in light red fill with dark red text.

d. Make all columns wide enough to fit their data and headings.

e. Use formatting enhancements, such as fonts, font sizes, and text attributes, to make the worksheet more attractive.

f. Center-align the column labels.

g. Use conditional formatting so that entries for Year of Membership Expiration that are between 2011 and 2013 appear in a bold, contrasting color.

h. Adjust any items as necessary, then check the spelling.

i. Change the name of the Sheet 1 tab to one that reflects the sheet's contents, then add a tab color of your choice.

j. Enter your name in an empty cell, then save your work.

k. Before printing, preview the worksheet, make any final changes you think necessary, then print a copy. Compare your work to the sample shown in Figure C-30.

l. Close the workbook, then exit Excel.

FIGURE C-30

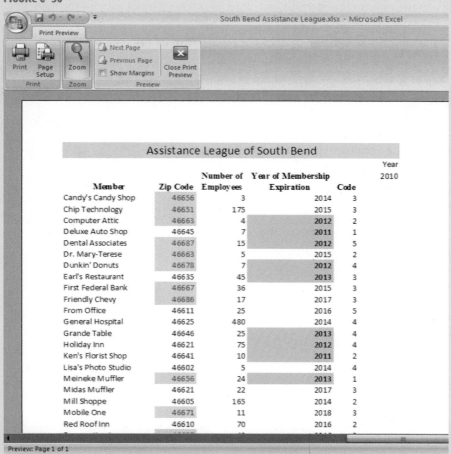

▼ INDEPENDENT CHALLENGE 3

Fine Line Writing Instruments is a Chicago-based company that manufactures high-quality pens and markers. As the finance manager, one of your responsibilities is to analyze the monthly reports from your five district sales offices. Your boss, Joanne Bennington, has just asked you to prepare a quarterly sales report for an upcoming meeting. Because several top executives will be attending this meeting, Joanne reminds you that the report must look professional. In particular, she asks you to emphasize the company's surge in profits during the last month and to highlight the fact that the Northeastern district continues to outpace the other districts.

a. Plan a worksheet that shows the company's sales during the first quarter. Assume that all pens are the same price. Make sure you plan to include:

- The number of pens sold (units sold) and the associated revenues (total sales) for each of the five district sales offices. The five sales districts are: Northeastern, Midwestern, Southeastern, Southern, and Western.
- Calculations that show month-by-month totals for January, February, and March, and a three-month cumulative total.
- Calculations that show each district's share of sales (percent of Total Sales).
- Labels that reflect the month-by-month data as well as the cumulative data.
- Formatting enhancements and data bars that emphasize the recent month's sales surge and the Northeastern district's sales leadership.

b. Ask yourself the following questions about the organization and formatting of the worksheet: What worksheet title and labels do you need, and where should they appear? How can you calculate the totals? What formulas can you copy to save time and keystrokes? Do any of these formulas need to use an absolute reference? How do you show dollar amounts? What information should be shown in bold? Do you need to use more than one font? Should you use more than one point size?

c. Start Excel, then save a new, blank workbook as **Fine Line Writing Instruments** to the drive and folder where you store your Data Files.

d. Build the worksheet with your own price and sales data. Enter the titles and labels first, then enter the numbers and formulas. You can use the information in Table C-4 to get started.

e. Adjust the column widths as necessary.

f. Change the height of row 1 to 33 points.

g. Format labels and values, and change the attributes and alignment if necessary.

h. Resize columns and adjust the formatting as necessary.

i. Add data bars for the monthly Units Sold columns.

j. Add a column that calculates a 25% increase in sales dollars. Use an absolute cell reference in this calculation. (*Hint*: Make sure the current formatting is applied to the new information.)

TABLE C-4

Fine Line Writing Instruments											
1st Quarter Sales Report											
		January		February		March		Total			
Office	Price	Units Sold	Sales	Units Sold	Sales	Units Sold	Sales	Units Sold	Sales		
Northeastern											
Midwestern											
Southeastern											
Southern											
Western											

▼ INDEPENDENT CHALLENGE 3 (CONTINUED)

Advanced Challenge Exercise

- Use the Format as Table feature to add a table style of your choice to the data.
- Insert a clip art image related to pens in an appropriate location, adjusting its size and position as necessary.
- Save your work.

l. Enter your name in an empty cell.

m. Check the spelling in the workbook, then save your work.

n. Preview, compare your work to Figure C-31, then print the worksheet in landscape orientation.

o. Close the workbook file, then exit Excel.

FIGURE C-31

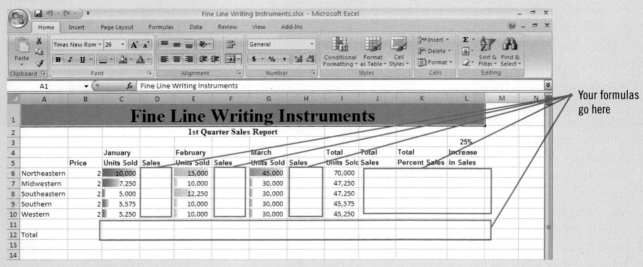

▼ REAL LIFE INDEPENDENT CHALLENGE

***Note*: This project requires an Internet connection.**

You are saving up to take an international trip you have always dreamed about. You plan to visit seven different countries over the course of two months, and budgeting an identical spending allowance in each country. To help work toward your goal, you want to create a worksheet that calculates the amount of native currency you will have in each country. You want the workbook to reflect the currency information for each country.

a. Start Excel, then save a new, blank workbook as **World Tour Budget** to the drive and folder where you store your Data Files.

b. Think of seven countries you would like to visit, then enter column and row labels for your worksheet. (*Hint*: You may wish to include row labels for each country, plus column labels for the country, the $1 equivalent in native currency, the total amount of native currency you'll have in each country, and the name of each country's monetary unit.)

c. Decide how much money you want to bring to each country (for example, $1000), and enter that in the worksheet.

d. Use your favorite search engine to find your own information sources on currency conversions for the countries you plan to visit.

e. Enter the cash equivalent to **$1** in U.S. dollars for each country in your list. Also include the name of the currency used in each country.

f. Create an equation that calculates the amount of native currency you will have in each country, using an absolute cell reference in the formula.

g. Format the entries in column B with three decimal places and in column C with two decimal places, using the correct currency unit for each country. (*Hint*: Use the Number tab in the Format cells dialog box; choose the appropriate currency format from the Symbol list, using two decimal places.)

h. Create a conditional format that changes the font attributes of the calculated amount in the "$1,000 US" column to bold and red if the amount exceeds **500 units** of the local currency.

i. Merge and center the title over the column headings.

j. Add any formatting attributes to the column headings, and resize the columns as necessary.

k. Add a background color to the title.

Advanced Challenge Exercise

- Modify the conditional format in the "$1,000 US" column so that entries between 1500 and 3999 display in red, boldface type, and entries above 4000 appear in blue, boldface type.
- Delete all the unused sheets in the workbook.
- Save your work as **World Tour Budget ACE** where you store your Data Files.
- If you have access to an e-mail account, e-mail this workbook to your instructor as an attachment.

l. Enter your name in the header of the worksheet.

m. Spell check, save, preview and compare your work to Figure C-32, then print the worksheet.

n. Close the workbook and exit Excel.

FIGURE C-32

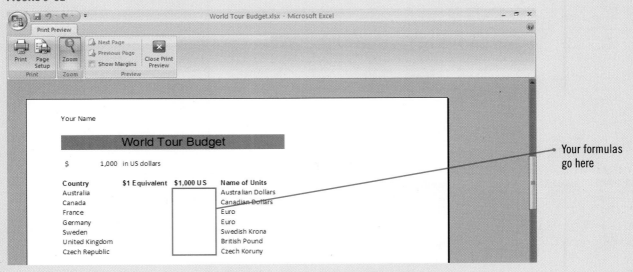

Your formulas go here

▼ VISUAL WORKSHOP

Open the file EX C-5.xlsx from the drive and folder where you store your Data Files, then save it as **Top Notch Personnel**. Use the skills you learned in this unit to format the worksheet so it looks like the one shown in Figure C-33. Create a conditional format in the Level column so that entries greater than 3 appear in red text. Create an additional conditional format in the Review Cycle column so that any value equal to 4 appears in green bold text. Replace the Accounting department label with Legal. (*Hint*: The only additional font used in this exercise is 16-point Times New Roman in row 1.) Enter your name in cell A25, check the spelling in the worksheet, then save and print your work.

FIGURE C-33

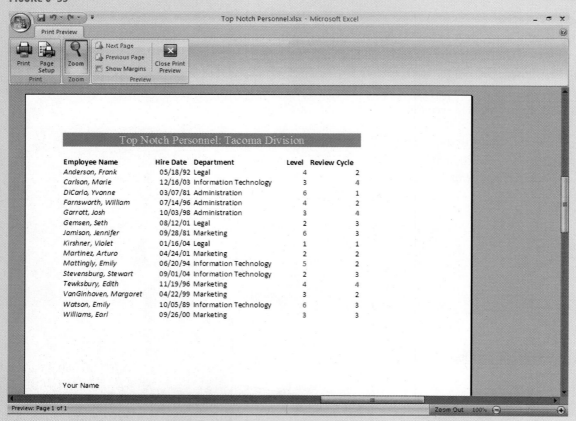

Working with Charts

Worksheets provide an effective layout for calculating and organizing data, but the grid layout is not always the best format for presenting your work to others. To display information so it's easier to interpret, you can create a chart. **Charts**, often called graphs, present information in a pictorial format, making it easier to see patterns, trends, and relationships. In this unit, you learn how to create a chart, how to edit the chart and change the chart type, how to add text annotations and arrows, and how to preview and print the chart. At the upcoming annual meeting, Grace Wong wants to emphasize a growth trend at Quest Specialty Travel. She asks you to create a chart showing the increase in company revenues over the past four quarters.

OBJECTIVES

Plan a chart

Create a chart

Move and resize a chart

Change the chart design

Change the chart layout

Format a chart

Annotate and draw on a chart

Create a pie chart

Planning a Chart

Before creating a chart, you need to plan the information you want your chart to show and how you want it to look. Planning ahead helps you to decide what type of chart to create and how to organize the data. Understanding the parts of a chart makes it easier to format it and change specific elements so that the chart best illustrates your data. In preparation for creating the chart for Grace's presentation, you identify your goals for the chart and plan it.

Use the following guidelines to plan the chart:

*   **Determine the purpose of the chart and identify the data relationships you want to communicate graphically**

    You want to create a chart that shows quarterly revenues throughout Quest Specialty Travel. This worksheet data is shown in Figure D-1. In the first quarter, the Marketing department launched an international advertising campaign. The campaign resulted in greatly increased sales starting in the second quarter. You want to create a chart for the annual meeting that illustrates the increase and compares sales across the quarters for each location.

*   **Determine the results you want to see, and decide which chart type is most appropriate**

    Different chart types display data in distinctive ways. For example, a pie chart compares parts to the whole, so it's useful for showing what proportion of a budget amount was spent on print ads relative to what was spent on direct mail or radio commercials. A line chart, in contrast, is best for showing trends over time. To choose the best chart type for your data, you should first decide how you want your data displayed and interpreted. Table D-1 describes several different types of charts you can create in Excel and their corresponding buttons on the Insert tab of the Ribbon. Because you want to compare QST revenues in multiple locations over a period of four quarters, you decide to use a column chart.

*   **Identify the worksheet data you want the chart to illustrate**

    Sometimes you use all the data in a worksheet to create a chart, while at other times you may need to select a range within the sheet. The worksheet from which you are creating your chart contains revenue data for the past year. You will need to use all the quarterly data contained in the worksheet.

*   **Understand the elements of a chart**

    The chart shown in Figure D-2 contains basic elements of a chart. In the figure, QST locations are on the horizontal axis (also called the **x-axis**) and monthly sales are on the vertical axis (also called the **y-axis**). The horizontal axis is also called the **category axis** because it often contains the names of data groups, such as locations, months, or years. The vertical axis is also called the **value axis** because it often contains numerical values that help you interpret the size of chart elements. (3-D charts also contain a **z-axis**, for comparing data across both categories and values.) The area inside the horizontal and vertical axes is the **plot area**. The **tick marks** at the left edge of the vertical axis and **gridlines** (extending across the plot area) create a scale of measure for each value. Each value in a cell you select for your chart is a **data point**. In any chart, a **data marker** visually represents each data point, which in this case is a column. A collection of related data points is a **data series**. In this chart, there are four data series (Quarter 1, Quarter 2, Quarter 3, and Quarter 4), so you include a **legend** to make it easy to identify them.

FIGURE D-1: Worksheet containing revenue data

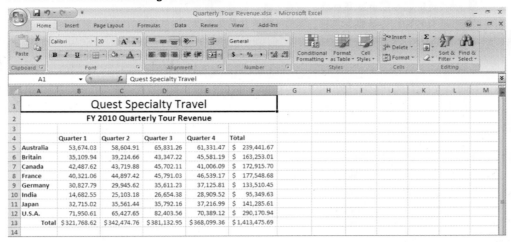

FIGURE D-2: Chart elements

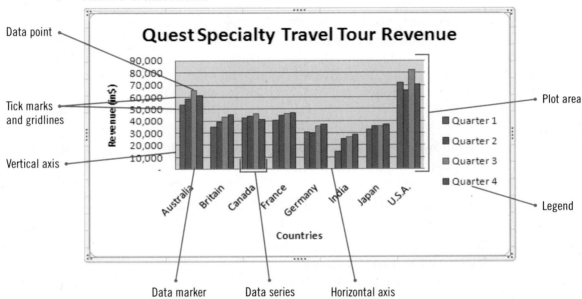

TABLE D-1: Common chart types

type	button	description
Column		Compares distinct object levels using a vertical format; the Excel default; sometimes referred to as a bar chart in other spreadsheet programs
Line		Compares trends over even time intervals; looks similar to an area chart, but does not emphasize total
Pie		Compares sizes of pieces as part of a whole; used for a single series of numbers
Bar		Compares distinct object levels using a horizontal format; sometimes referred to as a horizontal bar chart in other spreadsheet programs
Area		Shows how individual volume changes over time in relation to total volume
Scatter		Compares trends over uneven time or measurement intervals; used in scientific and engineering disciplines for trend spotting and extrapolation

Creating a Chart

To create a chart in Excel, you first select the range in a worksheet containing the data you want to chart. Once you've selected a range, you can use buttons on the Insert tab of the Ribbon to create and modify a chart. ▨▨▨▨ Using the worksheet containing the quarterly revenue data, you create a chart that shows the growth trend that occurred.

STEPS

1. **Start Excel, open the file EX D-1.xlsx from the drive and folder where you store your Data Files, then save it as Quarterly Tour Revenue**

   You want the chart to include the quarterly tour revenue figures, as well as quarter and country labels. You don't include the Total column and row because the quarterly figures make up the totals, and these figures would skew the chart.

2. **Select the range A4:E12, then click the Insert tab on the Ribbon**

   The Insert tab contains groups for inserting various types of objects, including charts. The Charts group includes buttons for each major chart type, plus an Other Charts button for additional chart types, such as stock charts for charting stock market data.

3. **Click the Column chart button, then click the Clustered Column button on the Column palette, as shown in Figure D-3**

   The chart is inserted in the center of the worksheet, and three contextual Chart Tools tabs open on the Ribbon: Design, Layout, and Format. On the Design tab, which is currently in front, you can quickly change the chart type, chart layout, and chart format and you can swap the data between the columns and rows. Currently, the countries are charted along the horizontal axis, with the quarterly revenues charted along the y-axis. This lets you easily compare quarterly revenues for each country.

4. **Click the Switch Row/Column button in the Data group on the Chart Tools Design tab**

   Clicking this button switches the data in the columns and rows, as shown in Figure D-4, so that the quarterly revenues are charted along the horizontal axis and the countries are plotted as the data points.

5. **Click the Undo button 🔄 on the Quick Access toolbar**

   The chart returns to its original configuration.

6. **Click the Chart Tools Layout tab, click the Chart Title button in the Labels group, then click Above Chart on the palette**

   A title placeholder appears above the chart.

7. **Click anywhere in the Chart Title text box, press [Ctrl][A] to select the text, type Quarterly Tour Revenue, then click anywhere in the chart to deselect the title**

   Adding a title helps identify the chart. This chart is known as an **embedded** chart because it's inserted directly in the current worksheet. The **sizing handles**, the small series of dots at the corners and sides of the chart's border, indicate that the chart is selected. See Figure D-5. Your chart might be in a different location on the worksheet and may look slightly different; you will move and resize it in the next lesson. Any time a chart is selected, as it is now, a blue border surrounds the worksheet data range, a purple border surrounds the row labels, and a green border surrounds the column labels. Embedding a chart in the current sheet is the default selection when creating a chart, but you can also place a chart on a different sheet in the workbook, or on a newly created chart sheet. A **chart sheet** is a sheet in a workbook that contains only a chart, which is linked to the workbook data.

8. **Save your work**

FIGURE D-3: Column chart palette

Clustered Column chart type

Column chart types

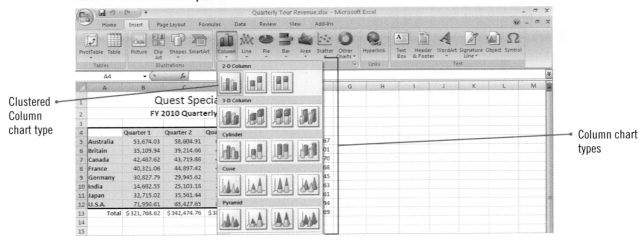

FIGURE D-4: Clustered Column chart with rows and columns switched

Undo button

Switch Row/Column button

Column labels

Row labels

Data range

Selected chart object

Chart Tools tabs

Legend

Quarter labels on horizontal axis

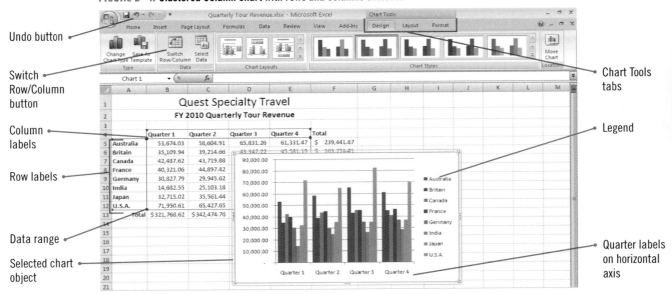

FIGURE D-5: Chart with rows and columns restored and title added

Title

Sizing handles

Country labels on horizontal axis

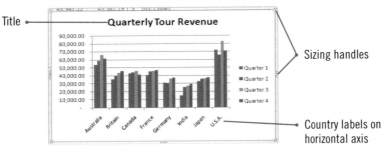

Using the contextual Chart Tools tabs

When a chart is selected, the three contextual Chart Tools tabs (Design, Layout, and Format) appear on the Ribbon. These tabs help guide you through developing and perfecting your chart. Using the Design tab, you can change overall color schemes and positioning of objects within the chart as well as the data range and configuration used for the chart. The Layout tab is used to add and modify chart elements, such as titles and labels, and for adding graphics, such as pictures, shapes, and text boxes. The Format tab lets you format objects such as shapes and text, arrange multiple objects so they are layered attractively, and resize any object to exact specifications. While these tabs organize chart tools in a logical order, it is not necessary to use them in the order in which they appear. In other words, you can jump from the Design tab to the Format tab, back to Design, then to Layout, if you wish.

Moving and Resizing a Chart

Charts are graphics, or drawn objects, and are not located in a specific cell or at a specific range address. An **object** is an independent element on a worksheet. You can select an object by clicking within its borders; sizing handles around the object indicate it is selected. You can move a selected chart object anywhere on a worksheet without affecting formulas or data in the worksheet. However, any data changed in the worksheet is automatically updated in the chart. You can resize a chart to improve its appearance by dragging its sizing handles. You can even move a chart to a different sheet, and it will still reflect the original data. Chart objects contain other objects, such as a title and legend, which you can move and resize. In addition to repositioning chart elements to set locations using commands on the Layout tab, you can freely move any object using the mouse. Simply select it, then drag it or cut and paste it to a new location. When the mouse pointer hovers over any chart object, the name of the selected object appears on screen as a ScreenTip. You want to resize the chart, position it below the worksheet data, and move the legend.

STEPS

QUICK TIP
If you want to delete a chart, select it, then press [Delete].

1. **Make sure the chart is still selected, then position the pointer over the chart**

   The pointer shape ⁺ℛ indicates that you can move the chart object or use a sizing handle to resize it. For a table of commonly used graphic object pointers, refer to Table D-2.

TROUBLE
If you do not drag a blank area on the chart, you might inadvertently move a chart element instead of the whole chart; if this happens, undo the action and try again.

2. **Position ⁺ℛ on a blank area near the top left edge of the chart, press and hold the left mouse button, drag the chart until its upper left corner is at the upper left corner of cell A16, then release the mouse button**

   As you drag the chart, you can see an outline representing the chart's perimeter. The chart appears in the new location.

3. **Position the pointer on the right-middle sizing handle until it changes to ⟷, then drag the right edge of the chart to the right edge of column G**

   The chart is widened. See Figure D-6.

QUICK TIP
To resize a chart object to exact specification, select the object, click the Chart Tools Format tab on the Ribbon, then enter the desired height and width in the Size group.

4. **Position the pointer over the upper-middle sizing handle until it changes to ↕, then drag it to the top edge of row 15**

5. **Scroll down if necessary so row 26 is visible, position the pointer over the lower-middle sizing handle until it changes to ↕, then drag the bottom border of the chart to the bottom border of row 26**

   You can move any object on a chart. You want to align the top of the legend with the top of the plot area.

QUICK TIP
Although the sizing handles on objects within a chart look different from the sizing handles that surround a chart, they function the same way.

6. **Click the legend to select it, press and hold [Shift], drag the legend up using ⁺ℛ so the dotted outline is approximately ¼" above the top of the plot area, then release [Shift]**

   When you click the legend, sizing handles appear around it and "Legend" appears as a ScreenTip when the pointer hovers over the object. As you drag, a dotted outline of the legend border appears. Pressing and holding the [Shift] key holds the horizontal position of the legend as you move it vertically.

7. **Click cell A12, type United States, click the Enter button ✓ on the formula bar, use AutoFit to resize column A, then press [Ctrl][Home]**

   The axis label changes to reflect the updated cell contents, as shown in Figure D-7. Changing any data in the worksheet modifies corresponding text or values in the chart. Because the chart is no longer selected, the Chart Tools tabs no longer appear on the Ribbon.

8. **Save your work**

FIGURE D-6: Moved and resized chart

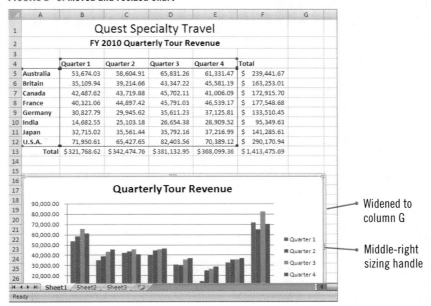

Widened to column G

Middle-right sizing handle

FIGURE D-7: Worksheet with modified legend and label

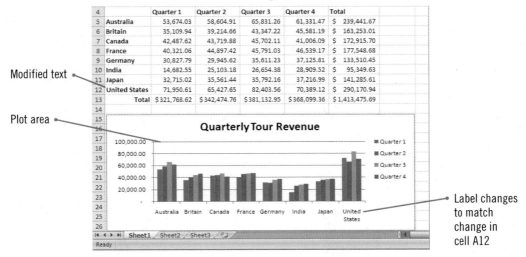

Modified text

Plot area

Label changes to match change in cell A12

TABLE D-2: Common graphic object pointers

name	pointer	use	name	pointer	use
Diagonal resizing	⤢ or ⤡	Change chart shape	I-beam	I	Edit chart text from corners
Draw	+	Create shapes	Move chart	⭭	Change chart location
Horizontal resizing	⇔	Change chart shape from left to right	Vertical resizing	↕	Change chart shape from top to bottom

Moving an embedded chart to a sheet

Suppose you have created an embedded chart that you decide would look better on a chart sheet. You can make this change without recreating the entire chart. To do so, first select the chart, click the Chart Tools Design tab, then click the Move Chart button in the Location group. The Move Chart dialog box opens. If the chart is embedded, click the New sheet option button, then click OK. If the chart is on its own sheet, click the Object in option button, then click OK.

Changing the Chart Design

Once you've created a chart, it's easy to modify the design. You can change data values in the worksheet, and the chart is automatically updated to reflect the new data. Each of the Chart Tools tabs can be used to make specific changes in a chart. Using the Chart Tools Design tab, you can change the chart type in the Type group, modify the data range and configuration in the Data group, change the layout of objects in the Chart Layouts group, choose from coordinating color schemes in the Chart Styles group, and move the location of the chart in the Location group. The layouts in the Chart Styles group offer preconfigured arrangements of objects in your chart, such as a legend, title, or gridlines; these layouts offer an alternative to manually making formatting and design changes. You look over your worksheet and realize the data for the United States in Quarter 2 and Quarter 4 is incorrect. After you correct this data, you want to see how the same data looks using different chart layouts and types.

STEPS

1. **Click cell C12, type 75432.29, press [Tab] twice, type 84295.27, then press [Enter]**
    In the worksheet, the United States entries for Quarter 2 and Quarter 4 reflect the increased sales figures. See Figure D-8. The totals in column F and row 13 are also updated.

QUICK TIP
You can see more layout choices by clicking the More button in the Chart Layouts group.

2. **Select the chart by clicking a blank area within the chart border, click the Chart Tools Design tab on the Ribbon, then click the Layout 3 button in the Chart Layouts group**
    The legend moves to the bottom of the chart. You prefer the original layout.

3. **Click the Undo button 🔄 on the Quick Access toolbar, then click the Change Chart Type button in the Type group**
    The Change Chart Type dialog box opens, as shown in Figure D-9, where you can choose from all available chart type categories and types. The left pane lists the available categories, and the right pane shows the individual chart types. An orange border surrounds the currently selected chart type.

QUICK TIP
If you plan to print a chart on a black-and-white printer, you may wish to change to a black-and-white chart style, so you can see how the output will look as you work.

4. **Click Bar in the left pane of the Change Chart Type dialog box, confirm that the Clustered Bar chart type is selected, then click OK**
    The column chart changes to a clustered bar chart. See Figure D-10. You look at the bar chart, then decide to see if the large increase in sales is more apparent if you use a three-dimensional column chart.

5. **Click the Change Chart Type button in the Type group, click Column in the left pane of the Change Chart Type dialog box, click 3-D Clustered Column (fourth from the left in the first row), then click OK**
    A three-dimensional column chart appears. You notice that the three-dimensional column format is more crowded than the two-dimensional format, but it gives you a sense of volume.

QUICK TIP
You can also use the Undo button on the Quick Access toolbar to return to a previous chart type.

6. **Click the Change Chart Type button in the Type group, click the Clustered Column button (first from the left, first row), then click OK**

7. **Click the Style 3 button in the Chart Styles group**
    The columns change to shades of blue. You prefer the previous color scheme.

8. **Click 🔄 in the Quick Access toolbar, then save your work**

Creating a Combination Chart

You can apply a chart type to an existing data series in a chart, to create a combination chart. In the existing chart, select the data series that you want plotted on a secondary axis, then open the Format dialog box (use the shortcut menu, or click Format Selection in the Current Selection group of the Format tab on the Ribbon). In the Format dialog box, click Series Options, if necessary, click the Secondary Axis option button under Plot Series On, then click Close. Click the Layout tab on the Ribbon, click Axes in the Axes group, then click the type of secondary axis you want and where you want it to appear. To finish, click the Change Chart Type button in the Type group on the Design tab, then select a chart type for the secondary axis.

FIGURE D-8: Worksheet with modified data

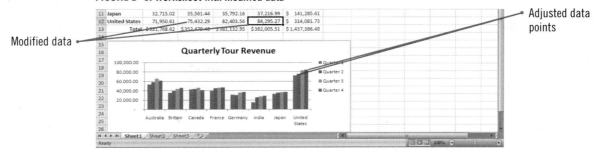

Modified data

Adjusted data points

FIGURE D-9: Change Chart Type dialog box

Currently selected chart type

Bar category

Chart type categories

FIGURE D-10: Column chart changed to bar chart

Change Chart Type button

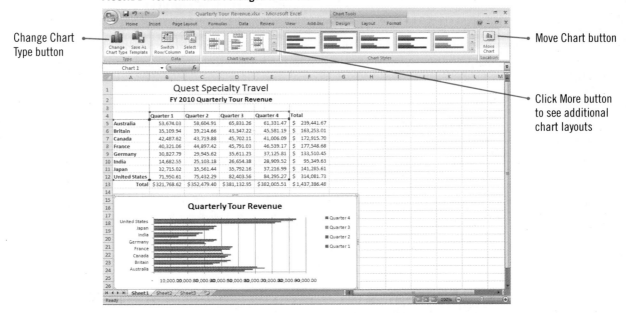

Move Chart button

Click More button to see additional chart layouts

Working with a 3-D chart

Excel includes true 3-D chart types as well as chart types formatted in 3-D. In a true 3-D chart, a third axis, called the **z-axis**, lets you compare data points across both categories and values. The z-axis runs along the depth of the chart, so it appears to advance from the back of the chart. To create a true 3-D chart, look for chart subtypes that begin with "3-D," such as 3-D Column. Charts that are formatted in 3-D contain only two axes but their graphics give the illusion of three-dimensionality. For example, the Clustered Column in 3-D chart displays columns in a 3-D format, but does not include a z-axis that you can modify. To create a chart that is only formatted in 3-D, look for chart subtypes that end with "in 3-D." In a 3-D chart, other

data series in the same chart can sometimes obscure columns or bars, but you can rotate the chart to obtain a better view. Right-click the chart, then click 3-D Rotation. The Format Chart Area dialog box opens, with the 3-D Rotation category active. This dialog box can also be used to modify fill, line, line style, shadow, and 3-D format. The 3-D Rotation options let you choose the orientation and perspective of the chart area, plot area, walls, and floor for a 3-D chart. You can use these rotation options to improve the appearance of plotted data within a chart. The 3-D Format options let you choose what three-dimensional effects you would like to apply to select chart elements. (Not all 3-D Format options are available on all charts.)

Changing the Chart Layout

Changing chart layout involves adding, removing, and modifying individual chart elements such as the chart title, plot area, gridlines, and data series. While the Chart Tools Design tab includes preconfigured chart layouts you can apply, the Chart Tools Layout tab makes it easy to create and modify individual chart objects. Using buttons on this tab, you can also add shapes and additional text to a chart, add and modify labels, change the display of axes, and modify the fill behind the plot area. You can also eliminate or change the look of gridlines. **Gridlines** are the horizontal and vertical lines in the chart that enable the eye to follow the value on an axis. You can create titles for the horizontal and vertical axes, add graphics, or add background color. You can even format the text you use in a chart. ▓▓▓▓ You want to make some layout changes in the chart, to make sure it's easy to interpret and improve its general appearance.

STEPS

1. **With the chart still selected, click the Chart Tools Layout tab on the Ribbon, click the Gridlines button in the Axes group, point to Primary Horizontal Gridlines, then click None**

   The gridlines that extend from the value axis tick marks across the chart's plot area are removed from the chart, as shown in Figure D-11.

2. **Click the Gridlines button in the Axes group, point to Primary Horizontal Gridlines, then click Major & Minor Gridlines**

   Both major and minor gridlines now appear in the chart. **Minor gridlines** show the values between the tick marks. You can change the color of the columns to better distinguish the data series.

3. **Click the Axis Titles button in the Labels group, point to Primary Horizontal Axis Title, click Title Below Axis, triple-click the axis title, then type Tour Countries**

   Descriptive text on the category axis helps readers understand the chart.

4. **Click the Axis Titles button in the Labels group, point to Primary Vertical Axis Title, then click Rotated Title**

   A placeholder for the vertical axis title is added to the left of the vertical axis.

5. **Triple-click the vertical axis title, then type Revenue (in $)**

   The text "Revenue (in $)" appears to the left of the vertical axis, as shown in Figure D-12.

6. **Right-click the horizontal axis labels ("Australia", "Britain", etc.), click the Font list on the Mini toolbar, click Times New Roman, click the Font Size list on the Mini toolbar, then click 8**

   The font of the horizontal axis text changes to Times New Roman, and the font size decreases, making more of the plot area visible.

7. **Right-click the vertical axis labels, click the Font list on the Mini toolbar, click Times New Roman, click the Font Size list on the Mini toolbar, then click 8**

8. **Right-click the chart title ("Quarterly Tour Revenue"), click Format Chart Title on the shortcut menu, click Border Color in the left pane, then click the Solid line option button in the right pane**

   Adding a solid border is the first step to creating a shadow box that surrounds the title. You can only add a shadow to a text box that has a border.

9. **Click Shadow in the left pane, click the Presets list arrow, click the Offset Diagonal Bottom Right (first row, first from the left) style in the Outer group, click Close, then save your work**

   A border with a drop shadow surrounds the title. Compare your work to Figure D-13.

FIGURE D-11: Gridlines removed from chart

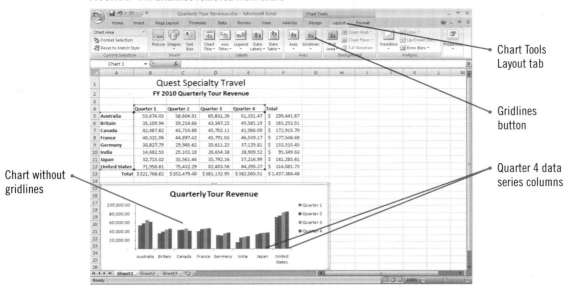

Chart Tools
Layout tab

Gridlines
button

Chart without
gridlines

Quarter 4 data
series columns

FIGURE D-12: Axes titles added to chart

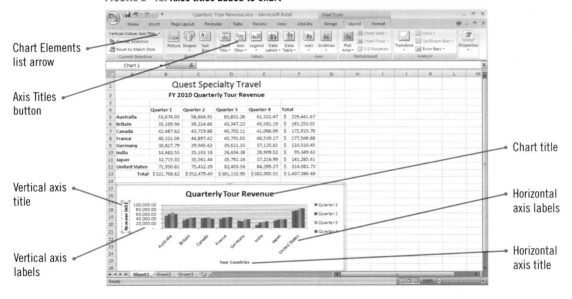

Chart Elements
list arrow

Axis Titles
button

Vertical axis
title

Vertical axis
labels

Chart title

Horizontal
axis labels

Horizontal
axis title

FIGURE D-13: Enhanced chart

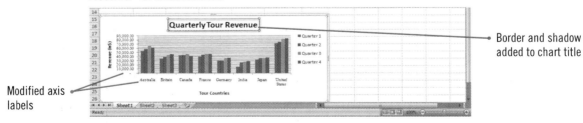

Modified axis
labels

Border and shadow
added to chart title

Adding data labels to a chart

There are times when your audience might benefit by seeing data labels on a chart. These labels can indicate the series name, category name, and/or the value of one or more data points. Once your chart is selected, you can add this information to your chart by clicking the Data Labels button in the Labels group in the Chart Tools Layout tab on the Ribbon. Once you have added the data labels, you can apply formatting to them or delete individual data labels. Delete individual data labels by clicking them until handles surround the set you want to delete, then press [Delete].

Formatting a Chart

Formatting a chart can make it easier to read and understand. Many formatting enhancements can be made using the Chart Tools Format tab. You can change colors in a specific data series or you can apply a style to a series using the Shape Styles group. Styles make it possible to apply multiple formats, such as an outline, fill color, and text color, all with a single click. You can also make individual selections of fill color, outline, and other effects using the Shape Styles group. WordArt, which lets you create curved or stylized text, can be created using the WordArt Styles group. ▧▧▧▧ You want to improve the appearance of the chart by creating titles for the horizontal and vertical axes and adding a drop shadow to the chart title.

STEPS

1. **With the chart selected, click the Chart Tools Format tab on the Ribbon, then click any column in the Quarter 4 data series**

    The Chart Tools Format tab opens, and handles surround each column in the Quarter 4 data series, indicating that the entire series is selected.

2. **Click the Format Selection button in the Current Selection group**

3. **Click Fill in the left pane of the Format Data Series dialog box, then click the Solid fill option button**

4. **Click the Color list arrow ▧ ▾, click Orange, Accent 6 (first row, tenth from the left) as shown in Figure D-14, then click Close**

    All the columns for the series become orange, and the legend changes to match the new color. You can also change the color of selected objects by applying a shape style.

5. **Click any column in the Quarter 3 data series**

    Handles surround each column in the Quarter 3 data series.

6. **Click the More button ▾ on the Shape Styles gallery, then hover the pointer over the Moderate Effect – Accent 3 button (fifth row, fourth from the left) as shown in Figure D-15**

7. **Click the Subtle Effect – Accent 3 button (fourth row, fourth from the left) in the palette**

    The color for the data series changes, as shown in Figure D-16.

8. **Save your work**

Changing alignment in axis text and titles

The buttons on the Chart Tools Layout tab provide a few options for aligning axis text and titles, but you can customize the position and rotation to exact specifications using the Format dialog box. You can modify the alignment of axis text to make it fit better within the plot area. With a chart selected, right-click the axis text you want to modify, then click Format Axis on the shortcut menu. The Format Axis dialog box opens for the selected element. Click Alignment, then select the appropriate option. You can create a custom angle by clicking the Text direction list arrow, clicking Horizontal, then selecting the number of degrees from the Custom angle text box. When you have made the desired changes, click Close.

FIGURE D-14: Format Data Series dialog box

Click Border Color to control line display

Click Shadow to control shadow settings

Orange, Accent 6

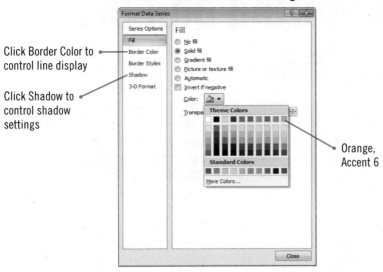

FIGURE D-15: Chart with formatted data series

Subtle Effect – Accent 3

Moderate Effect – Accent 3

In Step 6, point to this style

Live Preview of current style

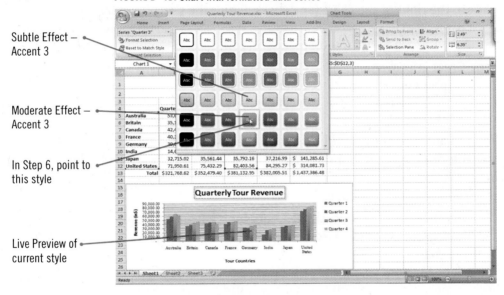

FIGURE D-16: Color of data series changed

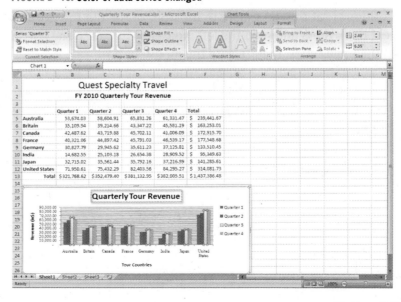

Annotating and Drawing on a Chart

You can add text annotations and graphics to a chart to point out critical information. **Text annotations** are labels that further describe your data. You can also draw lines and arrows that point to the exact locations you want to emphasize. Shapes such as arrows and boxes can be added from the Illustrations group on the Insert tab or from the Insert group on the Chart Tools Layout group on the Ribbon. These groups are also used to Insert pictures and clip art. ▰▰▰ You want to call attention to the India tour revenue increases, so you decide to add a text annotation and an arrow to this information in the chart.

STEPS

1. **Make sure the chart is selected, click the Chart Tools Layout tab, click the Text Box button in the Insert group, then move the pointer over the worksheet**

   The pointer changes to ↓, indicating that you can begin typing text by clicking.

2. **Click to the right of the chart (anywhere *outside* the chart boundary)**

   A text box is added to the worksheet, and the Drawing Tools Format tab opens, so that you can format the new object. First you need to type the text.

3. **Type Great improvement**

   The text appears in a selected text box on the worksheet and the chart is no longer selected, as shown in Figure D-17. Your text box may be in a different location; this is not important, because you'll move the annotation in the next step.

4. **Point to an edge of the text box so that the pointer changes to ⌖, drag the text box into the chart to the left of the chart title, as shown in Figure D-18, then release the mouse button**

   You want to add a simple arrow shape in the chart.

5. **Click the chart to select it, click the Chart Tools Layout tab, click the Shapes button in the Insert group, click the Arrow shape in the Lines category, then move the pointer over the chart**

   The pointer changes to ✛, and the status bar displays "Click and drag to insert an AutoShape." When you draw an arrow, the point farthest from where you start has the arrowhead. When ✛ is near the text box handles, the handles turn red. The red handles act as an anchor for the arrow.

6. **Position ✛ at the red square to the right of the t in the word "improvement" (in the text box), press and hold the left mouse button, drag the line to the Quarter 2 column in the India series, then release the mouse button**

   An arrow points to India's second quarter revenue, and the Drawing Tools Format tab displays options for working with this new object. You can resize, format, or delete it just like any other object in a chart.

7. **Click the Shape Outline list arrow in the Shape Styles group, point to Weight, then click 1½ pt**

   Compare your finished chart to Figure D-19.

8. **Save your work**

FIGURE D-17: **Text box added**

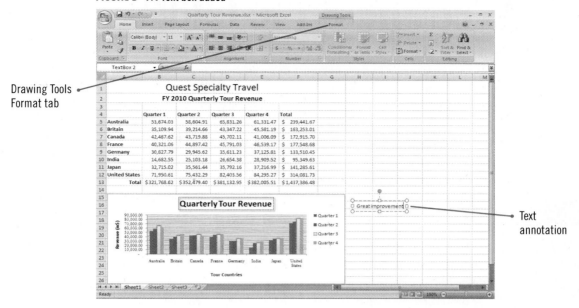

Drawing Tools
Format tab

Text
annotation

FIGURE D-18: **Text annotation on chart**

Text annotation

FIGURE D-19: **Drawn object added to chart**

Arrow added and
formatted

Adding SmartArt graphics

In addition to charts, annotations, and drawn objects, you can create a variety of diagrams using SmartArt. Diagram types include List, Process, Cycle, Hierarchy, Relationship, Matrix, and Pyramid. To insert SmartArt, click the SmartArt button in the Illustrations group on the Insert tab on the Ribbon. Click the category of SmartArt you want to create from the left panel, then click the style from the center panel. The right panel shows a sample of the selection you've chosen, as shown in Figure D-20. The diagram appears on the worksheet as an embedded object with sizing handles. An additional window opens where you can enter the diagram text.

FIGURE D-20: **Choose a SmartArt Graphic dialog box**

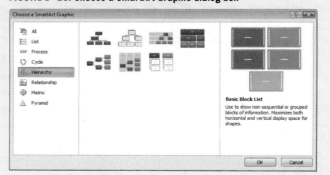

Creating a Pie Chart

You can create multiple charts based on the same worksheet data. While a column chart may illustrate certain important aspects of your worksheet data, you may find you want to create an additional chart to emphasize a different point. Depending on the type of chart you create, you have additional options for calling attention to trends and patterns. For example, if you create a pie chart, you can emphasize one data point by **exploding**, or pulling that slice away from, the pie chart. When you're ready to print a chart, you can preview it just as you do a worksheet, to check the output before committing it to paper. You can print a chart by itself or as part of the worksheet. At an upcoming meeting, Grace plans to discuss the total tour revenue and which countries need improvement. You want to create a pie chart she can use to illustrate total revenue. Finally, you want to print the worksheet and the charts.

STEPS

QUICK TIP

The Exploded Pie in 3-D button creates a pie chart in which all slices are exploded.

1. **Select the range A5:A12, press and hold [Ctrl], select the range F5:F12, click the Insert tab, click the Pie button in the Charts group, then click the Pie in 3-D button in the gallery**

   The new chart appears in the center of the worksheet. You can move the chart and quickly format it using a Chart Layout.

2. **Drag the chart so its top left corner is at the top left corner of cell G1, then click the Layout 2 button in the Chart Layouts group**

QUICK TIP

If the Format Data Series command displays instead of Format Data Point, double-click the data point for the slice you want exploded before right-clicking.

3. **Click the slice for the India data point, click again so it is the only data point selected, right-click, then click Format Data Point**

   The Format Data Point dialog box opens, as shown in Figure D-21. You can use the Point Explosion slider to control the distance a pie slice moves or you can type a value in the Point Explosion text box.

4. **Double-click 0 in the Point Explosion text box, type 40, then click Close**

   Compare your chart to Figure D-22. You decide to preview the chart and data before you print.

5. **Drag the bottom edge of the chart so it is close to the top of row 15, if necessary**

6. **Click cell A1, switch to Page Layout view, type Your Name in the left-hand header box, then click cell A1**

   You decide the chart and data would fit better on the page if they were printed in **landscape** orientation—that is, with the text running the long way on the page.

7. **Click the Page Layout tab, click the Orientation button in the Page Setup group, then click Landscape**

QUICK TIP

To preview only a chart, select the chart, click the Office button, point to Print, then click Print Preview.

8. **Open the Print Preview window, click the Page Setup button on the Print Preview tab, click the Fit to option button, make sure the contents are set to fit to 1 page wide by 1 page tall, then click OK**

   The data and chart are positioned horizontally on a single page. See Figure D-23. The printer you have selected may affect the appearance of your preview screen, and if you do not have a color printer installed, the image will appear in black & white.

9. **Click the Print button on the Print Preview tab, print one copy of the page, save and close the workbook, then exit Excel**

FIGURE D-21: **Format Data Point dialog box**

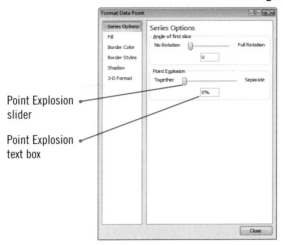

Point Explosion
slider

Point Explosion
text box

FIGURE D-22: **Exploded pie slice**

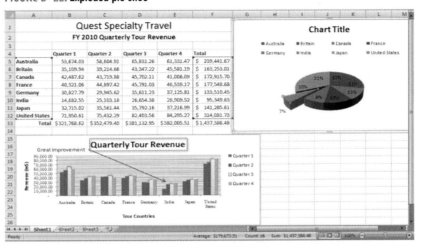

FIGURE D-23: **Landscape view of completed charts**

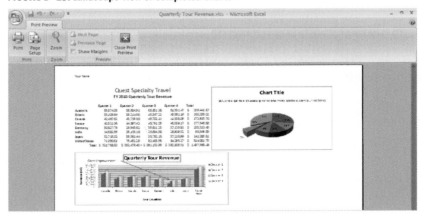

Using the Page Setup dialog box for a chart

When a chart is selected (or a chart sheet is active) and the Print Preview window is open, you can make modifications by clicking Page Setup in the Print group on the Print Preview tab. The Page Setup dialog box does not display all the options normally available. For example, the Center on page options (in the Margins tab) are not always available, and the Scaling options (in the Page tab) are grayed out.

You can also use the Show Margins checkbox in the Preview group of the Print Preview tab to accurately position a chart on the page. Margin lines appear on the screen and show you exactly how the margins appear on the page. The exact placement appears in the status bar when you press and hold the mouse button on the margin line. You can drag the lines to the exact settings you want.

Practice

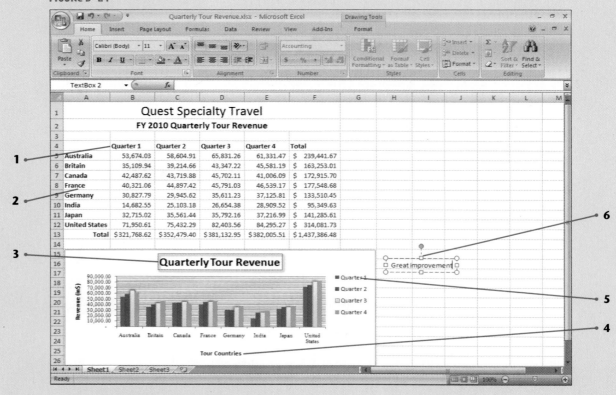

If you have a SAM user profile, you may have access to hands-on instruction, practice, and assessment of the skills covered in this unit. Log in to your SAM account (http://sam2007.course.com/) to launch any assigned training activities or exams that relate to the skills covered in this unit.

▼ CONCEPTS REVIEW

Label each element of the Excel chart shown in Figure D-24.

FIGURE D-24

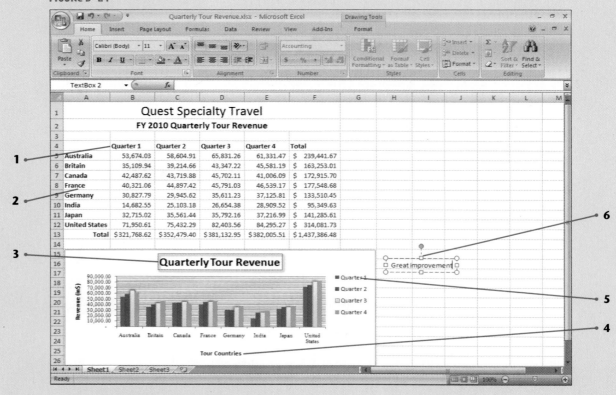

Match each chart type with the statement that best describes it.

7. Line	a. Compares trends over even time intervals
8. Pie	b. Shows how volume changes over time
9. Area	c. Compares data over time the Excel default
10. Column	d. Displays a column and line chart using different scales of measurement
11. Combination	e. Compares data as parts of a whole

Select the best answer from the list of choices.

12. Which tab on the Ribbon do you use to create a chart?

   a. Design   **c.** Page Layout

   b. Insert   **d.** Format

13. Which tab appears only when a chart is selected?

   a. Insert   **c.** Review

   b. Chart Tools Format   **d.** Page Layout

14. Which pointer do you use to resize a chart object?

   a. $+$ **c.** ↓

   b. I   **d.** ↕

15. How do you move an embedded chart to a chart sheet?

   a. Click a button on the Chart Tools Design tab.

   b. Drag the chart to the sheet tab.

   c. Delete the chart, switch to a different sheet, then create a new chart.

   d. Use the Copy and Paste buttons on the Ribbon.

16. The object in a chart that identifies patterns used for each data series is a(n):

   a. Data marker.   **c.** Organizer

   b. Data point.   **d.** Legend.

17. A collection of related data points in a chart is called a:

   a. Data series.   **c.** Cell address.

   b. Data tick.   **d.** Value title.

▼ SKILLS REVIEW

1. Plan a chart.

   a. Start Excel, open the Data File EX D-2.xlsx from the drive and folder where you store your Data Files, then save it as **Departmental Software Usage**.

   b. Describe the type of chart you would use to plot this data.

   c. What chart type would you use to compare total company expenses by department?

   d. What term is used to describe each value in a worksheet range selected for a chart?

2. Create a chart.

   a. In the worksheet, select the range containing all the data and headings.

   b. Click the Insert tab, if necessary.

   c. Create a clustered column chart, then add the chart title **Software Usage, by Department** above the chart.

   d. Save your work.

3. Move and resize a chart.

   a. Make sure the chart is still selected.

   b. Move the chart beneath the data.

   c. Resize the chart so it extends to the left edge of column I.

   d. Use the Chart Tools Layout tab to move the legend below the charted data.

   e. Resize the chart so its bottom edge is at the top of row 25.

   f. Save your work.

4. Change the chart design.

   a. Change the value in cell B3 to **25**. Observe the change in the chart.

   b. Select the chart.

   c. Use the Chart Layouts group on the Chart Tools Design tab to change to Layout 7, then undo the change.

   d. Use the Change Chart Type button on the Chart Tools Design tab to change the chart to a clustered bar chart.

   e. Change the chart to a 3-D clustered column chart , then change it back to a clustered column chart.

   f. Save your work.

5. **Change the chart layout.**

   a. Use the Layout tab to turn off the displayed gridlines in the chart.

   b. Change the font used in the horizontal and vertical axes labels to Times New Roman.

   c. Turn on the major gridlines for both the horizontal and vertical axes.

   d. Change the chart title's font to Times New Roman, with a font size of 20.

   e. Enter **Departments** as the horizontal axis title.

   f. Enter **Number of Users** as the vertical axis title. (*Hint*: Use a rotated title)

   g. Change the font size of the horizontal axis to 10, if necessary, and the font to Times New Roman.

   h. Change the font size of the vertical axis labels to 10, if necessary, and the font to Times New Roman.

   i. Change Personnel in the column heading to **Human Resources**. (*Hint*: Change the label in the worksheet, then resize the column.)

   j. Change the font size of the legend to 14.

   k. Add an offset diagonal bottom-right outer drop shadow to the chart title. (*Hint*: Use a solid line border in the default color.)

   l. Save your work.

6. **Format a chart.**

   a. Make sure the chart is selected, then select the Format tab, if necessary.

   b. Change the color of the Excel data series to Olive Green, Accent 3 Darker 50%.

   c. Change the shape effect of the Excel data series to Bevel – Circle.

   d. Save your work.

7. **Annotate and draw on a chart.**

   a. Make sure the chart is selected, then create the text annotation **Needs more users**.

   b. Position the text annotation so the 'N' in 'Needs' is positioned approximately below the 't' in 'Software'.

   c. Use the Shapes group on the Insert tab to create a 1½ pt weight arrow that points to the Excel users in the Design Department.

   d. Deselect the chart.

   e. Save your work.

8. **Create a pie chart.**

   a. Select the range A1:F2, then create a 3-D pie chart.

   b. Drag the 3-D pie chart beneath the existing chart.

   c. Change the chart title to **Excel Users**.

   d. Apply Chart Style 26 to the chart.

   e. Explode the Human Resources slice from the pie chart at 25%.

   f. In the worksheet, enter your name in the left section of the header.

▼ SKILLS REVIEW (CONTINUED)

g. View the worksheet and charts in the Print Preview window, make sure all the contents fit on one page, then compare your work to Figure D-25.

h. Save your work.

i. Close the workbook, then exit Excel.

FIGURE D-25

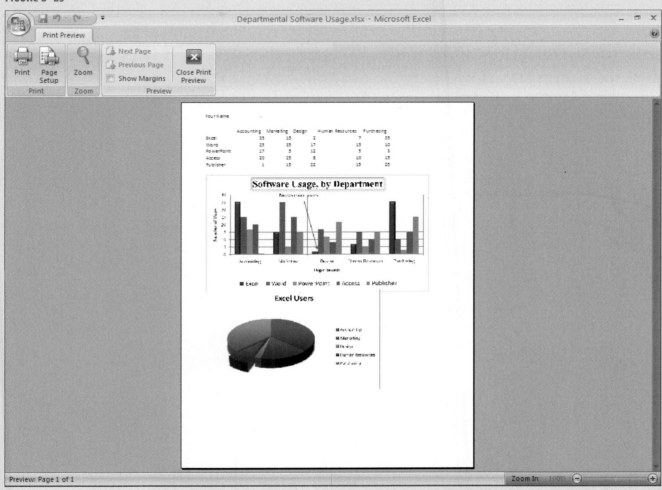

▼ INDEPENDENT CHALLENGE 1

You are the operations manager for the Springfield Theater Group in Massachusetts. Each year the group applies to various state and federal agencies for matching funds. For this year's funding proposal, you need to create charts to document the number of productions in previous years.

a. Start Excel, open the file EX D-3.xlsx from the drive and folder where you store your Data Files, then save it as **Springfield Theater Group**.

b. Take some time to plan your charts. Which type of chart or charts might best illustrate the information you need to display? What kind of chart enhancements do you want to use? Will a 3-D effect make your chart easier to understand?

c. Create a clustered column chart for the data.

d. If you wish, change at least one of the colors used in a data series.

e. Make the appropriate modifications to the chart to make it easy to read and understand, and visually attractive. Include chart titles, legends, and value and category axis titles, using the suggestions in Table D-3.

TABLE D-3

suggested chart enhancements for a column chart	
Title	Types and Number of Plays
Legend	Year 1, Year 2, Year 3, Year 4
Vertical axis title	Number of Plays
Horizontal axis title	Play Types

f. Create at least two additional charts for the same data to show how different chart types display the same data. Place each new chart on its own sheet in the workbook, and name the sheet according to the type of chart you created. One of the additional charts should be a pie chart; the other is up to you. Modify each new chart as necessary to improve its appearance and effectiveness. Compare your chart to the sample in Figure D-26.

FIGURE D-26

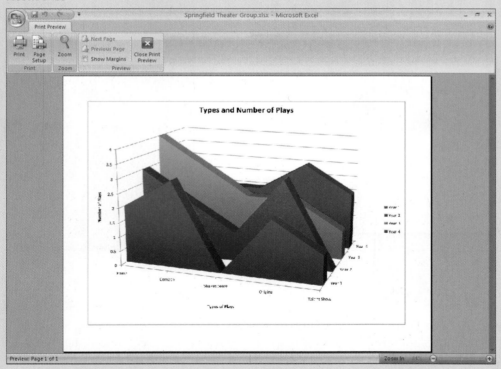

g. Enter your name in the worksheet header.

h. Save your work. Before printing, preview the workbook in Print Preview, then adjust any items as necessary.

i. Print the worksheet (charts and data).

j. Close the workbook, then exit Excel.

▼ INDEPENDENT CHALLENGE 2

FIGURE D-27

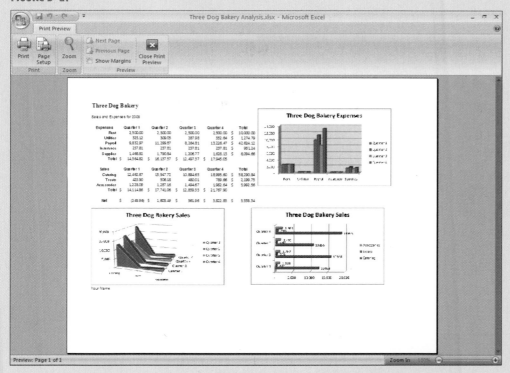

You work at Three Dog Bakery, a locally-owned bakery for dogs. One of your responsibilities at the bakery is to manage the company's sales and expenses using Excel. Another is to convince the current staff that Excel can help them make daily operating decisions more easily and efficiently. To do this, you've decided to create charts using the previous year's operating expenses, including rent, utilities, and payroll. The manager will use these charts at the next monthly meeting.

a. Start Excel, open the Data File EX D-4.xlsx from the drive and folder where you store your Data Files, then save it as **Three Dog Bakery Analysis**.

b. Decide which data in the worksheet should be charted. What type of chart or charts are best suited for the information you need to show? What kinds of chart enhancements are necessary?

c. Create a 3-D column chart (with the data series in rows) on the worksheet, showing the expense data for all four quarters. (*Hint*: Do not include the totals.)

d. Change the scale of the vertical axis (Expense data) so no decimals are displayed. (*Hint*: Right-click the scale you want to modify, click Format Axis, click Number category, change the number of decimal places, then click Close.)

e. Using the sales data, create two charts on this worksheet that illustrate trends in the data. (*Hint*: Move each chart to a new location on the worksheet, then deselect it before creating the next one.)

f. In one chart of the sales data, add data labels, then add chart titles as you see fit.

g. Make any necessary formatting changes to make the charts look more attractive, then enter your name in a worksheet cell.

h. Save your work.

i. Before printing, preview each chart, and adjust any items as needed. Fit the charts to a single page, then print one copy. Compare your work to the sample in Figure D-27.

j. Close the workbook, then exit Excel.

▼ INDEPENDENT CHALLENGE 3

FIGURE D-28

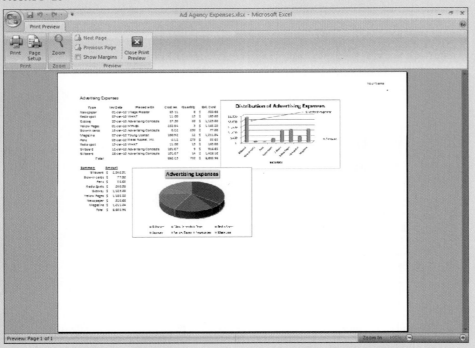

You are working as an account representative at the Inspiration Ad Agency. You have been examining the expenses charged to clients of the firm. The board of directors wants to examine certain advertising expenses and has asked you to prepare charts that can be used in this evaluation. In particular, you want to see how dollar amounts compare among the different expenses, and you also want to see how expenses compare with each other proportional to the total budget.

a. Start Excel, open the Data File EX D-5.xlsx from the drive and folder where you store your Data Files, then save it as **Ad Agency Expenses**.

b. Choose three types of charts that seem best suited to illustrate the data in the range A16:B24. What kinds of chart enhancements are necessary?

c. Create at least two different types of charts that show the distribution of advertising expenses. (*Hint*: Move each chart to a new location on the same worksheet.) One of the charts should be a 3-D pie chart.

d. Add annotated text and arrows highlighting important data, such as the largest expense.

e. Change the color of at least one data series in at least one of the charts.

f. Add chart titles and category and value axis titles where appropriate. Format the titles with a font of your choice. Place a drop shadow around the chart title in at least one chart.

g. Add your name to a section of the header, then save your work.

h. View the file in Print Preview. Adjust any items as needed. Be sure the charts are all visible on the page. Compare your work to the sample in Figure D-28.

Advanced Challenge Exercise

■ Explode a slice from the 3-D pie chart.

■ Add a data label to the exploded pie slice.

■ Change the number format of labels in the non-pie charts so no decimals are displayed.

■ Modify the scale of the vertical axis in one of the charts. (*Hint*: Right-click the vertical axis, click Format Axis, then click Axis Options.)

■ Save your work, then view it in Print Preview.

i. Print the charts, close the workbook, then exit Excel.

▼ REAL LIFE INDEPENDENT CHALLENGE

FIGURE D-29

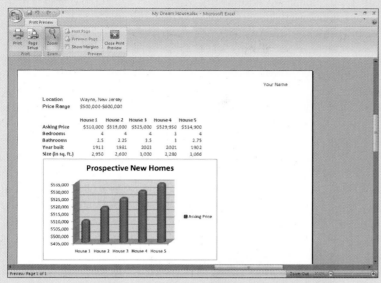

Note: This project requires an Internet connection.

A cash inheritance from a distant relative has finally been deposited in your bank account, and you have decided to quit your job and relocate to the town of your dreams. You have a good idea where you'd like to live and decide to use the Web to see what sort of houses are currently available.

a. Start Excel, then save a new, blank workbook as **My Dream House** to the drive and folder where you save your Data Files.

b. Decide on where you would like to live, and use your favorite search engine to find information sources on homes for sale in that area.

c. Determine a price range and features within the home. Find data for at least five homes that meet your location and price requirements, and enter them in the worksheet. See Table D-4 below for suggested data layout.

d. Format the data so it looks attractive and professional.

e. Create any type of column chart, using only the House and Asking Price data. Place it on the same worksheet as the data. Include a descriptive title.

f. Change the colors in the chart, using the Chart Style of your choice.

g. Enter your name in a section of the header.

TABLE D-4

location					
price range					
	House 1	House 2	House 3	House 4	House 5
Asking price					
Bedrooms					
Bathrooms					
Year built					
Size (in sq. ft.)					

h. Save the workbook. Preview the chart(s) and change margins and/or orientation as necessary. Compare your work to the sample chart shown in Figure D-29.

i. Print your worksheet(s), including the data and chart(s), making setup modifications as necessary.

Advanced Challenge Exercise

■ Change the chart type to a Clustered Column chart.

■ Create a combination chart that plots the asking price on one axis and the size of the home on the other axis. (*Hint*: Use Help to get tips on how to chart with a secondary axis.)

j. Close the workbook, then exit Excel.

▼ VISUAL WORKSHOP

Open the Data File EX D-6.xlsx from the drive and folder where you store your Data Files, then save it as **Projected Project Revenue**. Modify the worksheet data so it looks like Figure D-30, then create and modify two charts to match the ones shown in the figure. You will need to make formatting, layout, and design changes once you create the charts. Enter your name in the left section of the header, then save, preview, and print your results.

FIGURE D-30

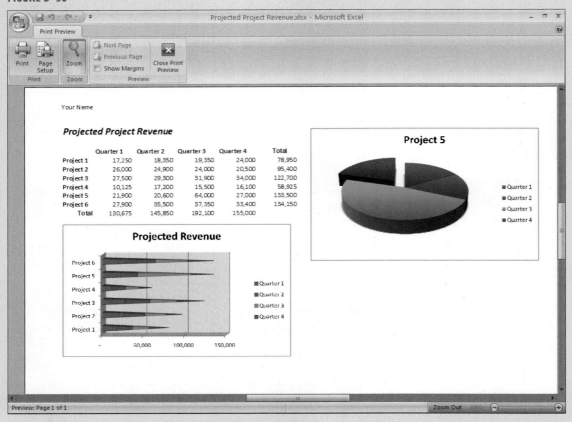

Analyzing Data Using Formulas

As you have learned, formulas and functions help you to analyze worksheet data. As you learn how to use different types of formulas and functions, you will discover more valuable uses for Excel. In this unit, you will gain a deeper understanding of Excel formulas and learn how to use several Excel functions. Kate Morgan, QST's vice president of sales, uses Excel formulas and functions to analyze sales data for the U.S. region and to consolidate sales data from several worksheets. Because management is considering adding a new regional branch, Kate asks you to estimate the loan costs for a new office facility and to compare tour sales in the existing U.S. offices.

OBJECTIVES

Format data using text functions
Sum a data range based on conditions
Consolidate data using a formula
Check formulas for errors
Construct formulas using named ranges
Build a logical formula with the IF function
Build a logical formula with the AND function
Calculate payments with the PMT function

Formatting Data Using Text Functions

Often, data you import needs restructuring or reformatting to be understandable and attractive, or to match the formatting of other data in your worksheet. Instead of handling these tasks manually in each cell, you can use Excel conversion tools and text functions to perform these tasks automatically for a range of cell data. The Convert Text to Columns feature breaks data fields in one column into separate columns. Your data elements should be separated by a **delimiter**, or separator, such as a space, comma, or semicolon. The text function PROPER capitalizes (converts to a proper noun) the first letter in a string of text as well as any text following a space. For example, if cell A1 contains the text string marketing department, then =PROPER(A1) would display Marketing Department. The CONCATENATE function is used to join two or more strings into one text string. ▰▰▰▰ Kate has received the U.S. sales representatives' data from the human resources department. She asks you to use text formulas to format the data into a more useful layout.

STEPS

1. **Start Excel, open the file EX E-1.xlsx from the drive and folder where you store your Data Files, then save it as Sales Data**

2. **On the Sales Reps sheet, select the range A4:A15, click the Data tab, then click the Text to Columns button in the Data Tools group**
   The Convert Text to Columns Wizard opens, as shown in Figure E-1. The data fields on your worksheet are separated by commas, which will act as delimiters.

3. **If necessary, click the Delimited option button to select it, click Next, in the Delimiters area of the dialog box click the Comma check box to select it if necessary, click any other selected check boxes to deselect them, then click Next**
   You instructed Excel to separate your data at the comma delimiter.

4. **Click the Text option button in the Column data format area, click the General column to select it in the Data preview area, click the Text option button in the Column data format area, then click Finish**
   The data are separated into three columns of text. You want to format the letters to the correct cases.

5. **Click cell D4, click the Formulas tab, click the Text button in the Function Library group, click PROPER, with the insertion point in the Text text box, click cell A4, then click OK**
   The name is copied from cell A4 to cell D4 with the correct uppercase letters for proper names. The remaining names and the cities are still in lowercase letters.

6. **Drag the fill handle to copy the formula in cell D4 to cell E4, then copy the formulas in cells D4:E4 into the range D5:E15**
   You want to format the years data to be more descriptive.

7. **Click cell F4, click the Text button in the Function Library group, click CONCATENATE, with the insertion point in the Text1 text box, click cell C4, press [Tab], with the insertion point in the Text2 text box, press [Spacebar], type Years, then click OK**

8. **Copy the formula in cell F4 into the range F5:F15, click the Insert tab, click the Header & Footer button in the Text group, click the Go to Footer button in the Navigation group, enter your name in the center text box, click cell A1, then click the Normal button ▦ in the status bar**

9. **Save your file, then print the worksheet and compare your work to Figure E-2**

FIGURE E-1: Convert Text to Columns dialog box

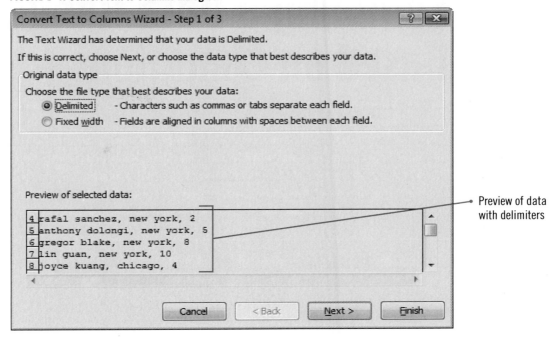

Preview of data with delimiters

FIGURE E-2: Worksheet with data formatted in columns

			United States Sales Representatives		
			Name	Office	Years of Service
rafal sanchez	new york	2	Rafal Sanchez	New York	2 Years
anthony dolongi	new york	5	Anthony Dolongi	New York	5 Years
gregor blake	new york	8	Gregor Blake	New York	8 Years
lin guan	new york	10	Lin Guan	New York	10 Years
joyce kuang	chicago	4	Joyce Kuang	Chicago	4 Years
garrin cunha	chicago	7	Garrin Cunha	Chicago	7 Years
cathy jaques	chicago	5	Cathy Jaques	Chicago	5 Years
alyssa maztta	chicago	4	Alyssa Maztta	Chicago	4 Years
april radka	miami	6	April Radka	Miami	6 Years
jose costello	miami	7	Jose Costello	Miami	7 Years
joyce haddad	miami	4	Joyce Haddad	Miami	4 Years
summer zola	miami	7	Summer Zola	Miami	7 Years

Using text functions

Other commonly used text functions include UPPER, LOWER, and SUBSTITUTE. The UPPER function converts text to all uppercase letters, the LOWER function converts text to all lowercase letters, and SUBSTITUTE replaces text in a text string. For example, if cell A1 contains the text string Today is Wednesday, then =LOWER(A1) would produce today is wednesday, =UPPER(A1) would produce

TODAY IS WEDNESDAY, and =SUBSTITUTE(A1, "Wednesday", "Tuesday") would result in Today is Tuesday.

If you want to copy and paste data formatted using text functions, you need to select Values Only from the Paste Options drop-down list to paste the cell values rather than the text formulas.

Summing a Data Range Based on Conditions

You have learned how to use the SUM, COUNT, and AVERAGE functions for data ranges. You can also use Excel functions to sum, count, and average data in a range based on criteria, or conditions, you set. The SUMIF function conditionally totals cells in a sum range that meet given criteria. For example, you can total the values in a column of sales where a sales rep name equals Joe Smith (the criterion). Similarly, the COUNTIF function counts cells and the AVERAGEIF function averages cells in a range based on a specified condition. The format for the SUMIF function appears in Figure E-3. ▓▓▓▓ Kate asks you to analyze the New York branch's January sales data to provide her with information about each tour.

STEPS

1. **Click the NY sheet tab, click cell G7, click the Formulas tab, click the More Functions button in the Function Library group, point to Statistical, then click COUNTIF**

   The Function Arguments dialog box opens, as shown in Figure E-4. You want to count the number of times Pacific Odyssey appears in the Tour column. The formula you use will say, in effect, "Examine the range I specify, then count the number of cells in that range that contain "Pacific Odyssey." You will specify absolute addresses for the range so you can copy the formula.

2. **With the insertion point in the Range text box, select the range A6:A25, press [F4], press [Tab], with the insertion point in the Criteria text box, click cell F7, then click OK**

   The number of Pacific Odyssey tours, 4, appears in cell G7. You want to calculate the total sales revenue for the Pacific Odyssey tours.

3. **Click cell H7, click the Math & Trig button in the Function Library group, scroll down the list of functions, then click SUMIF**

   The Function Arguments dialog box opens. You want to enter two ranges and a criterion; the first range is the one where you want Excel to search for the criteria entered. The second range contains the corresponding cells that will be totaled when the criterion you want Excel to search for in the first range is met.

4. **With the insertion point in the Range text box, select the range A6:A25, press [F4], press [Tab], with the insertion point in the Criteria text box, click cell F7, press [Tab], with the insertion point in the Sum_range text box, select the range B6:B25, press [F4], then click OK**

   Your formula asks Excel to search the range A6:A25, and where it finds the value shown in cell F7 (that is, when it finds the value Pacific Odyssey), add the corresponding amounts from column B. The revenue for the Pacific Odyssey tours, 12403, appears in cell H7. You want to calculate the average price paid for the Pacific Odyssey tours.

5. **Click cell I7, click the More Functions button in the Function Library group, point to Statistical, then click AVERAGEIF**

6. **With the insertion point in the Range text box, select the range A6:A25, press [F4], press [Tab], with the insertion point in the Criteria text box, click cell F7, press [Tab], with the insertion point in the Average_range text box, select the range B6:B25, press [F4], then click OK**

   The average price paid for the Pacific Odyssey tours, 3101, appears in cell I7.

7. **Select the range G7:I7, then drag the fill handle to fill the range G8:I10**

   Compare your results with those in Figure E-5.

8. **Add your name to the center of the footer, save the workbook, then preview and print the worksheet**

FIGURE E-3: Format of SUMIF function

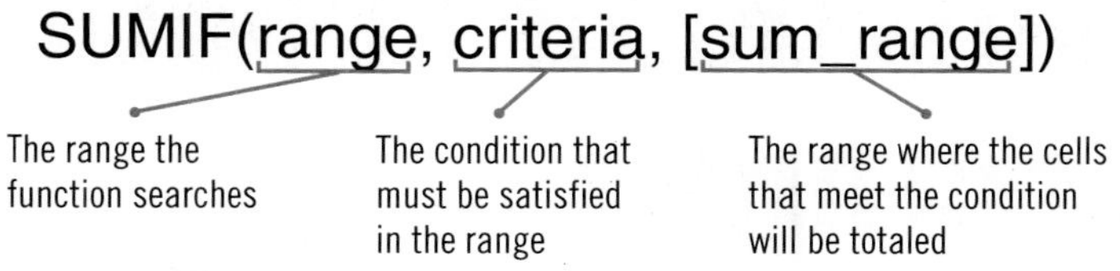

SUMIF(range, criteria, [sum_range])
The range the function searches
The condition that must be satisfied in the range
The range where the cells that meet the condition will be totaled

FIGURE E-4: COUNTIF function in the Function Arguments dialog box

Function Arguments
COUNTIF
Range
= reference
Criteria
= any
=
Counts the number of cells within a range that meet the given condition.
Range is the range of cells from which you want to count nonblank cells.
Formula result =
Help on this function
OK
Cancel

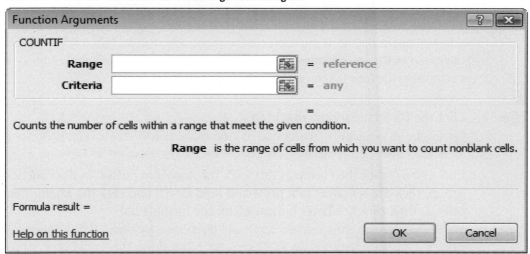

FIGURE E-5: Worksheet with conditional statistics

	A	B	C	D	E	F	G	H	I
4									
5	Tour	Price	Sale Date	Sales Representative					
6	Pacific Odyssey	$ 3,105	1/3/2010	Rafal Sanchez		Tour	Tours Sold	Revenue	Average Price
7	Essential India	$ 3,933	1/4/2010	Anthony Dolongi		Pacific Odyssey	4	12403	3101
8	Old Japan	$ 2,100	1/4/2010	Gregor Blake		Old Japan	5	10505	2101
9	Essential India	$ 3,955	1/6/2010	Lin Guan		Down Under Exodus	5	14016	2803
10	Pacific Odyssey	$ 3,090	1/8/2010	Anthony Dolongi		Essential India	6	23583	3931
11	Down Under Exodus	$ 2,800	1/10/2010	Anthony Dolongi					
12	Old Japan	$ 2,099	1/12/2010	Gregor Blake					
13	Down Under Exodus	$ 2,804	1/13/2010	Rafal Sanchez					
14	Old Japan	$ 2,103	1/14/2010	Rafal Sanchez					
15	Down Under Exodus	$ 2,810	1/16/2010	Lin Guan					
16	Pacific Odyssey	$ 3,110	1/17/2010	Anthony Dolongi					
17	Essential India	$ 3,920	1/17/2010	Lin Guan					
18	Old Japan	$ 2,108	1/18/2010	Gregor Blake					
19	Down Under Exodus	$ 2,798	1/19/2010	Lin Guan					
20	Essential India	$ 3,875	1/19/2010	Lin Guan					
21	Old Japan	$ 2,095	1/21/2010	Gregor Blake					
22	Essential India	$ 3,945	1/23/2010	Rafal Sanchez					
23	Down Under Exodus	$ 2,804	1/27/2010	Gregor Blake					
24	Pacific Odyssey	$ 3,098	1/27/2010	Lin Guan					
25	Essential India	$ 3,955	1/29/2010	Rafal Sanchez					

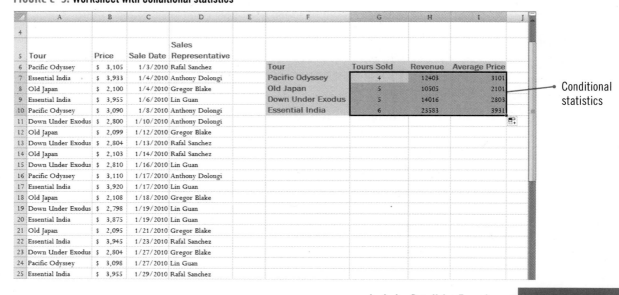

Conditional statistics

Consolidating Data Using a Formula

When you want to summarize similar data that exists in different sheets or workbooks, you can **consolidate**, or combine and display, the data in one sheet. For example, you might have entered departmental sales figures on four different store sheets that you want to consolidate on one summary sheet, showing total departmental sales for all stores. The best way to consolidate data is to use cell references to the various sheets on a consolidation, or summary, sheet. Because they reference other sheets that are usually behind the summary sheet, such references effectively create another dimension in the workbook and are called **3-D references**, as shown in Figure E-6. You can reference, or **link** to, data in other sheets and in other workbooks. Linking to a worksheet or workbook is a better method than retyping calculated results from the worksheet or workbook because the data values on which calculated totals depend might change. If you reference the values, any changes to the original values are automatically reflected in the consolidation sheet. ▓▓▓▓▓ Kate asks you to prepare a January sales summary sheet comparing the total U.S. revenue for the tours sold in the month.

STEPS

QUICK TIP

You can also consolidate data using named ranges. For example, you might have entered team sales figures using the names team1, team2, and team3 on different sheets that you want to consolidate on one summary sheet. As you enter the summary formula you can click the Formulas tab, click the Use in Formula button in the Defined Names group, and select the range name.

1. **Click the US Summary Jan sheet tab**

   Because the US Summary Jan sheet (which is the consolidation sheet) will contain the reference to the data in the other sheets, the cell pointer must reside there when you initiate the reference.

2. **Click cell B7, click the Formulas tab, click the AutoSum button in the Function Library group, click the NY sheet tab, press and hold [Shift] and click the Miami sheet tab, click cell G7, then click the Enter button ✔ on the formula bar**

   The US Summary Jan sheet becomes active, and the formula bar reads =SUM(NY:Miami!G7), as shown in Figure E-7. NY:Miami references the NY, Chicago, and Miami sheets. The ! (exclamation point) is an **external reference indicator**, meaning that the cells referenced are outside the active sheet; G7 is the actual cell reference you want to total in the external sheets. The result, 12, appears in cell B7 of the US Summary Jan sheet; it is the sum of the number of Pacific Odyssey tours sold and referenced in cell G7 of the NY, Chicago, and Miami sheets. Because the Revenue data is in the column to the right of the Tours Sold column on the NY, Chicago, and Miami sheets, you can copy the tours sold summary formula, with its relative addresses, into the cell that holds the revenue summary information.

3. **Drag the fill handle to copy the formula in cell B7 to cell C7**

   The result, 37405, appears in cell C7 of the US Summary Jan sheet, showing the sum of the Pacific Odyssey tour revenue referenced in cell H7 of the NY, Chicago, and Miami sheets.

QUICK TIP

You can also use a summary worksheet to consolidate yearly sales figures. Place data for each quarter on a separate sheet. On a summary sheet, use a row for each quarter that references each quarter's sales. Then sum the quarterly information to display total yearly sales.

4. **In the US Summary Jan sheet, with the range B7:C7 selected, drag the fill handle to fill the range B8:C10**

   You can test a consolidation reference by changing one cell value on which the formula is based and seeing if the formula result changes.

5. **Click the Chicago sheet tab, edit cell A6 to read Pacific Odyssey, then click the US Summary Jan sheet tab**

   The number of Pacific Odyssey tours sold is automatically updated to 13 and the revenue is increased to 40280, as shown in Figure E-8.

6. **Click the Insert tab, click the Header & Footer button in the Text group, click the Go to Footer button, enter your name in the center text box, click cell A1, then click the Normal button ▦ in the status bar**

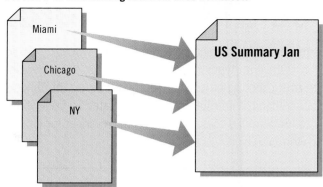

FIGURE E-6: Consolidating data from three worksheets

FIGURE E-7: Worksheet showing total Pacific Odyssey tours sold

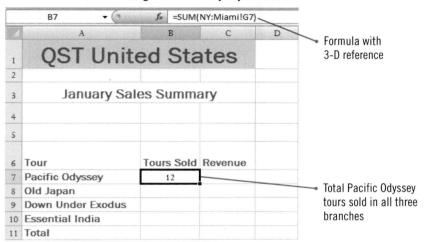

Formula with 3-D reference

Total Pacific Odyssey tours sold in all three branches

FIGURE E-8: US Summary Jan worksheet with updated totals

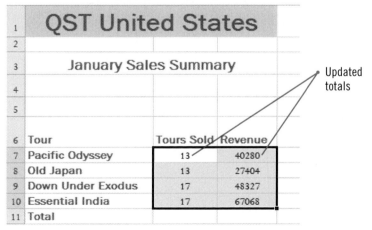

Updated totals

Linking data between workbooks

Just as you can link data between cells in a worksheet and between sheets in a workbook, you can link workbooks so that changes made in referenced cells in one workbook are reflected in the consolidation sheet in the other workbook. To link a single cell between workbooks, open both workbooks, select the cell to receive the linked data, type = (the equal sign), select the cell in the other workbook containing the data to be linked, then press [Enter]. Excel automatically inserts the name of the referenced workbook in the cell reference. For example, if the linked data is contained in cell C7 of worksheet New in the Products workbook, the cell entry reads ='[Product.xlsx]New'!$C$7. To perform calculations, enter formulas on the consolidation sheet using cells in the supporting sheets. If you are linking more than one cell, you can copy the linked data to the Clipboard, select the upper left cell in the workbook to receive the link, click the Home tab, click the Paste list arrow, then click Paste Link.

Checking Formulas for Errors

When formulas result in errors, Excel displays an error value based on the error type. See Table E-1 for a description of the error types and error codes that might appear in worksheets. The IFERROR function simplifies the error-checking process for your worksheets. This function displays a message or value that you specify, rather than the one automatically generated by Excel, if there is an error in a formula.  Kate asks you to use formulas to compare the tour revenues for January. You will use the IFERROR function to help catch formula errors.

STEPS

1. **Click cell B11, click the Formulas tab, click the AutoSum button in the Function Library group, then click the Enter button** ☑ **on the formula bar**

   The number of tours sold, 60, appears in cell B11.

2. **Drag the fill handle to copy the formula in cell B11 into cell C11**

   The tour revenue total of 183079 appears in cell C11. You decide to enter a formula to calculate the percentage of revenue the Pacific Odyssey tour represents by dividing the individual tour revenue figures by the total revenue figure. To help with error checking, you decide to enter the formula using the IFERROR function.

3. **Click cell B14, click the Logical button in the Function Library group, click IFERROR, with the insertion point in the Value text box, click cell C7, type /, click cell C11, press [Tab], in the Value_if_error text box, type ERROR, then click OK**

   The percentage of Pacific Odyssey tour revenue of 22.00% appears in cell B14. You want to be sure that your error message will display properly, so you decide to test it by intentionally creating an error. You copy and paste the formula—which has a relative address in the denominator, where an absolute address should be used.

4. **Drag the fill handle to copy the formula in cell B14 into the range B15:B17**

   The ERROR value appears in cells B15:B17, as shown in Figure E-9. The errors are a result of the relative address for C11 in the denominator of the copied formula. Changing the relative address of C11 in the copied formula to an absolute address of $C$11 will correct the errors.

   QUICK TIP
   You can also check formulas for errors using the buttons in the Formula Auditing group on the Formulas tab.

5. **Double-click cell B14, select C11 in the formula, press [F4], then click** ☑ **on the formula bar**

   The formula now contains an absolute reference to cell C11.

6. **Copy the corrected formula in cell B14 into the range B15:B17**

   The tour revenue percentages now appear in all four cells, without error messages, as shown in Figure E-10.

7. **Save the workbook, print the worksheet, then close the workbook**

Correcting circular references

A cell with a circular reference contains a formula that refers to its own cell location. If you accidentally enter a formula with a circular reference, a warning box opens, alerting you to the problem. Click OK to open a Help window explaining how to find the circular reference. In simple formulas, a circular reference is easy to spot. To correct it, edit the formula to remove any reference to the cell where the formula is located.

FIGURE E-9: Worksheet with error codes

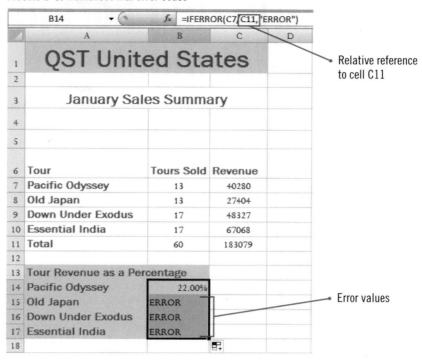

Relative reference to cell C11

Error values

FIGURE E-10: Worksheet with tour percentages

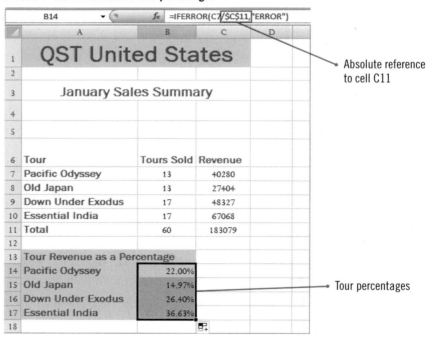

Absolute reference to cell C11

Tour percentages

TABLE E-1: Understanding error values

error value	cause of error	error value	cause of error
#DIV/0!	A number is divided by 0	#NAME?	Formula contains text error
#NA	A value in a formula is not available	#NULL!	Invalid intersection of areas
#NUM!	Invalid use of a number in a formula	#REF!	Invalid cell reference
#VALUE!	Wrong type of formula argument or operand	#####	Column is not wide enough to display data

Constructing Formulas Using Named Ranges

To make your worksheet easier to follow, you can assign names to cells and ranges. You can also use names in formulas to make them easier to build and to reduce formula errors. For example, a formula named revenue-cost is easier to understand than the formula A5-A8. Names can use uppercase or lowercase letters as well as digits, but cannot have spaces. After you name a cell or range, you can define its **scope**, or the worksheets where it can be used. When defining a name's scope, you can limit its use to a worksheet or make it available to the entire workbook. If you move a named cell or range, its name moves with it, and if you add or remove rows or column to the worksheet the ranges are adjusted to their new position in the worksheet. When used in formulas, names become absolute cell references by default. ▓▓▓▓ Kate asks you to calculate the number of days before each tour departs. You will use range names to construct the formula.

STEPS

1. **Open the file EX E-2.xlsx from the drive and folder where you store your Data Files, then save it as Tours**

2. **Click cell B4, click the Formulas tab if necessary, click the Define Name button in the Defined Names group**

   The New Name dialog box opens, as shown in Figure E-11. You can name ranges containing dates to make formulas that perform date calculations easier to build.

3. **Type current_date in the Name text box, click the Scope list arrow, click April Tours, then click OK**

   The name assigned to cell B4, current_date, appears in the Name box. Because its scope is the April Tours worksheet, the range name current_date will appear on the name list on that worksheet only. You can also name ranges that contain dates.

4. **Select the range B7:B13, click the Define Name button in the Defined Names group, enter tour_date in the Name text box, click the Scope list arrow, click April Tours, then click OK**

   Now you can use the named range and named cell in a formula. The formula =tour_date–current_date is easier to understand than =B7-$B$4.

5. **Click cell C7, type =, click the Use in Formula button in the Defined Names group, click tour_date, type –, click the Use in Formula button, click current_date, then click the Enter button ✓ on the formula bar**

   The number of days before the Pacific Odyssey tour departs, 10, appears in cell C7. You can use the same formula to calculate the number of days before the other tours depart.

6. **Drag the fill handle to copy the formula in cell C7 into the range C8:C13, then compare your formula results with those in Figure E-12**

7. **Save the workbook**

FIGURE E-11: New Name dialog box

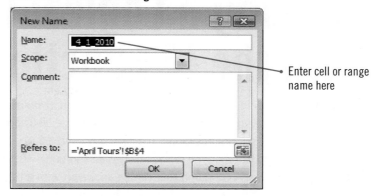

Enter cell or range name here

FIGURE E-12: Worksheet with days before departure

Name box

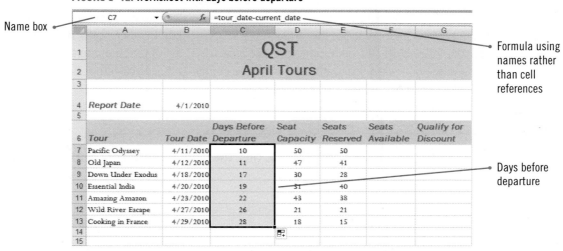

Formula using names rather than cell references

Days before departure

Inside Figure E-12 the worksheet:

C7 — =tour_date-current_date

QST
April Tours

	Tour	Tour Date	Days Before Departure	Seat Capacity	Seats Reserved	Seats Available	Qualify for Discount
4	Report Date	4/1/2010					
7	Pacific Odyssey	4/11/2010	10	50	50		
8	Old Japan	4/12/2010	11	47	41		
9	Down Under Exodus	4/18/2010	17	30	28		
10	Essential India	4/20/2010	19	51	40		
11	Amazing Amazon	4/23/2010	22	43	38		
12	Wild River Escape	4/27/2010	26	21	21		
13	Cooking in France	4/29/2010	28	18	15		

Managing workbook names

You can use the Name Manager to create, delete, and edit names in a workbook. Click the Name Manager button in the Defined Names group on the Formulas tab to open the Name Manager dialog box, as shown in Figure E-13. Click the New button to create a new named cell or range, click Edit to change a highlighted cell name, and click Delete to remove a highlighted name. Click Filter to see options for displaying specific criteria for displaying names.

FIGURE E-13: Name Manager dialog box

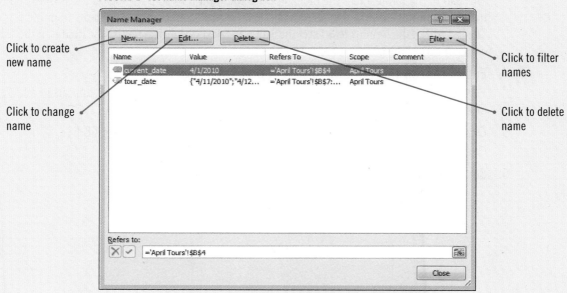

Click to create new name

Click to change name

Click to filter names

Click to delete name

Name Manager contents:

Name	Value	Refers To	Scope	Comment
current_date	4/1/2010	='April Tours'!$B$4	April Tours	
tour_date	{"4/11/2010";"4/12...	='April Tours'!$B$7:...	April Tours	

Refers to: ='April Tours'!$B$4

Building a Logical Formula with the IF Function

You can build a logical formula using an IF function. A **logical formula** makes calculations based on criteria that you create, called **stated conditions**. For example, you can build a formula to calculate bonuses based on a person's performance rating. If a person is rated a 5 (the stated condition) on a scale of 1 to 5, with 5 being the highest rating, he or she receives an additional 10% of his or her salary as a bonus; otherwise, there is no bonus. A condition that can be answered with a true or false response is called a **logical test**. The IF function has three parts, separated by commas: a condition or logical test, an action to take if the logical test or condition is true, and an action to take if the logical test or condition is false. Another way of expressing this is: IF(test_cond,do_this,else_this). Translated into an Excel IF function, the formula to calculate bonuses might look like this: IF(Rating=5,Salary*0.10,0). In other words, if the rating equals 5, multiply the salary by 0.10 (the decimal equivalent of 10%), then place the result in the selected cell; if the rating does not equal 5, place a 0 in the cell. When entering the logical test portion of an IF statement, you typically use some combination of the comparison operators listed in Table E-2. Kate asks you to use an IF function to calculate the number of seats available for each tour in April.

STEPS

1. **Click cell F7, on the Formulas tab, click the Logical button in the Function Library group, then click IF**

   The Function Arguments dialog box opens. You want the function to calculate the seats available as follows: If the seat capacity is greater than the number of seats reserved, calculate the number of seats that are available (capacity–number reserved), and place the result in cell F7; otherwise, place the text "None" in the cell.

2. **With the insertion point in the Logical_test text box, click cell D7, type >, click cell E7, then press [Tab]**

   The symbol (>) represents "greater than." So far, the formula reads "If the seating capacity is greater than the number of reserved seats,". The next part of the function tells Excel the action to take if the capacity exceeds the reserved number of seats.

3. **With the insertion point in the Value_if_true text box, click cell D7, type –, click cell E7, then press [Tab]**

   This part of the formula tells the program what you want it to do if the logical test is true. Continuing the translation of the formula, this part means "Subtract the number of reserved seats from the seat capacity." The last part of the formula tells Excel the action to take if the logical test is false (that is, if the seat capacity does not exceed the number of reserved seats).

4. **Enter None in the Value_if_false text box, then click OK**

   The function is complete, and the result, None (the number of available seats), appears in cell F7, as shown in Figure E-14.

5. **Drag the fill handle to copy the formula in cell F7 into the range F8:F13**

   Compare your results with Figure E-15.

6. **Save the workbook**

FIGURE E-14: Worksheet with IF function

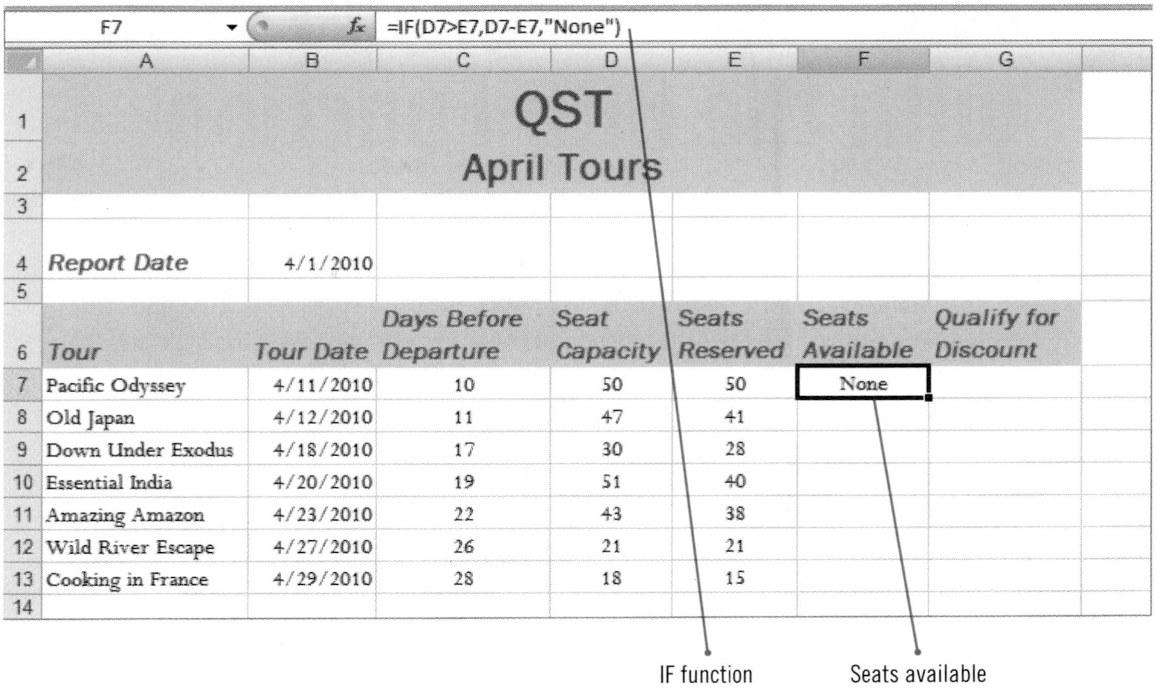

| | F7 | fx | =IF(D7>E7,D7-E7,"None") |

	A	B	C	D	E	F	G
1				QST			
2				April Tours			
3							
4	*Report Date*	4/1/2010					
5							
6	*Tour*	*Tour Date*	*Days Before Departure*	*Seat Capacity*	*Seats Reserved*	*Seats Available*	*Qualify for Discount*
7	Pacific Odyssey	4/11/2010	10	50	50	None	
8	Old Japan	4/12/2010	11	47	41		
9	Down Under Exodus	4/18/2010	17	30	28		
10	Essential India	4/20/2010	19	51	40		
11	Amazing Amazon	4/23/2010	22	43	38		
12	Wild River Escape	4/27/2010	26	21	21		
13	Cooking in France	4/29/2010	28	18	15		
14							

IF function   Seats available

FIGURE E-15: Worksheet showing seats available

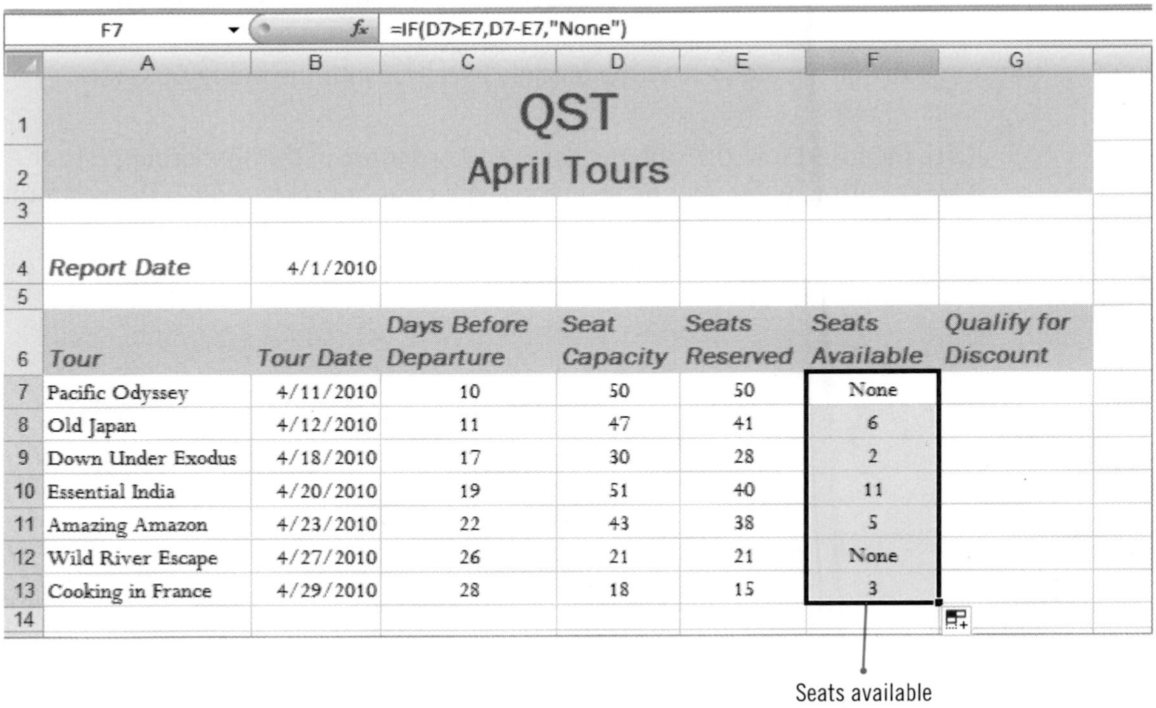

| | F7 | fx | =IF(D7>E7,D7-E7,"None") |

	A	B	C	D	E	F	G
1				QST			
2				April Tours			
3							
4	*Report Date*	4/1/2010					
5							
6	*Tour*	*Tour Date*	*Days Before Departure*	*Seat Capacity*	*Seats Reserved*	*Seats Available*	*Qualify for Discount*
7	Pacific Odyssey	4/11/2010	10	50	50	None	
8	Old Japan	4/12/2010	11	47	41	6	
9	Down Under Exodus	4/18/2010	17	30	28	2	
10	Essential India	4/20/2010	19	51	40	11	
11	Amazing Amazon	4/23/2010	22	43	38	5	
12	Wild River Escape	4/27/2010	26	21	21	None	
13	Cooking in France	4/29/2010	28	18	15	3	
14							

Seats available

TABLE E-2: Comparison operators

operator	meaning	operator	meaning
<	Less than	<=	Less than or equal to
>	Greater than	>=	Greater than or equal to
=	Equal to	<>	Not equal to

Building a Logical Formula with the AND Function

You can also build a logical function using the AND function. The AND function evaluates all of its arguments and **returns**, or displays, TRUE if every logical test in the formula is true. The AND function returns a value of FALSE if one or more of its logical tests is false. The AND function arguments can include text, numbers, or cell references. ██████ Kate wants you to analyze the tour data to find tours that qualify for discounting. You will use the AND function to check for tours with seats available and that depart within 21 days.

STEPS

1. **Click cell G7, click the Logical button in the Function Library group, then click AND**
   The Function Arguments dialog box opens. You want the function to evaluate the discount qualification as follows: There must be seats available and the tour must depart within 21 days.

> **TROUBLE**
> If you get a formula error, check to be sure that you typed the quotation marks around None.

2. **With the insertion point in the Logical1 text box, click cell F7, type < >, type "None", then press [Tab]**
   The symbol (<>) represents "not equal to." So far, the formula reads "If the number of seats available is not equal to None,"—in other words, if it is an integer. The next logical test checks the number of days before the tour departs.

3. **With the insertion point in the Logical2 text box, click cell C7, type <21, then click OK**
   The function is complete, and the result, FALSE, appears in cell G7, as shown in Figure E-16.

4. **Drag the fill handle to copy the formula in cell G7 into the range G8:G13**
   Compare your results with Figure E-17.

5. **Click the Insert tab, click the Header & Footer button in the Text group, click the Go to Footer button, enter your name in the center text box, click cell A1, then click the Normal button ▦ in the status bar**

6. **Save the workbook, then preview and print the worksheet**

Using the OR and NOT logical functions

The OR logical function has the same syntax as the AND function, but rather than returning TRUE if every argument is true, the OR function will return TRUE if any of its arguments are TRUE. It will only return FALSE if all of its arguments are FALSE. The NOT logical function reverses the value of its argument. For example NOT(TRUE) reverses its argument of TRUE and returns FALSE. This can be used in a worksheet to ensure that a cell is not equal to a particular value. See Table E-3 for examples of the AND, OR, and NOT functions.

TABLE E–3: Examples of AND, OR, and NOT functions with cell values A1=10 and B1=20

function	formula	result
AND	=AND(A1>5,B1>25)	FALSE
OR	=OR(A1>5,B1>25)	TRUE
NOT	=NOT(A1=0)	TRUE

FIGURE E-16: Worksheet with AND function

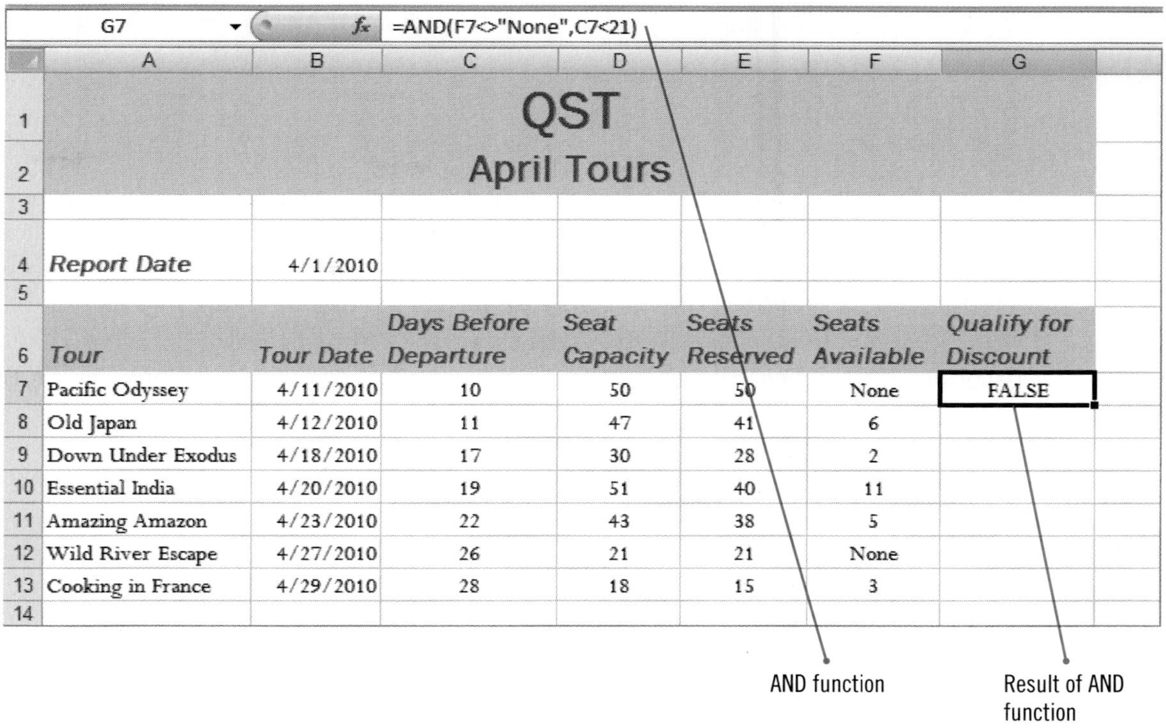

	G7		*fx*	=AND(F7<>"None",C7<21)			
	A	B	C	D	E	F	G
1			QST				
2			April Tours				
3							
4	*Report Date*	4/1/2010					
5							
6	*Tour*	*Tour Date*	*Days Before Departure*	*Seat Capacity*	*Seats Reserved*	*Seats Available*	*Qualify for Discount*
7	Pacific Odyssey	4/11/2010	10	50	50	None	FALSE
8	Old Japan	4/12/2010	11	47	41	6	
9	Down Under Exodus	4/18/2010	17	30	28	2	
10	Essential India	4/20/2010	19	51	40	11	
11	Amazing Amazon	4/23/2010	22	43	38	5	
12	Wild River Escape	4/27/2010	26	21	21	None	
13	Cooking in France	4/29/2010	28	18	15	3	
14							

AND function   Result of AND function

FIGURE E-17: Worksheet with discount status evaluated

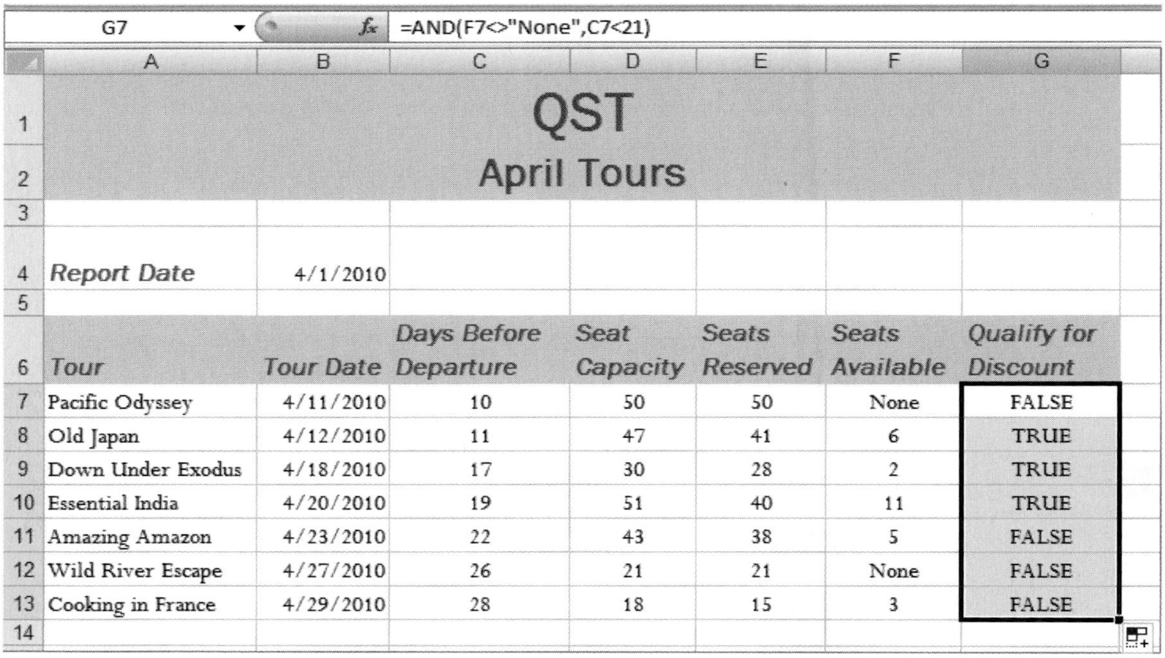

	G7		*fx*	=AND(F7<>"None",C7<21)			
	A	B	C	D	E	F	G
1			QST				
2			April Tours				
3							
4	*Report Date*	4/1/2010					
5							
6	*Tour*	*Tour Date*	*Days Before Departure*	*Seat Capacity*	*Seats Reserved*	*Seats Available*	*Qualify for Discount*
7	Pacific Odyssey	4/11/2010	10	50	50	None	FALSE
8	Old Japan	4/12/2010	11	47	41	6	TRUE
9	Down Under Exodus	4/18/2010	17	30	28	2	TRUE
10	Essential India	4/20/2010	19	51	40	11	TRUE
11	Amazing Amazon	4/23/2010	22	43	38	5	FALSE
12	Wild River Escape	4/27/2010	26	21	21	None	FALSE
13	Cooking in France	4/29/2010	28	18	15	3	FALSE
14							

Calculating Payments with the PMT Function

PMT is a financial function that calculates the periodic payment amount for money borrowed. For example, if you want to borrow money to buy a car, and you know the principal amount, interest rate, and loan term, the PMT function can calculate your monthly payment. Say you want to borrow $20,000 at 6.5% interest and pay the loan off in five years. The Excel PMT function can tell you that your monthly payment will be $391.32. The main parts of the PMT function are: PMT(rate, nper, pv). See Figure E-18 for an illustration of a PMT function that calculates the monthly payment in the car loan example. ░░░░ For several months, QST's United States region has been discussing opening a new branch in San Francisco. Kate has obtained quotes from three different lenders on borrowing $259,000 to begin the expansion. She obtained loan quotes from a commercial bank, a venture capitalist, and an investment banker. She wants you to summarize the information using the Excel PMT function.

STEPS

1. **Click the Loan sheet tab, click cell F5, click the Formulas tab, click the Financial button in the Function Library group, scroll down the list of functions, then click PMT**

2. **With the insertion point in the Rate text box, click cell D5 on the worksheet, type /12, then press [Tab]**

   You must divide the annual interest by 12 because you are calculating monthly, not annual, payments.

3. **With the insertion point in the Nper text box, click cell E5; click the Pv text box, click cell B5, then click OK**

   The payment of (5445.81) in cell F5 appears in red, indicating that it is a negative amount. Excel displays the result of a PMT function as a negative value to reflect the negative cash flow the loan represents to the borrower. To show the monthly payment as a positive number, you can place a minus sign in front of the Pv cell reference in the function. The Fv and Type arguments are optional: The argument Fv is the future value, or the total amount you want to obtain after all payments. If you omit it, Excel assumes the Fv is 0. The Type argument indicates when the payments are made; 0 is the end of the period, and 1 is the beginning of the period. The default is the end of the period.

4. **Double-click cell F5 and edit it so it reads =PMT(D5/12,E5,-B5), then click the Enter button ☑ on the formula bar**

   A positive value of $5,445.81 now appears in cell F5, as shown in Figure E-19. You can use the same formula to generate the monthly payments for the other loans.

5. **With cell F5 selected, drag the fill handle to fill the range F6:F7**

   A monthly payment of $8,266.30 for the venture capitalist loan appears in cell F6. A monthly payment of $11,826.41 for the investment banker loan appears in cell F7. The loans with shorter terms have much higher payments. You will not know the entire financial picture until you calculate the total payments and total interest for each lender.

6. **Click cell G5, type =, click cell E5, type *, click cell F5, then press [Tab], in cell H5, type =, click cell G5, type –, click cell B5, then click ☑**

7. **Copy the formulas in cells G5:H5 into the range G6:H7, then click cell A1**

   Your worksheet appears as shown in Figure E-20. You can experiment with different interest rates, loan amounts, or terms for any one of the lenders; the PMT function generates a new set of values automatically.

8. **Add your name to the center section of the footer, save the workbook, preview and print the worksheet, then close the workbook and exit Excel**

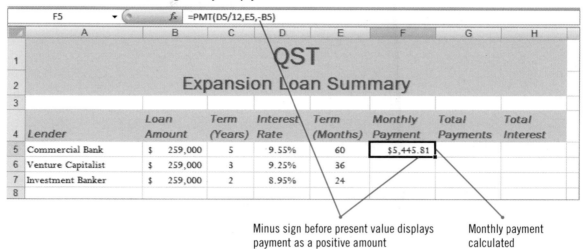

FIGURE E-18: Example of PMT function for car loan

$$PMT(0.065/12, 60, 20000) = \$391.32$$

Interest rate per period (rate) | Number of payments (nper) | Present value of loan amount (pv) | Monthly payment calculated

FIGURE E-19: PMT function calculating monthly loan payment

F5   fx   =PMT(D5/12,E5,-B5)

	A	B	C	D	E	F	G	H
1				QST				
2				Expansion Loan Summary				
3								
4	Lender	Loan Amount	Term (Years)	Interest Rate	Term (Months)	Monthly Payment	Total Payments	Total Interest
5	Commercial Bank	$ 259,000	5	9.55%	60	$5,445.81		
6	Venture Capitalist	$ 259,000	3	9.25%	36			
7	Investment Banker	$ 259,000	2	8.95%	24			
8								

Minus sign before present value displays payment as a positive amount   Monthly payment calculated

FIGURE E-20: Completed worksheet

	A	B	C	D	E	F	G	H
1				QST				
2				Expansion Loan Summary				
3								
4	Lender	Loan Amount	Term (Years)	Interest Rate	Term (Months)	Monthly Payment	Total Payments	Total Interest
5	Commercial Bank	$ 259,000	5	9.55%	60	$5,445.81	$ 326,748.77	$ 67,748.77
6	Venture Capitalist	$ 259,000	3	9.25%	36	$8,266.30	$ 297,586.78	$ 38,586.78
7	Investment Banker	$ 259,000	2	8.95%	24	$11,826.41	$ 283,833.78	$ 24,833.78
8								

Copied formula calculates total payments and interest for remaining two loan options

Calculating future value with the FV function

You can use the FV (Future Value) function to determine the amount of money a given monthly investment will amount to, at a given interest rate, after a given number of payment periods. The syntax is similar to that of the PMT function: FV(rate,nper,pmt,pv,type). The rate is the interest paid by the financial institution, the nper is the number of periods, and the pmt is the amount that you deposit. For example, suppose you want to invest $1000 every month for the next 12 months into an account that pays 12% a year, and you want to know how much you will have at the end of 12 months (that is, its future value). You enter the function FV(.01,12,-1000), and Excel returns the value $12,682.50 as the future value of your investment. As with the PMT function, the units for the rate and nper must be consistent. If you made monthly payments on a three-year loan at 6% annual interest, you use the rate .06/12 and 36 periods (12*3). The arguments pv and type are optional; pv is the present value, or the total amount the series of payments is worth now. If you omit it, Excel assumes the pv is 0. The "type" argument indicates when the payments are made; 0 is the end of the period, and 1 is the beginning of the period. The default is the end of the period.

Practice

If you have a SAM user profile, you may have access to hands-on instruction, practice, and assessment of the skills covered in this unit. Log in to your SAM account (http://sam2007.course.com/) to launch any assigned training activities or exams that relate to the skills covered in this unit.

▼ CONCEPTS REVIEW

FIGURE E-21

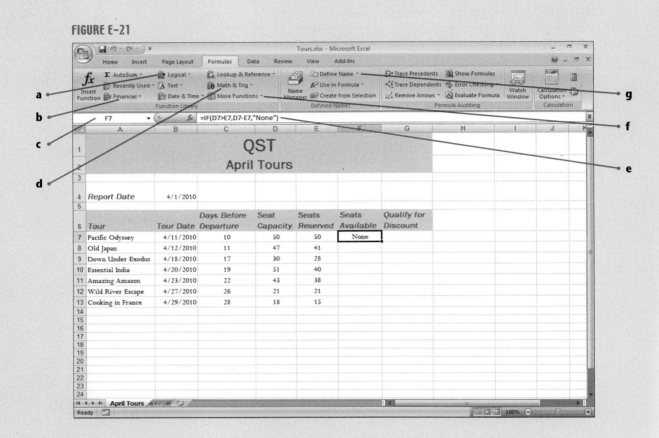

1. Which element points to the area where the name of a selected cell or range is displayed?
2. Which element points to a logical formula?
3. Which element do you click to add a statistical function to a worksheet?
4. Which element do you click to name a cell or range?
5. Which element do you click to insert an IF function into a worksheet?
6. Which element do you click to add a PMT function to a worksheet?
7. Which element do you click to add a SUMIF function to a worksheet?

Match each term with the statement that best describes it.

8. SUMIF
9. PROPER
10. test_cond
11. FV
12. PV

a. Function used to change the first letter of a string to uppercase
b. Function used to determine the future amount of an investment
c. Part of the PMT function that represents the loan amount
d. Part of the IF function in which the conditions are stated
e. Function used to conditionally total cells

Select the best answer from the list of choices.

13. **When you enter the rate and nper arguments in a PMT function, you must:**
   a. Use monthly units instead of annual units.
   b. Multiply both units by 12.
   c. Divide both values by 12.
   d. Be consistent in the units used.

14. **To express conditions such as less than or equal to, you can use a(n):**
   a. Statistical function.
   b. PMT function.
   c. Text formula.
   d. Comparison operator.

15. **Which of the following statements is false?**
   a. If you move a named cell or range, its name moves with it.
   b. Named ranges make formulas easier to build.
   c. Names cannot contain spaces.
   d. When used in formulas, names become relative cell references by default.

16. **Which of the following is an external reference indicator in a formula?**
   a. :
   b. &
   c. !
   d. =

▼ SKILLS REVIEW

1. **Format data using text functions.**
   a. Start Excel, open the file EX E-3.xlsx from the drive and folder where you store your Data Files, then save it as **Reviews**.
   b. On the Managers worksheet, select the range A2:A9 and, using the Text to Columns button on the Data tab, separate the names into two text columns. (*Hint*: The delimiter is a space.)
   c. In cell D2, enter the text formula to convert the first letter of the department in cell C2 to uppercase, then copy the formula in cell D2 into the range D3:D9.
   d. In cell E2, enter the text formula to convert all letters of the department in cell C2 to uppercase, then copy the formula in cell E2 into the range E3:E9.
   e. In cell F2, use the text formula to convert all letters of the department in cell C2 to lowercase, then copy the formula in cell F2 into the range F3:F9.
   f. In cell G2, use the text formula to substitute "Human Resources" for "hr" in cell F2. (*Hint*: In the Function Arguments dialog box, Text is F2, Old_text is hr, and New_text is Human Resources.) Copy the formula in cell G2 into the range G3:G9 to change the other cells containing hr to Human Resources. (Note that the marketing and sales entries will not change because the formula searches for the text hr).
   g. Save your work, then enter your name in the worksheet footer. Compare your screen to Figure E-22.
   h. Display the formulas in the worksheet, then print the worksheet.
   i. Redisplay the formula results.

FIGURE E-22

	A	B	C	D	E	F	G
1	Name		Department	PROPER	UPPER	LOWER	SUBSTITUTE
2	Paul	Keys	hR	Hr	HR	hr	Human Resources
3	Shimada	Story	hR	Hr	HR	hr	Human Resources
4	Kim	Hadley	MarKeting	Marketing	MARKETING	marketing	marketing
5	Albert	Ny	MarKeting	Marketing	MARKETING	marketing	marketing
6	Reggie	Delgado	saLEs	Sales	SALES	sales	sales
7	Harry	DePaul	saLEs	Sales	SALES	sales	sales
8	Mel	Abbott	hR	Hr	HR	hr	Human Resources
9	Jody	Wallace	MarKeting	Marketing	MARKETING	marketing	marketing
10							

2. **Sum a range of data conditionally.**
   a. Make the HR sheet active.
   b. In cell B20, use the COUNTIF function to count the number of employees with a rating of 5.
   c. In cell B21, use the AVERAGEIF function to average the salaries of employees with a rating of 5.
   d. In cell B22, enter the SUMIF function that totals the salaries of employees with a rating of 5.
   e. Format cells B21 and B22 with the Number format using commas and no decimals. Save your work.

3. Consolidate data using a formula.

a. Make the Summary sheet active.

b. In cell B4, use the AutoSum function to total cell F15 on the HR and Accounting sheets.

c. Format cell B4 with the Accounting number format.

d. Enter your name in the worksheet footer, then save your work. Compare your screen to Figure E-23.

e. Display the formula in the worksheet, then print the worksheet.

f. Redisplay the formula results in the worksheet.

4. Check formulas for errors.

a. Make the HR sheet active.

b. In cell I6, use the IFERROR function to display "ERROR" in the event that the formula F6/F15 results in a formula error. (*Note*: This formula will generate an intentional error, which you will correct in a moment.)

c. Copy the formula in cell I6 into the range I7:I14.

d. Correct the formula in cell I6 by making the denominator, F15, an absolute address.

e. Copy the new formula in cell I6 into the range I7:I14.

f. Format the range I6:I14 as percentage with two decimal places.

g. Save your work.

5. Construct formulas using named ranges.

a. On the HR sheet, name the range C6:C14 **review_date** and limit the scope of the name to the HR worksheet.

b. In cell E6, enter the formula **=review_date+183**, using the Use in Formula button to enter the cell name.

c. Copy the formula in cell E6 into the range E7:E14.

d. Use the Name Manager to add a comment of "Date of last review" to the review_date name. (*Hint*: In the Name Manager dialog box, click the review_date name, then click Edit to enter the comment.)

e. Save your work.

6. Build a logical formula with the IF function.

a. In cell G6, use the Function Arguments dialog box to enter the formula **=IF(D6=5,F6*0.05,0)**

b. Copy the formula in cell G6 into the range G7:G14.

c. In cell G15, use AutoSum to total the range G6:G14.

d. Format the range G6:G15 with the Currency number format, using the $ symbol and no decimal places.

e. Save your work.

7. Build a logical formula with the AND function.

a. In cell H6, use the Function Arguments dialog box to enter the formula **=AND(G6>0,B6>5)**.

b. Copy the formula in cell H6 into the range H7:H14.

c. Enter your name in the worksheet footer, save your work, compare your worksheet to Figure E-24, then print the worksheet.

d. Make the Accounting sheet active.

e. In cell H6, indicate if the employee needs more development hours to reach the minimum of 5: Use the Function Arguments dialog box for the NOT function to enter **B6>5** in the Logical text box. Copy the formula in cell H6 into the range H7:H14.

f. In cell I6, indicate if the employee needs to enroll in a quality class, as indicated by a rating less than 5 and having less than 5 development hours: Use the Function Arguments dialog box for the OR function to enter **D6<>5** in the Logical1 text box and **B6<=5** in the Logical2 text box. Copy the formula in cell I6 into the range I7:I14.

FIGURE E-23

	A	B
1	Payroll Summary	
2		
3		Salary
4	TOTAL	$ 565,787.00
5		
6		

FIGURE E-24

	A	B	C	D	E	F	G	H	I
1				Human Resources Department					
2				Merit Pay					
3									
4									
5	Last Name	Professional Development Hours	Review Date	Rating	Next Review	Salary	Bonus	Pay Bonus	Percentage of Total
6	Barry	5	2/1/2010	4	8/3/2010	19,840	$0	FALSE	7.21%
7	Gray	8	3/1/2010	5	8/31/2010	26,700	$1,335	TRUE	9.71%
8	Greenwood	1	7/1/2010	3	12/31/2010	33,200	$0	FALSE	12.07%
9	Hemsley	3	4/1/2010	5	10/1/2010	25,500	$1,275	FALSE	9.27%
10	Kim	9	3/1/2010	3	8/31/2010	37,500	$0	FALSE	13.63%
11	Manchevski	8	5/1/2010	5	10/31/2010	36,500	$1,825	TRUE	13.27%
12	Marley	10	6/1/2010	4	12/1/2010	37,500	$0	FALSE	13.63%
13	Smith	6	1/1/2010	3	7/3/2010	28,600	$0	FALSE	10.40%
14	Storey	1	9/1/2010	5	3/3/2011	29,700	$1,485	FALSE	10.80%
15						Total $ 275,040	$5,920		
16									
17									
18	Department Statistics								
19		Rating of 5							
20	Number		4						
21	Average Salary	29,600							
22	Total Salary	118,400							
23									

▼ SKILLS REVIEW (CONTINUED)

g. Enter your name in the worksheet footer, save your work, compare your screen to Figure E-25, then print the worksheet.

8. **Calculate payments with the PMT function.**

   a. Make the Loan sheet active.

   b. In cell B9, determine the monthly payment using the loan information shown: Use the Function Arguments dialog box to enter the formula =PMT(B5/12,B6,-B4).

   c. In cell B10, enter the formula =B9*B6.

   d. In cell B11, enter the formula =B10-B4, then compare your screen to Figure E-26.

   e. Enter your name in the worksheet footer, save the workbook, then print the worksheet.

   f. Close the workbook, then exit Excel.

FIGURE E-25

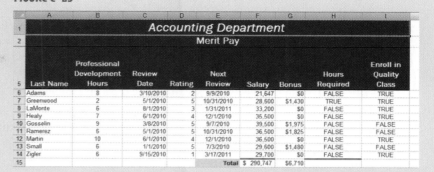

	Last Name	Professional Development Hours	Review Date	Rating	Next Review	Salary	Bonus	Hours Required	Enroll in Quality Class
6	Adams	8	3/10/2010	2	9/9/2010	21,647	$0	FALSE	TRUE
7	Greenwood	2	5/1/2010	5	10/31/2010	28,600	$1,430	TRUE	TRUE
8	LaMonte	6	8/1/2010	3	1/31/2011	33,200	$0	FALSE	TRUE
9	Healy	7	6/1/2010	4	12/1/2010	35,500	$0	FALSE	TRUE
10	Gosselin	9	3/8/2010	5	9/7/2010	39,500	$1,975	FALSE	FALSE
11	Ramerez	6	5/1/2010	5	10/31/2010	36,500	$1,825	FALSE	FALSE
12	Martin	10	6/1/2010	4	12/1/2010	36,500	$0	FALSE	TRUE
13	Small	6	1/1/2010	5	7/3/2010	29,600	$1,480	FALSE	FALSE
14	Zigler	6	9/15/2010	1	3/17/2011	29,700	$0	FALSE	TRUE
15					Total	$ 290,747	$6,710		

▼ INDEPENDENT CHALLENGE 1

As the accounting manager of Travel Well, a travel insurance company, you are reviewing the accounts payable information for your advertising accounts and prioritizing the overdue invoices for your collections service. You will analyze the invoices and use logical functions to emphasize priority accounts.

FIGURE E-26

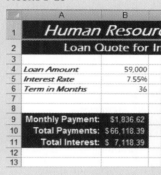

a. Start Excel, open the file EX E-4.xlsx from the drive and folder where you store your Data Files, then save it as **Ad Accounts**.

b. Name the range B7:B13 **invoice_date** and give the name a scope of the accounts payable worksheet.

c. Name the cell B4 **current_date** and give the name a scope of the accounts payable worksheet.

d. Enter a formula using the named range invoice_date in cell E7 that calculates the invoice due date by adding 30 to the invoice date.

e. Copy the formula in cell E7 to the range E8:E13.

f. In cell F7, enter a formula using the named range invoice_date and the named cell current_date that calculates the invoice age by subtracting the invoice date from the current date.

g. Copy the formula in cell F7 to the range F8:F13.

h. In cell G7, enter an IF function that calculates the number of days an invoice is overdue, assuming that an invoice must be paid in 30 days. (*Hint*: The Logical_test should check to see if the age of the invoice is greater than 30, the Value_if_true should calculate the current date minus the invoice due date, and the Value_if_false should be 0). Copy the IF function into the range G8:G13.

i. In cell H7, enter an AND function to prioritize the overdue invoices that are more than $1000 for collection services. (*Hint:* The Logical1 condition should check to see if the number of days overdue is more than 0 and the Logical2 condition should check if the amount is more than 1000). Copy the AND function into the range H8:H13.

j. Enter your name in the worksheet footer, then save, preview, and print the worksheet.

k. Close the workbook, then exit Excel.

Advanced Challenge Exercise

- Use the "Refers to:" text box in the Name Manager dialog box to verify that the names in the worksheet refer to the correct ranges.
- Use the filter in the Name Manager dialog box to verify that your names are scoped to the worksheet and not the workbook.
- Use the filter in the Name Manager dialog box to verify that your names are defined, free of errors, and not part of a table.

▼ INDEPENDENT CHALLENGE 2

You are an auditor with a certified public accounting firm. Goals, a manufacturer of ice skating products based in Quebec, has contacted you to audit its first-quarter sales records. The management at Goals is considering opening a branch in Great Britain and needs its sales records audited to prepare the business plan. Specifically, they want to show what percent of annual sales each category represents. You will use a formula on a summary worksheet to summarize the sales for January, February, and March and to calculate the overall first-quarter percentage of the sales categories.

    a. Start Excel, open the file EX E-5.xlsx from the drive and folder where you store your Data Files, then save it as **Goals Sales**.

    b. In cell B10 of the Jan, Feb, and Mar sheets, enter the formulas to calculate the sales totals for the month.

    c. For each month, in cell C5, create a formula calculating the percent of sales for the Sticks sales category. Use a function to display "ERROR" if there is a mistake in the formula. Verify that the percent appears with two decimal places. Copy this formula as necessary to complete the % of Sales data for all sales categories on all sheets. If any cells display "ERROR", fix the formulas in those cells.

    d. In column B of the Summary sheet, use formulas to total the sales categories for the Jan, Feb, and Mar worksheets.

    e. Locate the first-quarter sales total in cell B10 of the Summary sheet. Calculate the percent of each sales category on the Summary sheet. Use a function to display "ERROR" if there is a mistake in the formula. Copy this formula as necessary. If any cells display "ERROR", fix the formulas in those cells.

    f. Enter your name in the Summary worksheet footer, then save, preview, and print the worksheet.

    g. On the Products sheet, separate the product list in cell A1 into separate columns of text data. (*Hint*: The products are delimited with commas.) Widen the columns as necessary. Use the second row to display the products with the first letter of each word in uppercase, as shown in Figure E-27.

    h Enter your name in the Products worksheet footer, then save, preview, and print the worksheet.

    i. Close the workbook, then exit Excel.

FIGURE E-27

	A	B	C	D	E	F
1	sticks	ice skates	apparel	pads	equipment bags	
2	Sticks	Ice Skates	Apparel	Pads	Equipment Bags	
3						

▼ INDEPENDENT CHALLENGE 3

As the owner of Best Dressed, a clothing boutique with a growing clientele, you are planning to expand your business into a neighboring city. Because you will have to purchase additional inventory and renovate your new rental space, you decide to take out a $20,000 loan to finance your expansion expenses. You check three loan sources: the Small Business Administration (SBA), your local bank, and a consortium of investors. The SBA will lend you the money at 7.5% interest, but you have to pay it off in three years. The local bank offers you the loan at 8.25% interest over four years. The consortium offers you a 7% loan, but they require you to pay it back in two years. To analyze all three loan options, you decide to build a loan summary worksheet. Using the loan terms provided, build a worksheet summarizing your options.

    a. Start Excel, open a new workbook, then save it as **Dress Shop Loan**.

    b. Using Figure E-28 as a guide, enter labels and worksheet data for the three loan sources. (*Hint*: The Aspect theme is used with Orange Accent 1 as the fill color in the first two rows and Orange, Accent 1, Darker 25% as the text color in the calculation area.)

    c. Enter the monthly payment formula for your first loan source (making sure to show the payment as a positive amount), copy the formula as appropriate, then name the range containing the monthly payment formulas **Monthly_Payment** with a scope of the workbook.

FIGURE E-28

	A	B	C	D	E	F	G
1				Best Dressed			
2				Loan Options			
3							
4	Loan Source	Loan Amount	Interest Rate	# Payments	Monthly Payment	Total Payments	Total Interest
5	SBA	20,000	7.50%	36			
6	Bank	20,000	8.25%	48			
7	Investors	20,000	7.00%	24			
8							

▼ INDEPENDENT CHALLENGE 3 (CONTINUED)

d. Name the cell range containing the number of payments **Number_Payments** with the scope of the workbook.

e. Enter the formula for total payments for your first loan source using the named ranges Monthly_Payment and Number_Payments, then copy the formula as necessary.

f. Name the cell range containing the formulas for Total payments **Total_Payments**. Name the cell range containing the loan amounts **Loan_Amount**.

g. Enter the formula for total interest for your first loan source using the named ranges Total_Payments and Loan_Amount, then copy the formula as necessary.

h. Format the worksheet using formatting appropriate to the worksheet purpose, then enter your name in the worksheet footer.

i. Save, preview, and print the worksheet in landscape orientation, on a single page.

Advanced Challenge Exercise

- Turn on the print gridlines option for the worksheet.
- Turn on the printing of row and column headings.
- Print the worksheet formulas with the worksheet gridlines and headings on one page.
- Display the worksheet values.

j. Close the workbook then exit Excel.

▼ REAL LIFE INDEPENDENT CHALLENGE

You decide to create a weekly log of your daily aerobic exercise. As part of this log, you record your aerobic activity along with the number of minutes spent working out. If you do more than one activity in a day, for example, if you bike and walk, record each as a separate event. Along with each activity, you record the location where you exercise. For example, you may walk in the gym or outdoors. You will use the log to analyze the amount of time that you spend on each type of exercise.

a. Start Excel, open the file EX E-6.xlsx from the drive and folder where you store your Data Files, then save it as **Workout**.

b. Use the structure of the worksheet to record your aerobic exercise activities. Change the data in columns A, B, C, D, and F to reflect your activities, locations, and times. If you do not have any data to enter, use the provided worksheet data.

c. Use a SUMIF function in the column G cells to calculate the total minutes spent on each activity.

d. Enter an AVERAGEIF function in the column H cells to average the number of minutes spent on each activity.

e. Enter a COUNTIF function in the column I cells to calculate the number of sessions spent on each activity.

Advanced Challenge Exercise

- Enter one of your activities with a specific location, such as Walk Outdoors, in a column F cell, then enter the SUMIFS function in the adjacent column G cell that calculates the total number of minutes spent on that activity in the specific location (such as walking ...outdoors).
- Enter the AVERAGEIFS function in the corresponding column H cell that calculates the average number of minutes spent on the activity in the specified location.
- Enter the COUNTIFS function in the corresponding column I cell that calculates the number of days spent on the activity in the specific location.

f. Enter your name in the worksheet footer, then save, preview, and print the worksheet.

g. Close the workbook, then exit Excel.

▼ VISUAL WORKSHOP

Open the file EX E-7.xlsx from the drive and folder where you store your Data Files, then save it as **Quarterly Sales Summary**. Create the worksheet shown in Figure E-29 using the data in columns B, C, and D. (*Hints:* Use AND formulas to determine if a person is eligible for a bonus, and use IF formulas to enter the bonus amounts. An employee with a performance rating of seven or higher and who meets the sales quota receives a bonus of one percent of the sales. If the rating is less than seven, or if the sales amounts are less than the quota, no bonus is awarded.) Enter your name in the worksheet footer, then preview and print the worksheet.

FIGURE E-29

	A	B	C	D	E	F
1			Bonus Pay Summary			
2						
3	Last Name	Quota	Sales	Performance Rating	Eligible	Bonus Amount
4	Allen	$100,000	$125,400	7	TRUE	$1,254
5	Gray	$80,000	$75,420	3	FALSE	$0
6	Greenwood	$90,000	$83,540	9	FALSE	$0
7	Hanson	$120,000	$132,980	5	FALSE	$0
8	Kerns	$150,000	$147,650	8	FALSE	$0
9	Maloney	$140,000	$149,800	5	FALSE	$0
10	Martin	$135,000	$132,200	7	FALSE	$0
11	Smith	$100,000	$98,650	3	FALSE	$0
12	Storey	$90,000	$96,700	9	TRUE	$967
13						

Managing Workbook Data

As you analyze data using Excel, you will find that your worksheets and workbooks become more complex. In this unit, you will learn several Excel features to help you manage workbook data. In addition, you will want to share workbooks with coworkers, but you need to ensure that they can view your data while preventing unwarranted changes. You will learn how to save workbooks in different formats and how to prepare workbooks for distribution.  Kate Morgan, the vice president of sales at Quest Specialty Travel, asks for your help in analyzing yearly sales data from the Canadian branches. When the analysis is complete, she will distribute the workbook for branch managers to review.

OBJECTIVES

View and arrange worksheets

Protect worksheets and workbooks

Save custom views of a worksheet

Add a worksheet background

Prepare a workbook for distribution

Insert hyperlinks

Save a workbook for distribution

Group worksheets

Viewing and Arranging Worksheets

As you work with workbooks made up of multiple worksheets, you may need to compare data in the various sheets. To do this, you can view each worksheet in its own workbook window, called an **instance**, and display the windows in an arrangement that makes it easy to compare data. When you work with worksheets in separate windows, you are working with different views of the same worksheet; the data itself remains in one file. ▄▅▆▇▓ Kate asks you to compare the monthly store sales totals for the Toronto and Vancouver branches. Because the sales totals are on different worksheets, you want to arrange the worksheets side by side in separate windows.

STEPS

1. **Start Excel, open the file EX F-1.xlsx from the drive and folder where you store your Data Files, then save it as Store Sales**

2. **With the Toronto sheet active, click the View tab, then click the New Window button in the Window group**

   There are now two instances of the Store Sales workbook on the task bar: Store Sales.xlsx:1 and Store Sales.xlsx:2. The Store Sales.xlsx:2 window is active—you can see its button selected on the taskbar, and the filename in the title bar has :2 after it.

3. **Click the Vancouver sheet tab, click the Switch Windows button in the Window group, then click Store Sales.xlsx:1**

   The Store Sales.xlsx:1 instance is active. The Toronto sheet is active in the Store Sales.xlsx:1 workbook and the Vancouver sheet is active in the Store Sales.xlsx:2 workbook.

4. **Click the Arrange All button in the Window group**

   The Arrange Windows dialog box, shown in Figure F-1, provides configurations for displaying the worksheets. You want to view the workbooks vertically.

5. **Click the Vertical option button to select it, then click OK**

   The windows are arranged vertically, as shown in Figure F-2. You can activate a workbook by clicking one of its cells. You can also view only one of the workbooks by hiding the one you do not wish to see.

6. **Scroll horizontally to view the data in the Store Sales.xlsx:1 workbook, click anywhere in the Store Sales.xlsx:2 workbook, scroll horizontally to view the data in the Store Sales.xlsx:2 workbook, then click the Hide button in the Window group**

   When you hide the second instance, only the Store Sales.xlsx:1 workbook is visible.

7. **Click the Unhide button in the Window group; click Store Sales.xlsx:2, if necessary, in the Unhide dialog box; then click OK**

   The Store Sales.xlsx:2 book appears.

8. **Close the Store Sales.xlsx:2 instance, then maximize the Toronto worksheet in the Store Sales.xlsx workbook**

   Closing the Store Sales.xlsx:2 instance leaves only the first instance open, which is now named Store Sales.xlsx in the title bar.

FIGURE F-1: Arrange Windows dialog box

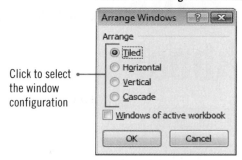

Click to select
the window
configuration

FIGURE F-2: Windows displayed vertically

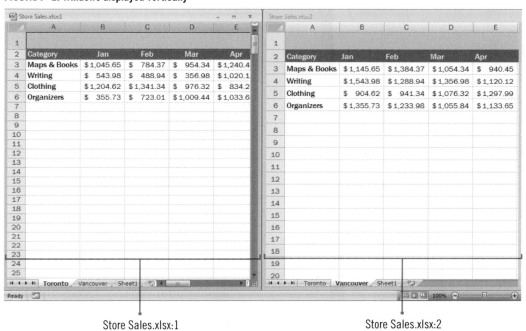

Store Sales.xlsx:1   Store Sales.xlsx:2

Splitting the worksheet into multiple panes

Excel lets you split the worksheet area into vertical and/or horizontal panes, so that you can click inside any one pane and scroll to locate information in that pane while the other panes remain in place, as shown in Figure F-3. To split a worksheet area into multiple panes, drag a split box (the small box at the top of the vertical scroll bar or at the right end of the horizontal scroll bar) in the direction you want the split to appear. To remove the split, move the pointer over the split until the pointer changes to a double-headed arrow, then double-click.

FIGURE F-3: Worksheet split into two horizontal and two vertical panes

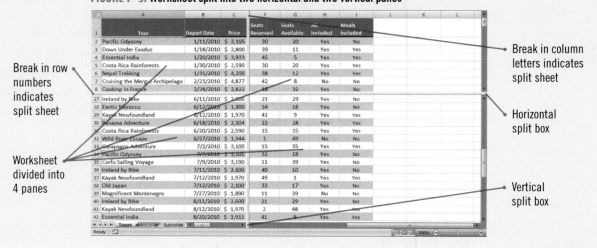

Break in row
numbers
indicates
split sheet

Worksheet
divided into
4 panes

Break in column
letters indicates
split sheet

Horizontal
split box

Vertical
split box

Protecting Worksheets and Workbooks

To protect sensitive information, Excel allows you to **lock** selected cells so that other people are able to view the data (values, numbers, labels, formulas, etc.) in those cells, but not change it. Excel locks all cells by default, but this protection does not take effect until you activate the Excel protection feature. A common worksheet protection strategy is to unlock cells in which data will be changed, sometimes referred to as the **data entry area**, and to lock cells in which the data should not be changed. Then, when you protect the worksheet, the unlocked areas can still be changed. ▀▀▀▀ Because the Toronto sales figures for January through March have been confirmed as final, Kate asks you to protect that area of the worksheet so the figures cannot be altered.

STEPS

1. **On the Toronto sheet, select the range E3:M6, click the Home tab, click the Format button in the Cells group, click Format Cells, then in the Format Cells dialog box click the Protection tab**

   The Locked check box in the Protection tab is already checked, as shown in Figure F-4. This check box is selected by default, meaning that all the cells in a new workbook start out locked. However, cell locking is not applied unless the protection feature is also activated. The protection feature is inactive by default. Because the April through December sales figures have not yet been confirmed as final and may need to be changed, you do not want those cells to be locked when the protection feature is activated.

2. **Click the Locked check box to deselect it, then click OK**

   The data remains unlocked until you set the protection in the next step.

3. **Click the Review tab, then click the Protect Sheet button in the Changes group**

   The Protect Sheet dialog box opens, as shown in Figure F-5. In the "Allow users of this worksheet to" list, you can select the actions that you want your worksheet users to be able to perform. The default options protect the worksheet while allowing users to select locked or unlocked cells only. You choose not to use a password.

4. **Verify that Protect worksheet and contents of locked cells is checked and that Select locked cells and Select unlocked cells are checked, then click OK**

   You are ready to test the new worksheet protection.

5. **In cell B3, type 1 to confirm that locked cells cannot be changed, then click OK**

   When you attempt to change a locked cell, a dialog box, shown in Figure F-6, reminds you of the protected cell's read-only status. **Read-only format** means that users can view but not change the data.

6. **Click cell F3, type 1, and notice that Excel allows you to begin the entry, press [Esc] to cancel the entry, then save the workbook**

   Because you unlocked the cells in columns E through M before you protected the worksheet, you can make changes to these cells. You decide to protect the workbook, but you want users to open the workbook without typing a password first.

7. **Click the Protect Workbook button in the Changes group, in the Protect Structure and Windows dialog box make sure the Structure check box is selected, click the Windows check box to select it, then click OK**

   You are ready to test the new workbook protection.

8. **Right-click the Toronto sheet tab**

   The Insert, Delete, Rename, Move or Copy, Tab Color, Hide, and Unhide menu options are not available. You decide to remove the workbook and worksheet protections.

9. **Click the Unprotect Workbook button in the Changes group, then click the Unprotect Sheet button to remove the worksheet protection**

FIGURE F-4: Protection tab in Format Cells dialog box

Click to remove
check mark

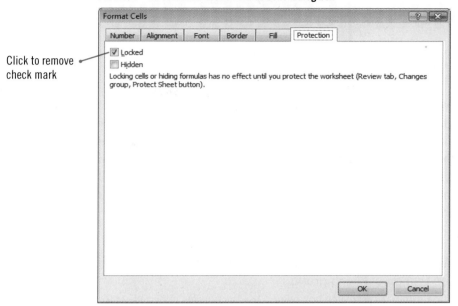

FIGURE F-5: Protect Sheet dialog box

Prevents locked
cells from
changes

Allows users to select
worksheet cells

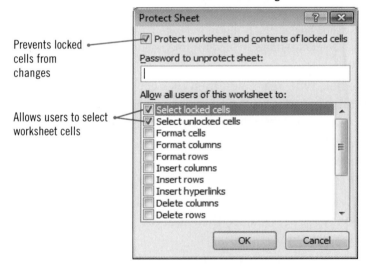

FIGURE F-6: Reminder of protected cell's read-only status

Freezing rows and columns

As the rows and columns of a worksheet fill up with data, you might need to scroll through the worksheet to add, delete, modify, and view information. You can temporarily freeze columns and rows so you can keep labeling information in view as you scroll. **Panes** are the columns and rows that **freeze**, or remain in place, while you scroll through your worksheet. To freeze panes you need to click the View tab, click the Freeze Panes button in the Window group then click Freeze Panes. Excel freezes the columns to the left and the rows above the selected cell. You can also select Freeze Top Row or Freeze First Column to freeze the top row or left worksheet column.

Saving Custom Views of a Worksheet

A **view** is a set of display and/or print settings that you can name and save, then access at a later time. By using the Excel Custom Views feature, you can create several different views of a worksheet without having to create separate sheets. For example, if you often hide columns in a worksheet, you can create two views, one that displays all of the columns and another with the columns hidden. You set the worksheet display first, then name the view. ▰▰▰▰▰ Because Kate wants to generate a sales report from the final sales data for January through March, she asks you to save the first-quarter sales data as a custom view. You begin by creating a view showing all of the worksheet data.

1. **With the Toronto sheet active, click the View tab, then click the Custom Views button in the Workbook Views group**

   The Custom Views dialog box opens. Any previously defined views for the active worksheet appear in the Views box. No views are defined for the Toronto worksheet. You decide to add a named view that shows all the worksheet columns.

   QUICK TIP
   To delete views from the active worksheet, select the view in the Custom Views dialog box, then click Delete.

2. **Click Add**

   The Add View dialog box opens, as shown in Figure F-7. Here, you enter a name for the view and decide whether to include print settings and hidden rows, columns, and filter settings. You want to include the selected options.

3. **In the Name box, type Year Sales, then click OK**

   You have created a view called Year Sales that shows all the worksheet columns. You want to set up another view that will hide the April through December columns.

4. **Select columns E through M, right-click the selected area, then click Hide on the shortcut menu**

   You are ready to create a custom view of the January through March sales data.

5. **Click cell A1, click the Custom Views button in the Workbook Views group, click Add, in the Name box type First Quarter, then click OK**

   You are ready to test the two custom views.

   TROUBLE
   If you receive the message "Some view settings could not be applied," turn off worksheet protection by clicking the Unprotect Sheet button in the Changes group of the Review tab.

6. **Click the Custom Views button in the Workbook Views group, click Year Sales in the Views list, then click Show**

   The Year Sales custom view displays all of the months' sales data. Now you are ready to test the First Quarter custom view.

7. **Click the Custom Views button in the Workbook Views group, then with First Quarter in the Custom Views dialog box selected, click Show**

   Only the January through March sales figures appear on the screen, as shown in Figure F-8.

8. **Return to the Year Sales view, then save your work**

FIGURE F-7: **Add View dialog box**

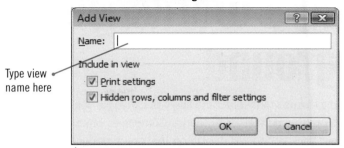

Type view
name here

Add View

Name: |

Include in view
- ☑ Print settings
- ☑ Hidden rows, columns and filter settings

OK   Cancel

FIGURE F-8: **First Quarter view**

January —
March sales
figures

Break in column
letters indicates
hidden columns

	A	B	C	D	N
1	QST Toronto				
2	Category	Jan	Feb	Mar	
3	Maps & Books	$ 1,045.65	$ 784.37	$ 954.34	
4	Writing	$ 543.98	$ 488.94	$ 356.98	
5	Clothing	$ 1,204.62	$ 1,341.34	$ 976.32	
6	Organizers	$ 355.73	$ 723.01	$ 1,009.44	
7					

Using Page Break Preview

The vertical and horizontal dashed lines in the Normal view of worksheets represent page breaks. Excel automatically inserts a page break when your worksheet data doesn't fit on one page. These page breaks are **dynamic**, which means they adjust automatically when you insert or delete rows and columns and when you change column widths or row heights. Everything to the left of the first vertical dashed line and above the first horizontal dashed line is printed on the first page. You can manually add or remove page breaks by clicking the Page Layout tab, clicking the Breaks button in the Page Setup group, then clicking the appropriate command. You can also view and change page breaks manually by clicking the View tab, then clicking the Page Break Preview button in the Workbook Views group, or by clicking the Page Break Preview button 🖳 on the status bar, then clicking OK. You can drag the blue page break lines to the desired location, as shown in Figure F-9. If you drag a page break to the right to include more data on a page, Excel shrinks the type to fit the data on that page. To exit Page Break Preview, click the Normal button in the Workbook Views group.

FIGURE F-9: **Page Break Preview window**

	A	B	C	D	E	F	G	H	I	J	K	L	M
1	QST Toronto												
2	Category	Jan	Feb	Mar	Apr	May	Jun	Jul	Aug	Sep	Oct	Nov	Dec
3	Maps & Books	$ 1,045.65	$ 784.37	$ 954.34	$ 1,240.45	$ 567.76	$ 1,240.76	$ 1,240.43	$ 1,240.34	$ 675.54	$ 1,240.54	$ 1,240.34	$ 1,240.34
4	Writing	$ 543.98	$ 488.94	$ 356.98	$ 1,020.12	$ 378.23	$ 392.41	$ 934.62	$ 145.89	$ 345.98	$ 435.78	$ 359.76	$ 289.88
5	Clothing	$ 1,204.62	$ 1,341.34	$ 976.32	$ 834.23	$ 1,022.35	$ 634.22	$ 1,309.22	$ 749.33	$ 1,209.04	$ 1,383.11	$ 1,456.21	$ 1,341.47
6	Organizers	$ 355.73	$ 723.01	$ 1,009.44	$ 1,033.65	$ 998.98	$ 1,003.48	$ 1,006.23	$ 942.56	$ 1,097.99	$ 865.11	$ 898.99	$ 1,012.75

Drag blue page
break lines to
change page
breaks

Adding a Worksheet Background

In addition to using a theme's font colors and fills, you can make your Excel data more attractive to view by adding a picture to the worksheet background. Companies often use their logo as a worksheet background. A worksheet background will display on the screen but will not print with the worksheet. If you want to add a worksheet background that appears on printouts, you can add a **watermark**, a translucent background design that prints behind your data. To add a watermark, you add the image to the worksheet header or footer. Kate asks you to add the Quest logo to the printed background of the Toronto worksheet. You will begin by adding the logo as a worksheet background.

1. **With the Toronto sheet active, click the Page Layout tab, then click the Background button in the Page Setup group**

    The Sheet Background dialog box opens.

2. **Navigate to the drive and folder where you store your Data Files, click Logo.gif, then click Insert**

    The Quest logo is tiled behind the worksheet data. It appears twice because the graphic is **tiled**, or repeated, to fill the background.

3. **Preview the Toronto worksheet, then click the Close Print Preview button**

    Because the logo is only for display purposes, it will not print with the worksheet, so is not visible in Print Preview. You want the logo to print with the worksheet, so you decide to remove the background and add the logo to the worksheet header.

4. **Click the Delete Background button in the Page Setup group, click the Insert tab, then click the Header & Footer button in the Text group**

    The Design tab of the Header & Footer Tools appears, as shown in Figure F-10. The Header & Footer group buttons add preformatted headers and footers to a worksheet. The Header & Footer Elements buttons allow you to add page numbers, the date, the time, pictures, and names to the header or footer. The Navigation group buttons move the insertion point from the header to the footer and back. The Options group buttons specify special circumstances for the worksheet's headers and footers. You want to add a picture to the header.

5. **With the insertion point in the center section of the header, click the Picture button in the Header & Footer Elements group, navigate to the drive and folder where you store your Data Files, click Logo.gif, then click Insert**

    A code representing a picture, &[Picture], appears in the center of the header.

6. **Click cell A1, then click the Normal button ⊞ on the Status Bar**

    You want to scale the worksheet data to print on one page.

7. **Click the Page Layout tab, click the Width list arrow in the Scale to Fit group, click 1 page, click the Height list arrow in the Scale to Fit group, click 1 page, then preview the worksheet**

    Your worksheet should look like Figure F-11.

8. **Click the Close Print Preview button, then save the workbook**

FIGURE F-10: Design tab of the Header & Footer tools

Click these buttons to customize the header and footer

Header & Footer Tools Design tab

Some cells may temporarily display ######### while header is added

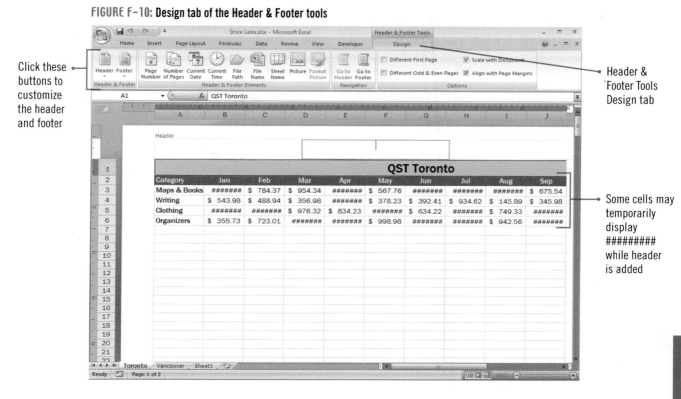

FIGURE F-11: Preview of Toronto worksheet with logo in the background

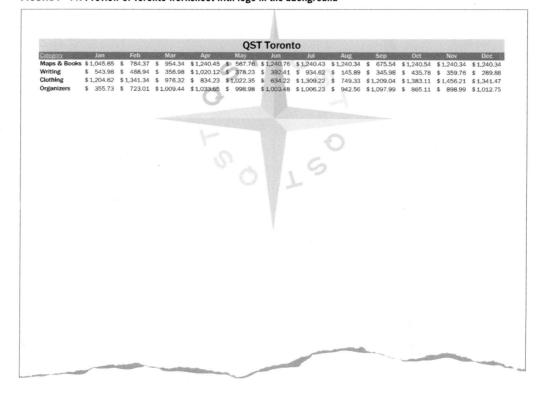

Category	Jan	Feb	Mar	Apr	May	Jun	Jul	Aug	Sep	Oct	Nov	Dec
Maps & Books	$1,045.65	$ 784.37	$ 954.34	$1,240.45	$ 567.76	$1,240.76	$1,240.43	$1,240.34	$ 675.54	$1,240.54	$1,240.34	$1,240.34
Writing	$ 543.98	$ 488.94	$ 356.98	$1,020.12	$ 378.23	$ 392.41	$ 934.62	$ 145.89	$ 345.98	$ 435.78	$ 359.76	$ 289.88
Clothing	$1,204.62	$1,341.34	$ 976.32	$ 834.23	$1,022.35	$ 634.22	$1,309.22	$ 749.33	$1,209.04	$1,383.11	$1,456.21	$1,341.47
Organizers	$ 355.73	$ 723.01	$1,009.44	$1,033.65	$ 998.98	$1,003.48	$1,006.23	$ 942.56	$1,097.99	$ 865.11	$ 898.99	$1,012.75

Excel 2007

Preparing a Workbook for Distribution

If you are collaborating with others and want to share a workbook with them, you might want to remove sensitive information, such as headers, footers, or hidden elements, before distributing the file. You can use the Document Inspector feature to find and remove hidden data and personal information in your workbooks. On the other hand, you might want to add helpful information, called **properties**, to a file to help others identify, understand, and locate it, such as keywords, the author's name, a title, the status, and comments. **Keywords** are terms users can search for that will help them locate your workbook. Properties are a form of **metadata**, information that describe data and are used in Microsoft Windows document searches. You enter properties in the Document Properties Panel. In addition, to insure that others do not make unauthorized changes to your workbook, you can mark a file as final, which changes it to a read-only file, which others can open but not alter. To protect the workbook and prepare it for distribution to the sales managers, Kate asks you to remove sensitive information, add document properties, and mark the workbook as final.

STEPS

1. **Click the Office button [image], point to Prepare, then click Inspect Document**

   The Document Inspector dialog box opens, as shown in Figure F-12. It lists items that you can have Excel evaluate for personal information. All the components are selected by default.

2. **Click Inspect**

   After inspecting your document, the inspector displays the inspection results. Areas with personal information have a ! in front of them. Headers and footers are also flagged. You want to keep the file's header and footer and remove personal information.

> **QUICK TIP**
> You can view a file's summary information by clicking the Document Properties list arrow in the Document Properties Panel, then clicking Advanced Properties.

3. **Click Remove All next to Document Properties and Personal Information, then click Close**

   You decide to add keywords to help the sales managers find the worksheet using the search words Toronto or Vancouver.

4. **Click [image], point to Prepare, then click Properties**

   The Document Properties Panel appears at the top of the worksheet, as shown in Figure F-13. You decide to add a title, status, keywords, and comments.

> **QUICK TIP**
> If you have Windows Rights Management Services (RMS) client software installed, you can use the Information Rights Management (IRM) feature to specify access permissions. Click the Office button, point to Prepare, point to Restrict Permission, then select permission options.

5. **In the Title text box type Store Sales, in the Keywords text box type Toronto Vancouver store sales, in the Status text box type DRAFT, then in the Comments text box type The first-quarter figures are final., then click the Close button on the Document Properties Panel**

   You are ready to mark the workbook as final.

6. **Click [image], point to Prepare, click Mark as Final, click OK, then click OK again**

   The workbook is saved as a read-only file. [Read-Only] appears in the title bar.

7. **Click cell B3, then type 1 to confirm that the cell cannot be changed**

   Marking a workbook as final prevents accidental changes to the workbook. However, it is not a strong form of workbook protection because a workbook recipient can remove this Final status and edit the document. You decide to remove the read-only status from the workbook so that it is again editable.

8. **Click [image], point to Prepare, then click Mark as Final**

   The title bar no longer displays [Read-Only] after the workbook title, indicating that you can now edit the workbook.

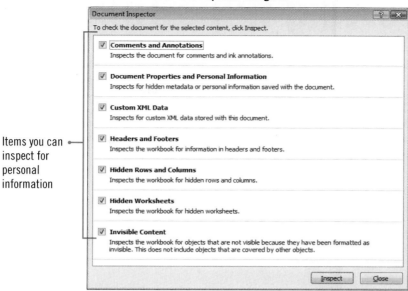

Items you can inspect for personal information

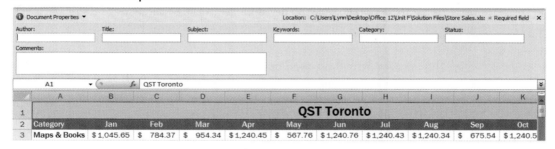

Adding a digital signature to a workbook

You can digitally sign a workbook to establish its validity and prevent it from being changed. You must obtain a valid certificate from a certificate authority to authenticate the workbook. To add a signature line in a workbook, click the Insert tab, click the Signature Line button in the Text group, then click OK. In the Signature Setup dialog box, enter information about the signer of the worksheet and then click OK. To add a signature, double-click the signature line, click OK, if prompted with a Get a Digital ID dialog box, click the Create your own digital ID option button, save your file if prompted, in the Sign dialog box click Select Image next to the sign box, browse to the location where your signature is saved, click Sign, then click OK. To add the certificate authenticating the workbook, click the Office button , point to Prepare, click Add a Digital Signature, then click OK. In the Sign dialog box click Sign, then click OK. The workbook will be saved as read-only and it will not be able to be changed by other users.

Sharing a workbook

You can make an Excel file a **shared workbook** so that several users can open and modify it at the same time. Click the Review tab, click the Share Workbook button in the Changes group, then on the Editing tab of the Share Workbook dialog box click "Allow changes by more than one user at the same time. This also allows workbook merging." If you get an error that the workbook cannot be shared because privacy is enabled, click the Office button, click Excel Options, click the Trust Center category on the left side of the dialog box, click Trust Center Settings, click Privacy Options in the list on the left, click the "Remove personal information from file properties on save" check box to deselect it, then click OK twice. When you share workbooks, it is often helpful to **track** modifications, or identify who made which changes. You can track all changes to a workbook by clicking the Track Changes button in the Changes group, and then clicking Highlight Changes. To resolve the tracked changes in a workbook, click the Track Changes button, then click Accept/Reject Changes. The changes are displayed one by one. You can accept the change or, if you disagree with any of the changes, you can reject them.

Inserting Hyperlinks

As you manage the content and appearance of your workbooks, you may want the workbook user to view information in another location. It might be nonessential information or data that is too detailed to place in the workbook itself. In these cases, you can create a hyperlink. A **hyperlink** is an object (a filename, word, phrase, or graphic) in a worksheet that, when you click it, displays, or "jumps to," another location, called the **target**. The target can also be a worksheet, another document, or a site on the World Wide Web. For example, in a worksheet that lists customer invoices, at each customer's name, you might create a hyperlink to an Excel file containing payment terms for each customer.  Kate wants managers who view the Store Sales workbook to be able to view the item totals for each sales category in the Toronto sheet. She asks you to create a hyperlink at the Category heading so that users can click the hyperlink to view the items for each category.

1. **Click cell A2 on the Toronto worksheet**

QUICK TIP

To remove a hyperlink or change its target, right-click it, then click Remove Hyperlink or Edit Hyperlink.

2. **Click the Insert tab if necessary, then click the Hyperlink button in the Links group**

    The Insert Hyperlink dialog box opens, as shown in Figure F-14. The icons under "Link to" on the left side of the dialog box let you specify the type of location you want the link to jump to: an existing file or Web page, a place in the same document, a new document, or an e-mail address. Because you want the link to display an already-existing document, the selected first icon, Existing File or Web Page, is correct, so you won't have to change it.

3. **Click the Look in list arrow, navigate to the location where you store your Data Files if necessary, then click Toronto Sales.xlsx in the file list**

    The filename you selected and its path appear in the Address text box. This is the document users will see when they click the hyperlink. You can also specify the ScreenTip that users see when they hold the pointer over the hyperlink.

4. **Click ScreenTip, type Items in each category, click OK, then click OK again**

    Cell A2 now contains underlined red text, indicating that it is a hyperlink. The color of a hyperlink depends on the worksheet theme colors. You need to change the text color of the hyperlink text so it is visible on the dark background. After you create a hyperlink, you should check it to make sure that it jumps to the correct destination.

QUICK TIP

If you link to a Web page, you must be connected to the Internet to test the link.

5. **Click the Home tab, click the Font Color list arrow A· in the Font group, click the White, Background 1 color (first color in the Theme Colors), move the pointer over the Category text, view the ScreenTip, then click once**

    After you click, the Toronto Sales workbook opens, displaying the Sales sheet, as shown in Figure F-15.

6. **Close the Toronto Sales workbook, then save the Store Sales workbook**

Returning to your document

After you click a hyperlink and view the destination document, you will often want to return to your original document that contains the hyperlink. To do this, you can add the Back button to the Quick Access Toolbar. However, the Back button does not appear in the Quick Access toolbar by default; you need to customize the toolbar. (If you are using a computer in a lab, check with your system administrator to see if you have permission to do this.) To customize the Quick Access toolbar, click the Office button, click Excel Options, click Customize in the Excel Options dialog box, click the "Choose Commands from" list arrow, select All Commands, click the Back button, click Add>>, then click OK.

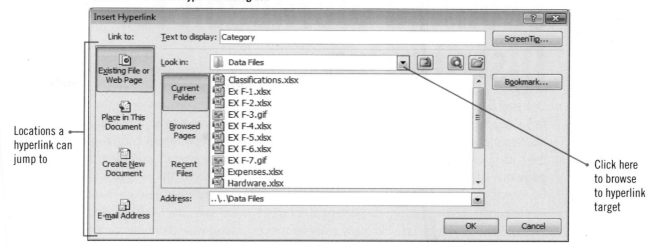

FIGURE F-14: Insert Hyperlink dialog box

Locations a hyperlink can jump to

Click here to browse to hyperlink target

FIGURE F-15: Target document

	A	B	C	D
1	QST Toronto			
2				
3	Travel Store Sales			
4				
5	Item	Total Sales	Category	
6	PopOut Maps	$ 2,619.82	Maps & Books	
7	Smart Packing Books	$ 3,934.77	Maps & Books	
8	Airport Guides	$ 4,941.62	Maps & Books	
9	Pack It Guides	$ 1,214.65	Maps & Books	
10	Travel Pens	$ 2,855.65	Writing	
11	Jounals	$ 2,836.92	Writing	
12	Plane Slippers	$ 2,099.15	Clothing	
13	Travel Socks	$ 1,108.26	Clothing	
14	Men's Sandals	$ 2,103.14	Clothing	
15	Women's Sandals	$ 1,954.29	Clothing	
16	Hats	$ 975.44	Clothing	
17	Men's T-Shirts	$ 3,112.76	Clothing	
18	Women's T-Shirts	$ 2,108.42	Clothing	
19	Cosmetics Folders	$ 2,798.53	Organizers	
20	Jewelry Cases	$ 2,108.42	Organizers	
21	Travel Cases	$ 2,095.75	Organizers	
22	Passport holders	$ 3,945.22	Organizers	

Sales   Sheet2   Sheet3

Ready

Using research tools

You can access resources online and locally on your computer using the Research task pane. To open the Research task pane, click the Review tab, then click the Research button in the Proofing group. You can click the Thesaurus button in the Proofing group for help with synonyms. You can click the Translate button in the Proofing group to translate your text into a selected language. The Search for text box in the Research pane allows you to specify a research topic. The Research pane has a drop-down list of the resources available to search for your topic.

Saving a Workbook for Distribution

One way to share Excel data is to place, or **publish**, the data on a network or on the Web so that others can access it using their Web browsers. To publish an Excel document to an **intranet** (a company's internal Web site) or the Web, you can save it in an **HTML (Hypertext Markup Language)** format, which is the coding format used for all Web documents. You can also save your Excel file as a **single file Web page** that integrates all of the worksheets and graphical elements from the workbook into a single file. This file format is called MHTML. In addition to distributing files on the Web, you may need to distribute your files to people working with an earlier version of Excel. You can save your files as Excel 97-2003 workbooks. Excel workbooks can be saved in many other formats to support wide distribution and to make them load faster. The most popular formats are listed in Table F-1. ▰▰▰▰ Kate asks you to create a workbook version that managers running an earlier version of Excel can open and modify. She also asks you to save the Store Sales workbook in MHT format so she can publish it on the Quest intranet for their sales managers to view.

STEPS

1. **Click the Office button ▣, point to Save As, click Excel 97-2003 Workbook, in the Save As dialog box, navigate to the drive and folder where you store your Data Files, then click Save**

   The Compatibility Checker appears on the screen, alerting you to the features that will be lost by saving in the earlier format. Some Excel 2007 features are not available in earlier versions of Excel.

2. **Click Continue, close the workbook, then reopen the Store Sales.xls workbook**

   [Compatibility Mode] appears in the title bar, as shown in Figure F-16. Compatibility mode prevents you from including Excel features in your workbook that are not supported in Excel 97-2003 workbooks. To exit compatibility mode, you need to save your file in one of the Excel 2007 formats and reopen the file.

3. **Click ▣, point to Save As, click Excel Workbook, if necessary navigate to the drive and folder where you store your Data Files, click Save, then click Yes when you are asked if you want to replace the existing file**

   [Compatibility Mode] remains displayed in the title bar. You decide to close the file and reopen it to exit compatibility mode.

4. **Close the workbook, then reopen the Store Sales.xlsx workbook**

   The title bar no longer displays [Compatibility mode]. You decide to save the file for Web distribution.

5. **Click ▣, click Save As, in the Save As dialog box, navigate to the drive and folder where you store your Data Files, change the filename to sales, then click the Save as type list arrow and click Single File Web Page (*.mht, *.mhtml)**

   The Save as type list box indicates that the workbook is to be saved as a Single File Web Page, which is in mhtml or mht format. To avoid problems when publishing your pages to a Web server, it is best to use lowercase characters, omit special characters and spaces, and limit your filename to eight characters with an additional three-character extension.

6. **Click Save, then click Yes**

   The dialog box indicated that some features may not be retained in the Web page file. Excel saves the workbook as an MHT file in the folder location you specified in the Save As dialog box. The MHT file is open on your screen, as shown in Figure F-17. It's a good idea to open an mht file in your browser to see how it will look to viewers.

7. **Close the sales.mht file in Excel, open Windows Explorer, open the sales.mht file, click the Vancouver sheet tab, then close your browser window**

FIGURE F-16: Workbook in compatibility mode

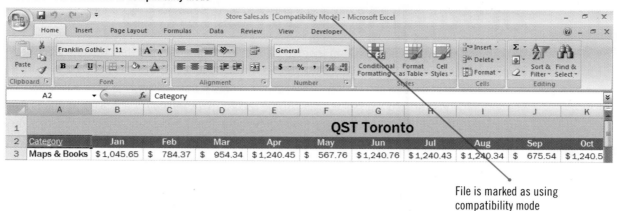

File is marked as using
compatibility mode

FIGURE F-17: Workbook saved as a single file web page

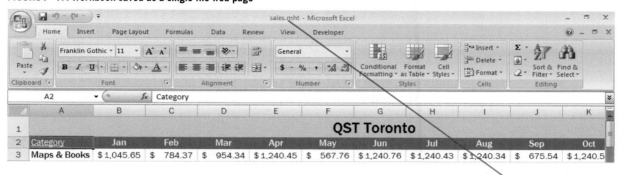

Web file with new name

TABLE F-1: Workbook formats

type of file	file extension(s)	Used for
Macro-enabled workbook	xlsm	Files that contain macros
Excel 97-2003 workbook	xls	Working with people using older versions of Excel
Single file Web page	mht, mhtml	Web sites with multiple pages and graphics
Web page	htm, html	Simple single-page Web sites
Excel template	xltx	Excel files that will be reused with small changes
Excel macro-enabled template	xltm	Excel files that will be used again and contain macros
Portable document format	pdf	Files with formatting that needs to be preserved
XML paper specification	xps	Files with formatting that needs to be preserved and files that need to be shared

Understanding Excel file formats

The default file format for Excel 2007 files is the Office Open XML format, which supports all Excel features. This format stores Excel files in small XML components which are zipped for compression. This default format has different types of files with their own extensions that are also often called formats themselves. The most often used format, xlsx , does not support macros. Macros, programmed instructions that perform tasks, can be a security risk. If your worksheet contains macros, you need to save it with an extension of xlsm so the macros will function in the workbook. If you use a workbook's text and formats repeatedly, you may want to save it as a template with the extension xltx. If your template contains macros, you need to save it with the xltm extension.

Grouping Worksheets

You can group worksheets to work on them as a collection so that data entered into one worksheet is automatically entered into all of the selected worksheets. This is useful for data that is common to every sheet of a workbook, such as headers and footers, or for column headings that will apply to all monthly worksheets in a yearly summary. Grouping worksheets can also be used to print multiple worksheets at one time.
Kate asks you to add the text Quest to the footer of both the Toronto and Vancouver worksheets. You will also add one-inch margins to the left and right sides of both worksheets.

STEPS

1. **Open the Store Sales.xlsx file from the drive and folder where you store your Data Files**

2. **With the Toronto sheet active, press and hold [Shift], click the Vancouver sheet, then release [Shift]**
    Both sheet tabs are selected, and the title bar now contains [Group], indicating that the worksheets are grouped together, so any changes you make to the Toronto sheet will also be made to the Vancouver sheet.

3. **Click the Insert tab, then click the Header & Footer button in the Text group**

4. **On the Header & Footer Tools Design tab, click the Go to Footer button in the Navigation group, type Quest in the center section of the footer, enter your name in the left section of the footer, click cell A1, then click the Normal button ▦ on the Status Bar**
    You decide to check the footers in Print Preview.

5. **With the worksheets still grouped, click the Office button 🌀, point to Print, click Print Preview, then click the Next Page button in the Preview group**
    Because the worksheets are grouped, both pages contain the footer with Quest and your name. The worksheets would look better with a wider top margin.

6. **Click the Close Print Preview button, click the Page Layout tab, click the Margins button in the Page Setup group, click Custom Margins, in the Top text box type 1, then click OK**

7. **Preview and print the worksheets**
    The Toronto worksheet is shown in Figure F-18; the Vancouver worksheet is shown in Figure F-19. You decide to ungroup the worksheets.

8. **Right-click the Toronto worksheet sheet tab, then click Ungroup Sheets**

9. **Save the workbook, then close it and exit Excel**

Creating a workspace

If you work with several workbooks at a time, you can group them so that you can open them in one step by creating a **workspace**, a file with an .xlw extension. Then, instead of opening each workbook individually, you can open the workspace. To create a workspace, open the workbooks you wish to group, then position and size them as you would like them to appear. Click the View tab, click the Save Workspace button in the Window group, type a name for the workspace file, navigate to the location where you want to store it, then click Save. Remember, however, that the workspace file does not contain the workbooks themselves, so you still have to save any changes you make to the original workbook files. If you work at another computer, you need to have the workspace file and all of the workbooks that are part of the workspace.

FIGURE F-18: **Toronto worksheet**

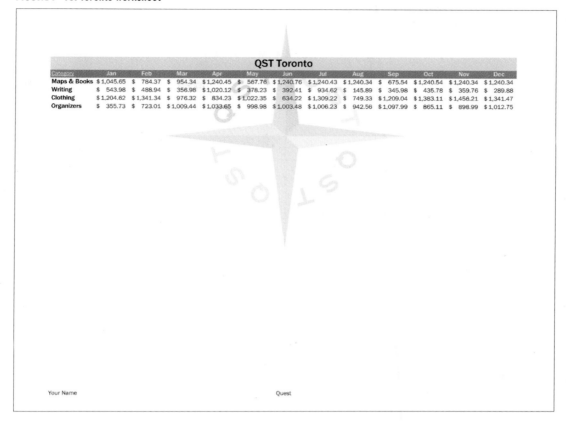

QST Toronto

Category	Jan	Feb	Mar	Apr	May	Jun	Jul	Aug	Sep	Oct	Nov	Dec
Maps & Books	$1,045.65	$ 784.37	$ 954.34	$1,240.45	$ 567.76	$1,240.76	$1,240.43	$1,240.34	$ 675.54	$1,240.54	$1,240.34	$1,240.34
Writing	$ 543.98	$ 488.94	$ 356.98	$1,020.12	$ 378.23	$ 392.41	$ 934.62	$ 145.89	$ 345.98	$ 435.78	$ 359.76	$ 289.88
Clothing	$1,204.62	$1,341.34	$ 976.32	$ 834.23	$1,022.35	$ 634.22	$1,309.22	$ 749.33	$1,209.04	$1,383.11	$1,456.21	$1,341.47
Organizers	$ 355.73	$ 723.01	$1,009.44	$1,033.65	$ 998.98	$1,003.48	$1,006.23	$ 942.56	$1,097.99	$ 865.11	$ 898.99	$1,012.75

Your Name   Quest

FIGURE F-19: **Vancouver worksheet**

QST Vancouver

Category	Jan	Feb	Mar	Apr	May	Jun	Jul	Aug	Sep	Oct	Nov	Dec
Maps & Books	$1,145.65	$1,384.37	$1,054.34	$ 940.45	$1,567.76	$1,040.76	$ 940.43	$1,140.34	$1,275.54	$ 940.54	$1,040.34	$1,040.34
Writing	$1,543.98	$1,288.94	$1,356.98	$1,120.12	$1,311.22	$1,392.41	$1,134.62	$1,145.89	$1,194.86	$ 835.78	$ 859.76	$ 889.88
Clothing	$ 904.62	$ 941.34	$1,076.32	$1,297.99	$ 922.35	$1,234.22	$1,509.22	$1,049.33	$1,009.04	$1,283.11	$1,126.21	$1,141.47
Organizers	$1,355.73	$1,233.98	$1,055.84	$1,133.65	$1,298.98	$1,303.48	$1,106.23	$ 842.56	$1,197.99	$ 965.11	$ 988.99	$1,112.75

Your Name   Quest

Practice

If you have a SAM user profile, you may have access to hands-on instruction, practice, and assessment of the skills covered in this unit. Log in to your SAM account (http://sam2007.course.com/) to launch any assigned training activities or exams that relate to the skills covered in this unit.

▼ CONCEPTS REVIEW

FIGURE F-20

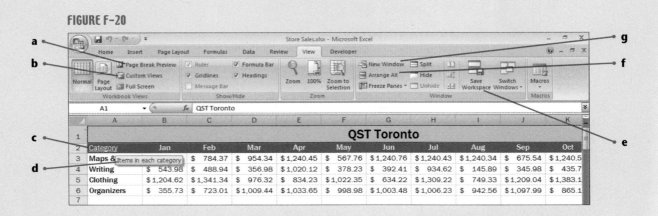

1. Which element do you click to organize windows in a specific configuration?
2. Which element points to a ScreenTip for a hyperlink?
3. Which element points to a hyperlink?
4. Which element do you click to open the active worksheet in a new window?
5. Which element do you click to name and save a set of display and/or print settings?
6. Which element do you click to group workbooks so that they open together as a unit?
7. Which element do you click to view and change the way worksheet data is distributed on printed pages?

Match each term with the statement that best describes it.

8. Data entry area	**a.** Web page format
9. Hyperlink	**b.** Portion of a worksheet that can be changed
10. Watermark	**c.** Translucent background design on a printed worksheet
11. HTML	**d.** An object that when clicked displays another worksheet or a Web page
12. Dynamic page breaks	**e.** Adjusted automatically when rows and columns are inserted or deleted

Select the best answer from the list of choices.

13. You can establish the validity of a workbook by adding a _____.
   - **a.** Keyword
   - **b.** Custom Views
   - **c.** Digital signature
   - **d.** Template

14. You can group several workbooks in a _____ so they can be opened together rather than individually.
   - **a.** Workgroup
   - **b.** Consolidated workbook
   - **c.** Workspace
   - **d.** Work unit

15. **Which of the following formats means that users can view but not change data in a workbook?**
    a. Macro
    b. PDF
    c. Read-only
    d. Template

16. **You can group noncontiguous worksheets by pressing and holding _____ while clicking the sheet tabs that you want to group.**
    a. [Ctrl]
    b. [Spacebar]
    c. [Alt]
    d. [F6]

▼ SKILLS REVIEW

1. **View and arrange worksheets.**
    a. Start Excel, open the file EX F-2.xlsx from the drive and folder where you store your Data Files, then save it as **Chicago Budget**.
    b. Activate the 2010 sheet if necessary, then open the 2011 sheet in a new window.
    c. Activate the 2010 sheet in the Chicago Budget.xlsx:1 workbook. Activate the 2011 sheet in the Chicago Budget.xlsx:2 workbook.
    d. View the Chicago Budget.xlsx:1 and Chicago Budget.xlsx:2 workbooks tiled horizontally. View the workbooks in a vertical arrangement.
    e. Hide the Chicago Budget.xlsx:2 instance, then unhide the instance. Close the Chicago Budget.xlsx:2 instance and maximize the Chicago Budget.xlsx workbook.
    f. Split the 2010 sheet into two horizontal panes. (*Hint*: Drag the Horizontal split box.) Remove the split by double-clicking it, then save your work.

2. **Protect worksheets and workbooks.**
    a. On the 2010 sheet, unlock the expense data in the range C9:F17.
    b. Protect the sheet without using a password.
    c. To make sure the other cells are locked, attempt to make an entry in cell D4. You should see the error message displayed in Figure F-21.
    d. Change the first-quarter mortgage expense to 4500.

    FIGURE F-21

    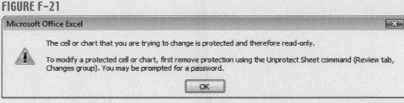

    e. Protect the workbook's structure and windows without applying a password. Right-click the 2010 and 2011 worksheets to verify that you cannot insert, delete, rename, move, copy, hide, or unhide the sheets, or change their tab color.
    f. Unprotect the workbook. Unprotect the 2010 worksheet.
    g. Save the workbook.

3. **Save custom views of a worksheet**
    a. Using the 2010 sheet, create a view of the entire worksheet called **Entire 2010 Budget**.
    b. Hide rows 8 through 19, then make a new view called **Income** showing only the income data.
    c. Use the Custom Views dialog box to display all of the data on the 2010 worksheet.
    d. Use the Custom Views dialog box to display only the income data on the 2010 worksheet.
    e. Use the Custom Views dialog box to return to the Entire 2010 Budget view.
    f. Save the workbook.

4. **Add a worksheet background.**
    a. Use EX F-3.gif as a worksheet background for the 2010 sheet.
    b. Delete the background image on the 2010 sheet.
    c. Add EX F-3.gif to the 2010 header.
    d. Preview the 2010 worksheet to verify that the background will print, then exit Print Preview and save the workbook.
    e. Add your name to the center section of the 2010 worksheet footer, then print the worksheet.

5. Prepare a workbook for distribution.

   a. Inspect the workbook and remove any document properties, personal information, and header and footer information.

   b. Use the Document Properties Panel to add a title of Quarterly Budget and the keywords café and Chicago.(*Hint*: Separate the keywords with a space.) If you are using your own computer, add your name in the Author text box.

   c. Mark the workbook as final and verify that [Read-Only] is in the title bar.

   d. Remove the final status of the workbook.

   e. Save the workbook.

6. Insert hyperlinks.

   a. On the 2010 worksheet, make cell A8 a hyperlink to the file **Expenses.xlsx** in your Data Files folder.

   b. Test the link, then print Sheet 1 of the Expenses workbook.

   c. Return to the Chicago Budget workbook, edit the hyperlink in cell A8, adding a ScreenTip that reads **Expense Details**, then verify that the ScreenTip appears.

   d. On the 2011 worksheet, enter the text **Based on 2010 budget** in cell A21.

   e. Make the text in cell A21 a hyperlink to cell A1 in the 2010 worksheet. (*Hint*: Use the Place in This Document button and note the cell reference in the Type the cell reference text box.)

   f. Test the hyperlink.

   g. Remove the hyperlink in cell A8 of the 2010 worksheet.

   h. Save the workbook.

7. Save a workbook for distribution.

   a. Save the Chicago Budget workbook as a single file Web page with the name chicago.mht. Close the chicago.mht file in Excel, then open the chicago.mht file in your Web browser. Close your browser window and reopen the Chicago Budget.xlsx file.

   b. If you have the PDF Add-in installed on your computer, save the Chicago Budget workbook as a PDF file.

   c. Save the Chicago Budget workbook as an Excel 97-2003 workbook and review the results of the Compatibility Checker.

   d. Close the Chicago Budget.xls file and reopen the Chicago Budget.xlsx file.

   e. Save the file as a macro-enabled template in the drive and folder where you store your Data Files. (*Hint*: Select the type Excel Macro-Enabled template xltm in the Save as type list.)

   f. Close the template file, then reopen the Chicago Budget.xlsx file.

8. Grouping worksheets.

   a. Group the 2010 and 2011 worksheets.

   b. Add your name to the center footer section of the worksheets.

   c. Save the workbook, then preview both sheets.

   d. Print both sheets, compare your sheets to Figure F-22, then ungroup the sheets.

   e. Close all open files and exit Excel.

FIGURE F-22

	A	B	C	D	E	F	G	H
1			Chicago 2010 Quarterly Café Budget					
2	Income	Description	1st QTR	2nd QTR	3rd QTR	4th QTR	TOTAL	% OF TOTAL
3		Coffee	$ 8,500	$ 8,700	$ 7,500	$ 8,100	$ 32,800	34.02%
4		Tea	$ 7,500	$ 6,800	$ 5,700	$ 6,800	$ 26,800	27.80%
5		Pastries	$ 9,100	$ 9,100	$ 8,700	$ 9,900	$ 36,800	38.17%
6		TOTAL	$ 25,100	$ 24,600	$ 21,900	$ 24,800	$ 96,400	100.00%
7								
8	Expenses							
9		Mortgage	$ 4,500	$ 4,300	$ 4,300	$ 4,300	$ 17,400	32.67%
10		Payroll	$ 5,500	$ 5,500	$ 5,500	$ 5,800	$ 22,300	41.87%
11		Pastries	$ 1,150	$ 1,150	$ 1,180	$ 1,150	$ 4,630	8.69%
12		Utilities	$ 580	$ 580	$ 580	$ 580	$ 2,320	4.36%
13		Phone	$ 490	$ 490	$ 490	$ 450	$ 1,920	3.60%
14		Coffee	$ 580	$ 580	$ 590	$ 580	$ 2,330	4.37%
15		Tea	$ 370	$ 370	$ 330	$ 370	$ 1,440	2.70%
16		Advertising	$ 230	$ 230	$ 230	$ 230	$ 920	1.73%
17		TOTAL	$ 13,400	$ 13,200	$ 13,200	$ 13,460	$ 53,260	100.00%
18								
19	Cash Flow		$ 11,700	$ 11,400	$ 8,700	$ 11,340	$ 43,140	
20								

	A	B	C	D	E	F	G	H
1			Chicago 2011 Quarterly Café Budget					
2	Income	Description	1st QTR	2nd QTR	3rd QTR	4th QTR	TOTAL	% OF TOTAL
3		Coffee	$ 8,800	$ 8,500	$ 7,500	$ 8,100	$ 32,900	33.64%
4		Tea	$ 7,700	$ 6,900	$ 5,700	$ 6,800	$ 27,100	27.71%
5		Pastries	$ 9,900	$ 9,300	$ 8,700	$ 9,900	$ 37,800	38.65%
6		TOTAL	$ 26,400	$ 24,700	$ 21,900	$ 24,800	$ 97,800	100.00%
7								
8	Expenses							
9		Mortgage	$ 4,300	$ 4,300	$ 4,300	$ 4,300	$ 4,300	31.85%
10		Payroll	$ 5,600	$ 5,600	$ 5,600	$ 5,600	$ 5,600	41.48%
11		Pastries	$ 1,250	$ 1,250	$ 1,250	$ 1,250	$ 1,250	9.26%
12		Utilities	$ 590	$ 590	$ 590	$ 590	$ 590	4.37%
13		Phone	$ 500	$ 500	$ 500	$ 500	$ 500	3.70%
14		Coffee	$ 590	$ 590	$ 590	$ 590	$ 590	4.37%
15		Tea	$ 390	$ 390	$ 390	$ 390	$ 390	2.89%
16		Advertising	$ 280	$ 280	$ 280	$ 280	$ 280	2.07%
17		TOTAL	$ 13,500	$ 13,500	$ 13,500	$ 13,500	$ 13,500	100.00%
18								
19	Cash Flow		$ 12,900	$ 11,200	$ 8,400	$ 11,300	$ 84,300	
20								
21	Based on 2010 Budget							
22								

▼ INDEPENDENT CHALLENGE 1

You manage Old City Photo, a photo supply company located in Montreal, Canada. You are organizing your first-quarter sales in an Excel worksheet. Because the sheet for the month of January includes the same type of information you need for February and March, you decide to enter the headings for all of the first-quarter months at the same time. You use a separate worksheet for each month and create data for three months.

a. Start Excel, create a new workbook, then save it as **Photo Sales.xlsx** in the drive and folder where you store your Data Files.

b. Name the first sheet January, name the second sheet February, and name the third sheet March.

c. Group the worksheets.

d. With the worksheets grouped, use Table F-2 as a guide to enter the row and column labels that need to appear on each of the three sheets. Add the headings in rows one and two. Center the first row across columns A and B. Enter the labels with the data in the range B3:B9 and the Total label in cell A10.

TABLE F-2

Old City Photo	
	Amount in $ (Canada)
Cameras	
Color Processing	
B & W Processing	
Film	
Digital Media	
Frames	
Darkroom Supplies	
TOTAL	

e. Enter the formula to sum the Amount column in cell B10. Ungroup the worksheets and enter your own data for each of the sales categories in the January, February, and March sheets.

f. Display each worksheet in its own window, then arrange the three sheets vertically.

g. Hide the window displaying the March sheet. Unhide the March sheet window.

h. Split the March window into two panes, the upper pane displaying rows one through five and the lower pane displaying rows six through ten. Scroll through the data in each pane, then remove the split.

i. Close the windows displaying Photo Sales.xlsx:2 and Photo Sales.xlsx:3, then maximize the Photo Sales.xlsx workbook.

j. Add the keywords **photo supplies** to your workbook, using the Document Properties Panel.

k. Group the worksheets again.

l. Add headers that include your name in the left section to all three worksheets.

m. With the worksheets still grouped, format the worksheets appropriately.

n. Ungroup the worksheets, then mark the workbook status as final.

o. Save the workbook, preview and print the three worksheets, then exit Excel.

▼ INDEPENDENT CHALLENGE 2

As the payroll manager at Media Communications, an advertising firm, you decide to organize the weekly timecard data using Excel worksheets. You use a separate worksheet for each week and track the hours for employees with different job classifications. A hyperlink in the worksheet provides pay rates for each classification and custom views limit the information that is displayed.

a. Start Excel, open the file EX F-4.xlsx from the drive and folder where you store your Data Files, then save it as **Timesheets**.

b. Compare the data in the workbook by arranging the Week 1, Week 2, and Week 3 sheets horizontally.

c. Maximize the Week 1 window. Unlock the hours data in the Week 1 sheet and protect the worksheet. Verify that the employee names, numbers, and classifications cannot be changed. Verify that the total hours data can be changed, but do not change the data.

d. Unprotect the Week 1 sheet and create a custom view called **Complete Worksheet** that displays all of the worksheet data.

e. Hide column E and create a custom view of the data in the range A1:D22. Give the view a name of **Employee Classifications**. Display each view, then return to the Complete Worksheet view.

▼ INDEPENDENT CHALLENGE 2 (CONTINUED)

f. Add a page break between columns D and E so that the Total Hours data prints on a second page. Preview the worksheet, then remove the page break. (*Hint*: Use the Breaks button on the Page Layout tab.)

g. Add a hyperlink to the Classification heading in cell D1 that links to the file Classifications.xlsx. Add a ScreenTip that reads Pay rates, then test the hyperlink. Compare your screen to Figure F-23.

h. Save the workbook as an Excel 97-2003 workbook, reviewing the Compatibility Checker information. Close the Timesheets.xls file, then reopen the Timesheets.xlsx workbook.

i. Group the three worksheets and add your name to the center section of the footer.

j. Save the workbook, then preview the grouped worksheets.

k. Ungroup the worksheets and add two-inch top and left margins to the Week 1 worksheet.

l. Hide the Week 2 and Week 3 worksheets.

m. Inspect the file and remove all document properties, personal information, headers, footers, and hidden worksheets.

n. Add the keyword hours to the workbook, save the workbook, then mark it as final.

FIGURE F-23

	A	B
1	**Media Communications**	
2	Classifications	Pay Rate
3	Associate	$37
4	Sr. Associate	$45
5	Assistant	$22
6	Sr. Assistant	$30
7		

Advanced Challenge Exercise

- Remove the final status from the workbook.
- If you have Windows Rights Management Services client software installed on your computer, restrict the permissions to the workbook by granting only yourself permission to change the workbook.
- If you have a valid certificate authority, add a digital signature to the workbook.
- Delete the hours data in the worksheet and save the workbook as an Excel Template.

o. Add your name to the center footer section, save the workbook, print the Week 1 worksheet, close the workbook and exit Excel.

▼ INDEPENDENT CHALLENGE 3

One of your responsibilities as the office manager at your technology training company is to order paper supplies for the office. You decide to create a spreadsheet to track these orders, placing each month's orders on its own sheet. You create custom views that will focus on the categories of supplies. A hyperlink will provide the supplier's contact information.

a. Start Excel, open the file EX F-5.xlsx from the drive and folder where you store your Data Files, then save it as **Supplies**.

b. Arrange the sheets for the three months horizontally to compare supply expenses, then close the extra workbook windows and maximize the remaining window.

c. Create a custom view of the entire January worksheet named **All Supplies**. Hide the paper, pens, and miscellaneous supply data and create a custom view displaying only the hardware supplies. Call the view **Hardware**.

d. Display the All Supplies view, group the worksheets, and create totals for the total costs in cell D28 on each month's sheet.

e. With the sheets grouped, add the sheet name to the center section of each sheet's header and your name to the center section of each sheet's footer.

f. Use the compatibility checker to view the unsupported features in earlier Excel formats.

g. Add a hyperlink in cell A1 of the January sheet that opens the file Hardware.xlsx. Add a ScreenTip of **Hardware Supplier**. Test the link, viewing the ScreenTip, then return to the Supplies workbook.

h. Create a workspace that includes the workbooks Supplies.xlsx and Hardware.xlsx in the tiled layout. Name the workspace **Office Supplies**. (*Hint*: Save Workspace is a button on the View tab in the Window group.)

i. Hide the Hardware.xlsx workbook.

j. Unhide the Hardware.xlsx workbook.

▼ INDEPENDENT CHALLENGE 3 (CONTINUED)

k. Close the Hardware.xlsx file and maximize the Supplies.xlsx worksheet.

l. Save the Supplies workbook as a macro-enabled workbook.

m. Print the January worksheet, close the workbook, and exit Excel.

▼ REAL LIFE INDEPENDENT CHALLENGE

Excel can be a useful tool in planning vacations. Whether you are planning a trip soon or in the distant future, you can use Excel to organize your travel budget. Use the table below as a guide in organizing your travel expenses. After your data is entered, you create custom views of the data, add a hyperlink and keywords, and save the file in an earlier version of Excel.

a. Start Excel, create a new workbook, then save it as **Travel Budget** in the drive and folder where you store your Data Files.

b. Enter your travel budget data using the relevant items from the Table F-3.

c. Add a hyperlink to your accommodations label that links to a Web page with information about the hotel, campground, B & B, or inn that you will stay at on your trip.

d. Create a custom view called **Entire Budget** that displays all of the budget information. Create a custom view named **Transportation** that displays only the transportation data. Check each view, then display the entire budget.

e. Add appropriate keywords to the workbook.

f. Add a footer that includes your name on the left side of the printout.

g. Unlock the price information in the worksheet. Protect the worksheet without using a password.

h. Save the workbook, then print the worksheet.

i. Save the workbook in Excel 97-2003 format.

j. Close the Travel Budget.xls file.

Advanced Challenge Exercise

- Open the Travel Budget.xlsx file and unprotect the worksheet.
- Enable the workbook to be changed by multiple people simultaneously.
- Set up the shared workbook so that all future changes will be tracked.
- Change the data for two of your dollar amounts.
- Review the tracked changes and accept the first change and reject the second change
- Save the workbook.

k. Exit Excel.

TABLE F-3

	Amount
Transportation	
Air	
Auto	
Train	
Cab	
Bus	
Accommodations	
Hotel	
Campground fees	
Bed & Breakfast	
Inn	
Meals	
Food	
Beverage	
Miscellaneous	
Admissions fees	
Souvenirs	

▼ VISUAL WORKSHOP

Start Excel, open the file EX F-6.xlsx from the drive and folder where you store your Data Files, then save it as **Summer Rentals**. Create the worksheet shown in Figure F-24. Enter your name in the footer, then print the worksheet. The text in cell A18 is a hyperlink to the Price Information workbook; the worksheet background is the Data File EX F-7.gif, and the picture in the header is the file EX F-7.gif.

FIGURE F-24

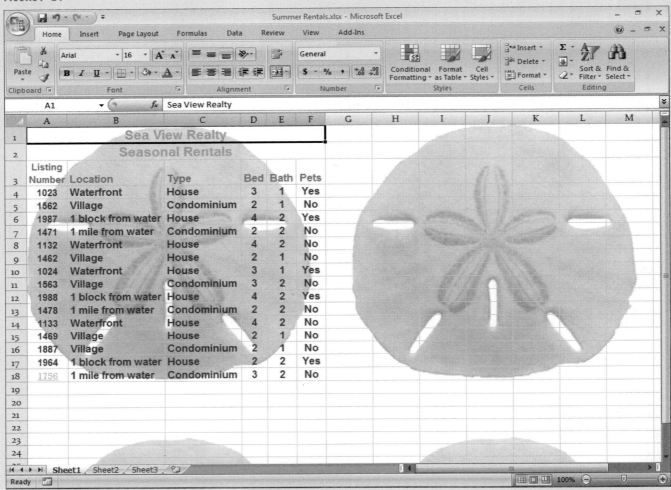

Using Tables

In addition to using Excel spreadsheet features, you can analyze and manipulate data in a table structure. An Excel **table** is an organized collection of rows and columns of similarly structured data in a worksheet. For example, a table might contain customer, sales, or inventory information. When you designate a particular range of worksheet data as a table, its formatting is extended when you add data and all table formulas are updated to include the new data. Without a table, you would have to manually adjust formatting and formulas every time data is added to a range. In this unit, you'll learn how to plan and create a table; add, change, find, and delete information in a table; and then sort, perform table calculations, and print a table. Quest uses tables to analyze tour data. The vice president of sales, Kate Morgan, asks you to help her build and manage a table of 2010 tour information.

OBJECTIVES

Plan a table
Create a table
Add table data
Find and replace table data
Delete table data
Sort table data
Use formulas in a table
Print a table

Planning a Table

When planning a table, consider what information you want your table to contain and how you want to work with the data, now and in the future. As you plan a table, you should understand its most important components. A table is organized into rows called records. A **record** contains data about an object, person, or other type of table item. Records are composed of fields. **Fields** are columns in the table; each field describes a characteristic of the record, such as a customer's last name or street address. Each field has a **field name**, which is a column label, such as "Address," that describes its contents. Tables usually have a **header row** as the first row that contains the field names. To plan your table, use the steps below. See Table G-1 for additional planning guidelines. ▒▒▒▒▓ Kate asks you to compile a table of the 2010 tours. Before entering the tour data into an Excel worksheet, you plan the table contents.

DETAILS

As you plan your table, use the following guidelines:

- **Identify the purpose of the table**

  Determine the kind of information the table should contain. You want to use the tours table to quickly find all departure dates of a particular tour. You also want to display the tours in order of departure date.

- **Plan the structure of the table**

  Determine the fields that are necessary to achieve the table's purpose. You have worked with the sales department to determine the type of information that they need to obtain about each tour. Figure G-1 shows a layout sketch for the table. Each row will contain one tour record. The columns represent fields that contain pieces of descriptive information you will enter for each tour, such as the name, departure date, and duration.

- **Document the table design**

  In addition to your table sketch, you should make a list of the field names that documents the type of data and any special number formatting required for each field. Field names should be as short as possible while still accurately describing the column info. When naming fields it is important to use text rather than numbers because numbers may be interpreted as parts of formulas. Your field names should be unique and not easily confused with cell addresses, such as the name D2. Your Tours table will contain eight field names, each one corresponding to the major characteristics of the 2010 tours. Table G-2 shows the documentation of the field names in your table.

TABLE G-1: Guidelines for planning a table

worksheet structure guidelines	row and column content guidelines
Tables can be created from any contiguous range of cells on your worksheet	Plan and design your table so that all rows have similar items in the same column
A table should not have any blank rows or columns	Do not insert extra spaces at the beginning of a cell because this can affect sorting and searching
Data in your table can be used independently of data outside of the table on the worksheet	Instead of blank rows or columns between your labels and your data, use formatting to make column labels stand out from the data
Data can be organized on a worksheet using multiple tables to define sets of related data	Use the same format for all cells below the field name in a column

Tour	Depart Date	Number of Days	Seat Capacity	Seats Reserved	Price	Air Included	Meals Included

Header row will contain
field names

Each tour will be
placed in a table row

TABLE G-2: **Table documentation**

field name	type of data	description of data
Tour	Text	Name of tour
Depart Date	Date	Date tour departs
Number of Days	Number with 0 decimal places	Duration of the tour
Seat Capacity	Number with 0 decimal places	Maximum number of people the tour can accommodate
Seats Reserved	Number with 0 decimal places	Number of reservations for the tour
Price	Accounting with 0 decimal places and $ symbol	Tour price (This price is not guaranteed until a 30% deposit is received)
Air Included	Text	Yes: Airfare is included in the price No: Airfare is not included in the price
Meals Included	Text	Yes: Breakfast and dinner included in the price No: Meals are not included in the price

Creating a Table

Once you have planned the table structure, the sequence of fields, and appropriate data types, you are ready to create the table in Excel. After you create a table, a Table Tools Design tab appears, containing a gallery of table styles. **Table styles** allow you to easily add formatting to your table by using preset formatting combinations that define fill color, borders, and type style and color. ▬▬▓▓▒ Kate asks you to build a table with the 2010 tour data. You begin by entering the field names. Then you enter the tour data that corresponds to each field name, create the table, and format the data using a table style.

STEPS

1. **Start Excel, open the file** EX G-1.xlsx **from the drive and folder where you store your Data Files, then save it as** 2010 Tours

2. **Beginning in cell A1 of the Practice sheet, enter each field name in a separate column, as shown in Figure G-2**

   Field names are usually entered in the first row of the table.

3. **Enter the information from Figure G-3 in the rows immediately below the field names, leaving no blank rows**

   The data appears in columns organized by field name.

4. **Select the range A1:H4, click the** Format button **in the Cells group, click** AutoFit Column Width, **then click cell A1**

   Resizing the column widths this way is faster than double-clicking the column divider lines.

5. **With cell A1 selected, click the** Insert tab, **then click the** Table button **in the Tables group, in the Create Table dialog box verify that your table data is in the range $A$1:$H$4 and make sure** My table has headers **is checked, then click** OK

   Filter list arrows, which let you display portions of your data, appear next to each column header. When you create a table, Excel automatically applies a default table style. The Table Tools Design tab appears and the Table Styles group displays a gallery of table formatting options. You decide to use a different table style from the gallery.

6. **Click the** Table Styles More button ⊽, **scroll to view all of the table styles, then move the mouse pointer over several styles without clicking**

   As you point to each table style, Live Preview shows you what your table will look like with the style applied. However, you only see a preview of each style; you need to click a style to apply it.

7. **Click the** Table Style Medium 7 **to apply it to your table, then click cell A1**

   Compare your table to Figure G-4.

Coordinating table styles with your document

The Table Styles gallery on the Table Tools Design tab has three style categories: Light, Medium, and Dark. Each category has numerous design types; for example, in some of the designs, the header row and total row are darker and the rows alternate colors. The available table designs use the current workbook theme colors so the table coordinates with your existing workbook content. If you select a different workbook theme and color scheme in the Themes group on the Page Layout tab, the Table Styles gallery uses those colors. You can modify gallery styles further by using the options in the Table Style Options group on the Table Tools Design tab; for example, if you select Header Row, the table styles in the gallery will all display distinctive header rows.

FIGURE G-2: Field names entered in row 1

	A	B	C	D	E	F	G	H	I
1	Tour	Depart Date	Number of Days	Seat Capacity	Seats Reserved	Price	Air Included	Meals Included	
2									

FIGURE G-3: Three records entered in the worksheet

	A	B	C	D	E	F	G	H	I
1	Tour	Depart Date	Number of Days	Seat Capacity	Seats Reserved	Price	Air Included	Meals Included	
2	Pacific Odyssey	1/11/2010	14	50	50	3105	Yes	No	
3	Old Japan	1/12/2010	21	47	41	2100	Yes	No	
4	Down Under Exodus	1/18/2010	10	30	28	2800	Yes	Yes	
5									

FIGURE G-4: Formatted table with three records

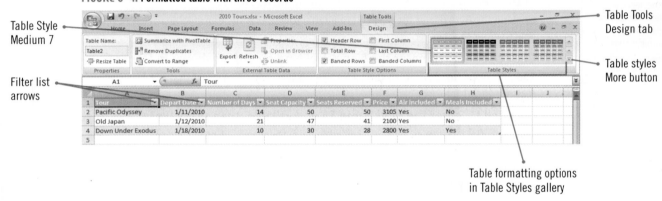

Table Style Medium 7

Filter list arrows

Table Tools Design tab

Table styles More button

Table formatting options in Table Styles gallery

Changing table style options

You can modify a table's appearance by using the check boxes in the Table Styles Options group on the Table Tools Design tab. For example, you can turn on or turn off the following options: **banding**, which creates different formatting for adjacent rows and columns; special formatting for first and last columns; Total Row, which calculates totals for each column; and Header Row, which displays or hides the header row. Use these options to modify a table's appearance either before or after applying a Table Style. For example, if your table has banded rows, you can select the Banded Columns check box to change the table to display with banded columns. Also, you may want to deselect the Header Row check box to hide a table's header row if a table will be included in a presentation. Figure G-5 shows the available table style options.

You can also create your own table style by clicking the Table Styles More button, then at the bottom of the Table Styles Gallery, clicking New Table Style. In the New Table Quick Style dialog box, name the style in the Name text box, click a table element, then

format selected table elements by clicking Format. You can also set a custom style as the default style for your tables by checking the Set as default table quick style for this document check box. You can click Clear at the bottom of the Table Styles gallery if you want to clear a table style.

FIGURE G-5: Table Styles Options

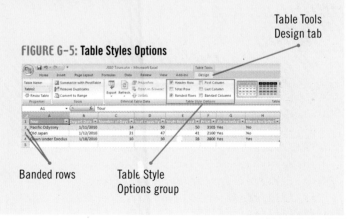

Table Tools Design tab

Banded rows

Table Style Options group

Adding Table Data

You can add records to a table by typing data directly below the last row of the table. After you press [Enter], the new row is added to the table and the table formatting is extended to the new data. When the active cell is the last cell of a table, you can add a new row by pressing [Tab]. You can add rows in any table location. If you decide you need additional data fields, you can add new columns to a table. Another way to expand a table is to drag the sizing handle in a table's lower-right corner; drag down to add rows and drag to the right to add columns. ⬛⬛⬛⬛ After entering all of the 2010 tour data, Kate decides to offer two additional tours. She also wants the table to display the number of available seats for each tour and whether visas are required for the destination.

STEPS

1. **Activate the 2010 Tours sheet**

   The sheet contains the 2010 tour data.

2. **Click cell A65 in the table, enter the data for the new Costa Rica Rainforest tour, as shown in Figure G-6, then press [Enter]**

   The new Costa Rica tour is part of the table. You want to enter a record about a new January tour above row 6.

3. **Click the inside left edge of cell A6 to select the table row data, click the Insert list arrow in the Cells group, then click Insert Table Rows Above**

   Clicking the left edge of the first cell in a table row selects the entire table row. A new blank row 6 is available to enter the new record.

4. **Click cell A6, then enter the Nepal Trekking record, as shown in Figure G-7**

   The new Nepal tour is part of the table. You want to add a new field that displays the number of available seats for each tour.

5. **Click cell I1, enter the field name Seats Available, then press [Enter]**

   The new field becomes part of the table and the header formatting extends to the new field. The AutoCorrect menu allows you to undo or stop the automatic table expansion, but in this case, you decide to leave this feature on. You want to add another new field to the table to display tours that require visas, but this time you will add the new field by resizing the table.

6. **Scroll down until cell I66 is visible, drag the sizing handle in the table's lower-right corner one column to the right to add column J to the table, as shown in Figure G-8.**

   The table range is now A1:J66 and the new field name is Column1.

7. **Click cell J1, enter Visa Required, then press [Enter]**

8. **Click the Insert tab, click the Header & Footer button in the Text group, enter your name in the center header text box, click cell A1, click the Normal button ▦ in the status bar, then save the workbook**

FIGURE G-6: New record in row 65

61	Galapagos Adventure	12/20/2010	14	15	1	$ 3,100	Yes	Yes	
62	Pacific Odyssey	12/21/2010	14	50	10	$ 3,105	Yes	No	
63	Essential India	12/30/2010	18	51	15	$ 3,933	Yes	Yes	
64	Old Japan	12/31/2010	21	47	4	$ 2,100	Yes	No	
65	Costa Rica Rainforests	1/30/2010	7	20	0	$ 2,590	Yes	Yes	
66									

New record
in row 65

FIGURE G-7: New record in row 6

	A	B	C	D	E	F	G	H
1	Tour	Depart Date	Number of Days	Seat Capacity	Seats Reserved	Price	Air Included	Meals Included
2	Pacific Odyssey	1/11/2010	14	50	50	$ 3,105	Yes	No
3	Old Japan	1/12/2010	21	47	41	$ 2,100	Yes	No
4	Down Under Exodus	1/18/2010	10	30	28	$ 2,800	Yes	Yes
5	Essential India	1/20/2010	18	51	40	$ 3,933	Yes	Yes
6	Nepal Trekking	1/31/2010	14	18	0	$ 4,200	Yes	Yes
7	Amazing Amazon	2/23/2010	14	43	38	$ 2,877	No	No
8	Cooking in France	2/28/2010	7	18	15	$ 2,822	Yes	No
9	Pearls of the Orient	3/12/2010	14	50	15	$ 3,400	Yes	No
10	Silk Road Travels	3/18/2010	18	25	19	$ 2,190	Yes	Yes

New record
in row 6

FIGURE G-8: Resizing a table using the resizing handles

60	Panama Adventure	12/18/2010	10	50	21	$ 2,304	Yes	Yes			
61	Galapagos Adventure	12/20/2010	14	15	1	$ 3,100	Yes	Yes			
62	Galapagos Adventure	12/20/2010	14	15	1	$ 3,100	Yes	Yes			
63	Pacific Odyssey	12/21/2010	14	50	10	$ 3,105	Yes	No			
64	Essential India	12/30/2010	18	51	15	$ 3,933	Yes	Yes			
65	Old Japan	12/31/2010	21	47	4	$ 2,100	Yes	No			
66	Costa Rica Rainforests	1/30/2010	7	20	0	$ 2,590	Yes	Yes			
67											
68											
69											

Drag sizing handle
to add column J

Finding and Replacing Table Data

From time to time, you need to locate specific records in your table. You can use the Excel Find feature to search your table for a particular record. You can also use the Replace feature to locate and replace existing entries or portions of entries with information you specify. If you don't know the exact spelling of the text you are searching for, you can use wildcards to help locate the records. **Wildcards** are special symbols that substitute for unknown characters. ▰▰▰▰ In response to feedback from the sales representatives about customers' lack of familiarity of Istria, Kate wants to replace "Istria" with "Croatia" in all of the tour names. She also wants to know how many Pacific Odyssey tours are scheduled for the year. You begin by searching for records with the text "Pacific Odyssey".

STEPS

1. **Click cell A1 if necessary, click the Home tab, click the Find & Select button in the Editing group, then click Find**

   The Find and Replace dialog box opens, as shown in Figure G-9. In this dialog box, you enter criteria that specify the records you want to find in the Find what text box. You want to search for records whose Tour field contains the label "Pacific Odyssey".

2. **Type Pacific Odyssey in the Find what text box, then click Find Next**

   A2 is the active cell because it is the first instance of Pacific Odyssey in the table.

3. **Click Find Next and examine the record for each found Pacific Odyssey tour until no more matching cells are found in the table and the active cell is A2 again, then click Close**

   There are four Pacific Odyssey tours.

4. **Return to cell A1, click the Find & Select button in the Editing group, then click Replace**

   The Find and Replace dialog box opens with the Replace tab selected and the insertion point in the Replace with text box, as shown in Figure G-10. You will search for entries containing "Istria" and replace them with "Croatia". You are not sure of the spelling of Istria, so you will use the * wildcard to help you locate the records containing the correct tour name.

QUICK TIP
You can also use the question mark (?) wildcard to represent any single character. For example, using "to?" as your search text would only find 3-letter words beginning with "to", such as "top" and "tot"; it would not find "tone" or "topography".

5. **Delete any text in the Find what text box, type Is* in the Find what text box, click the Replace with text box, then type Croatia**

   The asterisk (*) wildcard stands for one or more characters, meaning that the search text Is* will find words such as "Is", "Isn't", and "Islington". Because you notice that there are other table entries containing the text "is" with a lowercase "i" (in the Visa Required column heading), you need to make sure that only capitalized instances of the letter I are replaced.

6. **Click Options >>, click the Match case check box to select it, click Options <<, then click Find Next**

   Excel moves the cell pointer to the first occurrence of "Istria".

7. **Click Replace All, click OK, then click Close**

   The dialog box closes. Excel made two replacements, in cells A22 and A51. The Visa Required field heading remains unchanged because the "is" in "Visa" is lowercase.

8. **Save the workbook**

Using Tables

FIGURE G-9: **Find and Replace dialog box**

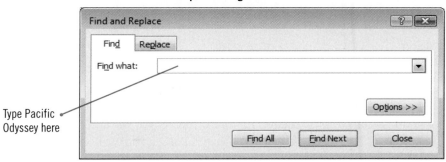

Type Pacific
Odyssey here

FIGURE G-10: **The Replace tab in the Find and Replace dialog box**

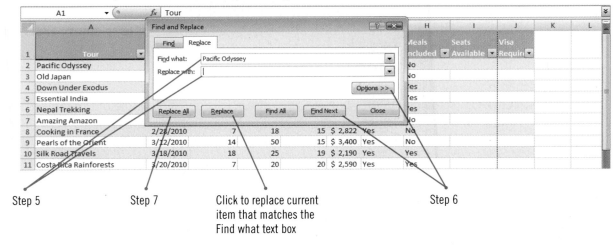

Step 5   Step 7   Click to replace current   Step 6
                                 item that matches the
                                 Find what text box

Using Find and Select features

You can also use the Find feature to navigate to a specific place in a workbook by clicking the Find & Select button in the Editing group, clicking Go To, typing a cell address, then clicking OK. Clicking the Find & Select button also allows you to find comments and conditional formatting in a worksheet by clicking Go to Special. You can use the Go to Special dialog box to select cells that contain different types of formulas, objects, or data validation. Some Go to Special commands also appear on the Find & Select menu. Using this menu, you can also change the mouse pointer shape to the Select Objects pointer so you can quickly select drawing objects when necessary. To return to the standard Excel pointer, press [Esc].

Deleting Table Data

In order to keep a table up to date, you need to be able to periodically remove records. You may even need to remove fields if the information stored in a field becomes unnecessary. You can delete table data using the Delete button or by dragging the sizing handle at the table's lower right corner. You can also easily delete duplicate records from a table. ▰▰▰ Kate is canceling the Old Japan tour that departs on 1/12/2010 and asks you to delete the record from the table. You will also remove any duplicate records from the table. Because the visa requirements are difficult to keep up with, Kate asks you to delete the field with visa information.

STEPS

1. **Click the left edge of cell A3 to select the table row data, click the Delete button list arrow in the Cells group, then click Delete Table Rows**

   The Old Japan tour is deleted and the Down Under Exodus tour moves up to row 3, as shown in Figure G-11. You can also delete a table row or a column using the Resize Table button in the Properties group of the Table Tools Design tab, or by right-clicking the row or column, pointing to Delete on the shortcut menu, then clicking Table Columns or Table Rows. You decide to check the table for duplicate records.

QUICK TIP

You can also remove duplicates from worksheet data by clicking the Data tab, then clicking the Remove Duplicates button in the Data Tools group.

2. **Click the Table Tools Design tab, then click the Remove Duplicates button in the Tools group**

   The Remove Duplicates dialog box opens, as shown in Figure G-12. You need to select the columns that the program should use to evaluate duplicates. Because you don't want to delete tours with the same destination but different departure dates, you will look for duplicate data in all of the columns.

3. **Make sure that "My data has headers" is checked and that all the columns headers are checked, then click OK**

   Two duplicate records are found and removed, leaving 63 rows in the table, including the header row. You want to remove the last column, which contains space for visa information.

4. **Click OK, scroll down until cell J63 is visible, drag the sizing handle of the table's lower-right corner one column to the left to remove column J from the table**

   The table range is now A1:I63 and the Visa Required field no longer appears in the table.

5. **Delete the contents of cell J1, return to cell A1, then save the workbook**

FIGURE G-11: Table with row deleted

	Tour	Depart Date	Number of Days	Seat Capacity	Seats Reserved	Price	Air Included	Meals Included	Seats Available	Visa Required
2	Pacific Odyssey	1/11/2010	14	50	50	$ 3,105	Yes	No		
3	Down Under Exodus	1/18/2010	10	30	28	$ 2,800	Yes	Yes		
4	Essential India	1/20/2010	18	51	40	$ 3,933	Yes	Yes		
5	Nepal Trekking	1/31/2010	14	18	0	$ 4,200	Yes	Yes		
6	Amazing Amazon	2/23/2010	14	43	38	$ 2,877	No	No		
7	Cooking in France	2/28/2010	7	18	15	$ 2,822	Yes	No		
8	Pearls of the Orient	3/12/2010	14	50	15	$ 3,400	Yes	No		
9	Silk Road Travels	3/18/2010	18	25	19	$ 2,190	Yes	Yes		
10	Costa Rica Rainforests	3/20/2010	7	20	20	$ 2,590	Yes	Yes		
11	Green Adventures in Ecuador	3/23/2010	18	25	22	$ 2,450	No	No		
12	African National Parks	4/7/2010	30	12	10	$ 4,870	Yes	Yes		
13	Experience Cambodia	4/10/2010	12	40	21	$ 2,908	Yes	No		
14	Old Japan	4/14/2010	21	47	30	$ 2,100	Yes	No		
15	Down Under Exodus	4/18/2010	10	30	20	$ 2,800	Yes	Yes		
16	Essential India	4/20/2010	18	51	31	$ 3,933	Yes	Yes		
17	Amazing Amazon	4/23/2010	14	43	30	$ 2,877	No	No		
18	Catalonia Adventure	5/9/2010	14	51	30	$ 3,100	Yes	No		
19	Treasures of Ethiopia	5/18/2010	10	41	15	$ 3,200	Yes	Yes		
20	Monasteries of Bulgaria	5/20/2010	7	19	11	$ 2,103	Yes	Yes		
21	Cooking in Croatia	5/23/2010	7	12	10	$ 2,110	No	No		
22	Magnificent Montenegro	5/27/2010	10	48	4	$ 1,890	No	No		
23	Catalonia Adventure	6/9/2010	14	51	15	$ 3,100	Yes	No		
24	Nepal Trekking	6/9/2010	14	18	18	$ 4,200	Yes	Yes		
25	Corfu Sailing Voyage	6/10/2010	21	12	10	$ 3,190	Yes	No		
26	Iceland by Bike	6/11/2010	10	15	10	$ 2,600	Yes	No		

Practice | **2010 Tours** | Sheet2

Ready   Average: 8612.8   Count: 8   Sum: 43064   100%

Row is deleted and tours move up one row

FIGURE G-12: Remove Duplicates dialog box

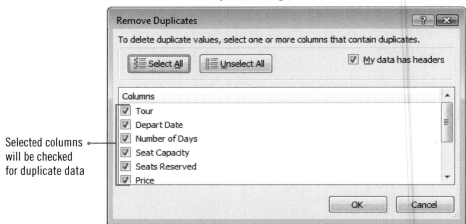

Selected columns will be checked for duplicate data

Sorting Table Data

Usually, you enter table records in the order in which you receive information, rather than in alphabetical or numerical order. When you add records to a table, you usually enter them at the end of the table. You can change the order of the records any time using the Excel **sort** feature. You can sort a table in ascending or descending order on one field using the filter list arrows next to the field name. In **ascending order**, the lowest value (the beginning of the alphabet or the earliest date) appears at the top of the table. In a field containing labels and numbers, numbers appear first in the sorted list. In **descending order**, the highest value (the end of the alphabet or the latest date) appears at the top of the table. In a field containing labels and numbers, labels appear first. Table G-3 provides examples of ascending and descending sorts. Because the data is structured as a table, Excel changes the order of the records while keeping each record, or row of information, together. ▓▓▒▒▒ Kate wants the tour data sorted by departure date, displaying tours that depart the soonest at the top of the table.

STEPS

1. **Click the** Depart Date filter list arrow, **then click** Sort Oldest to Newest

   Excel rearranges the records in ascending order by depart date, as shown in Figure G-13. The Depart Date filter list arrow has an upward pointing arrow indicating the ascending sort in the field. You can also sort the table on one field using the Sort & Filter button.

2. **Click the** Home tab, **click any cell in the Price column, click the** Sort & Filter button **in the Editing group, then click** Sort Largest to Smallest

   Excel sorts the table, placing those records with the higher price at the top. The Price filter list arrow now has a downward pointing arrow next to the filter list arrow, indicating the descending sort order. You can also rearrange the table data using a **multilevel sort**. This type of sort rearranges the table data using different levels. If you use two sort levels, the data is sorted by the first field and the second field is sorted within each grouping of the first field. Since you have many groups of tours with different departure dates, you want to use a multilevel sort to arrange the table data by tours and then by departure dates within each tour.

3. **Click the** Sort & Filter button **in the Editing group, then click** Custom Sort

   The Sort dialog box opens, as shown in Figure G-14.

4. **Click the** Sort by list arrow, **click** Tour, **click the** Order list arrow, **click** A to Z, **click** Add Level, **click the** Then by list arrow, **click** Depart Date, **click the second** Order list arrow, **click** Oldest to Newest **if necessary, then click** OK

   Figure G-15 shows the table sorted alphabetically in ascending order (A-Z) by Tour and, within each tour, in ascending order by the Depart Date.

5. **Save the workbook**

Sorting a table using conditional formatting

If conditional formats have been applied to a table, you can sort the table using conditional formatting to arrange the rows. For example, if cells are conditionally formatted with color, you can sort a field on Cell Color, using the color with the order of On Top or On Bottom in the Sort dialog box.

TABLE G-3: Sort order options and examples

option	alphabetic	numeric	date	alphanumeric
Ascending	A, B, C	7, 8, 9	1/1, 2/1, 3/1	12A, 99B, DX8, QT7
Descending	C, B, A	9, 8, 7	3/1, 2/1, 1/1	QT7, DX8, 99B, 12A

FIGURE G-13: Table sorted by depature date

Up arrow indicates ascending sort in the field

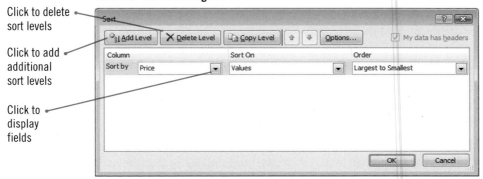

	Tour	Depart Date	Number of Days	Seat Capacity	Seats Reserved	Price	Air Included	Meals Included	Seats Available
2	Pacific Odyssey	1/11/2010	14	50	50	$ 3,105	Yes	No	
3	Down Under Exodus	1/18/2010	10	30	28	$ 2,800	Yes	Yes	
4	Essential India	1/20/2010	18	51	40	$ 3,933	Yes	Yes	
5	Costa Rica Rainforests	1/30/2010	7	20	0	$ 2,590	Yes	Yes	
6	Nepal Trekking	1/31/2010	14	18	0	$ 4,200	Yes	Yes	
7	Amazing Amazon	2/23/2010	14	43	38	$ 2,877	No	No	
8	Cooking in France	2/28/2010	7	18	15	$ 2,822	Yes	No	
9	Pearls of the Orient	3/12/2010	14	50	15	$ 3,400	Yes	No	
10	Silk Road Travels	3/18/2010	18	25	19	$ 2,190	Yes	Yes	
11	Costa Rica Rainforests	3/20/2010	7	20	20	$ 2,590	Yes	Yes	
12	Green Adventures in Ecuador	3/23/2010	18	25	22	$ 2,450	No	No	
13	African National Parks	4/7/2010	30	12	10	$ 4,870	Yes	Yes	
14	Experience Cambodia	4/10/2010	12	40	21	$ 2,908	Yes	No	
15	Old Japan	4/14/2010	21	47	30	$ 2,100	Yes	No	
16	Down Under Exodus	4/18/2010	10	30	20	$ 2,800	Yes	Yes	
17	Essential India	4/20/2010	18	51	31	$ 3,933	Yes	Yes	
18	Amazing Amazon	4/23/2010	14	43	30	$ 2,877	No	No	
19	Catalonia Adventure	5/9/2010	14	51	30	$ 3,100	Yes	No	
20	Treasures of Ethiopia	5/18/2010	10	41	15	$ 3,200	Yes	Yes	
21	Monasteries of Bulgaria	5/20/2010	7	19	11	$ 2,103	Yes	Yes	
22	Cooking in Croatia	5/23/2010	7	12	10	$ 2,110	No	No	
23	Magnificent Montenegro	5/27/2010	10	48	4	$ 1,890	No	No	
24	Catalonia Adventure	6/9/2010	14	51	15	$ 3,100	Yes	No	
25	Nepal Trekking	6/9/2010	14	18	18	$ 4,200	Yes	Yes	

FIGURE G-14: Sort dialog box

Click to delete sort levels

Click to add additional sort levels

Click to display fields

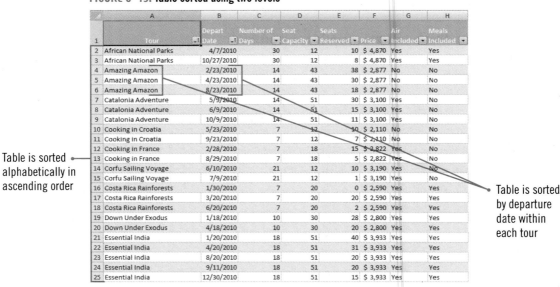

FIGURE G-15: Table sorted using two levels

	Tour	Depart Date	Number of Days	Seat Capacity	Seats Reserved	Price	Air Included	Meals Included
2	African National Parks	4/7/2010	30	12	10	$ 4,870	Yes	Yes
3	African National Parks	10/27/2010	30	12	8	$ 4,870	Yes	Yes
4	Amazing Amazon	2/23/2010	14	43	38	$ 2,877	No	No
5	Amazing Amazon	4/23/2010	14	43	30	$ 2,877	No	No
6	Amazing Amazon	8/23/2010	14	43	18	$ 2,877	No	No
7	Catalonia Adventure	5/9/2010	14	51	30	$ 3,100	Yes	No
8	Catalonia Adventure	6/9/2010	14	51	15	$ 3,100	Yes	No
9	Catalonia Adventure	10/9/2010	14	51	11	$ 3,100	Yes	No
10	Cooking in Croatia	5/23/2010	7	12	10	$ 2,110	No	No
11	Cooking in Croatia	9/23/2010	7	12	7	$ 2,110	No	No
12	Cooking in France	2/28/2010	7	18	15	$ 2,822	Yes	No
13	Cooking in France	8/29/2010	7	18	5	$ 2,822	Yes	No
14	Corfu Sailing Voyage	6/10/2010	21	12	10	$ 3,190	Yes	No
15	Corfu Sailing Voyage	7/9/2010	21	12	1	$ 3,190	Yes	No
16	Costa Rica Rainforests	1/30/2010	7	20	0	$ 2,590	Yes	Yes
17	Costa Rica Rainforests	3/20/2010	7	20	20	$ 2,590	Yes	Yes
18	Costa Rica Rainforests	6/20/2010	7	20	2	$ 2,590	Yes	Yes
19	Down Under Exodus	1/18/2010	10	30	28	$ 2,800	Yes	Yes
20	Down Under Exodus	4/18/2010	10	30	20	$ 2,800	Yes	Yes
21	Essential India	1/20/2010	18	51	40	$ 3,933	Yes	Yes
22	Essential India	4/20/2010	18	51	31	$ 3,933	Yes	Yes
23	Essential India	8/20/2010	18	51	20	$ 3,933	Yes	Yes
24	Essential India	9/11/2010	18	51	20	$ 3,933	Yes	Yes
25	Essential India	12/30/2010	18	51	15	$ 3,933	Yes	Yes

Table is sorted alphabetically in ascending order

Table is sorted by departure date within each tour

Specifying a custom sort order

You can identify a custom sort order for the field selected in the Sort by box. Click the Order list arrow in the Sort dialog box, click Custom List, then click the desired custom order. Commonly used custom sort orders are days of the week (Sun, Mon, Tues, Wed, etc.) and months (Jan, Feb, Mar, etc.); alphabetic sorts do not sort these items properly.

Using Formulas in a Table

Many tables are large, making it difficult to know from viewing them the "story" the table tells. The Excel table calculation features help you summarize table data so you can see important trends. After you enter a single formula into a table cell, the **calculated columns** feature fills in the remaining cells with the formula's results. The column continues to fill with the formula results as you enter rows in the table. This makes it easy to update your formulas because you only need to edit the formula once, and the change will fill in to the other column cells. The **structured reference** feature allows your formulas to refer to table columns by names that are automatically generated when you create the table. These names automatically adjust as you add or delete table fields. An example of a table reference is =[Sales]–[Costs], where Sales and Costs are field names in the table. Tables also have a specific area at the bottom called the **table total row** for calculations using the data in the table columns. The cells in this row contain a dropdown list of functions that can be used for the column calculation. The table total row adapts to any changes in the table size. ▟▓▟ Kate wants you to use a formula to calculate the number of available seats for each tour. You will also add summary information to the end of the table.

STEPS

1. **Click cell I2, then type =[**
    A list of the table field names is displayed, as shown in Figure G-16. Structured referencing allows you to use the names that Excel created when you defined your table to reference fields in a formula. You can choose a field by clicking it and pressing [TAB] or by double-clicking the field name.

2. **Click [Seat Capacity], press [Tab], then type]**
    Excel begins the formula, placing [Seat Capacity] in the cell in blue and framing the Seat Capacity data in a blue border.

3. **Type -[, double-click [Seats Reserved], then type]**
    Excel places [Seats Reserved] in the cell in green and outlines the Seats Reserved data in a green border.

4. **Press [Enter]**
    The formula result, 2, is displayed in cell I2. The table column also fills with the formula displaying the number of available seats for each tour.

5. **Click the AutoCorrect Options list arrow** ⬚ ▾
    Because the calculated columns option saves time, you decide to leave the feature on. You want to display the total number of available seats on all of the tours.

6. **Click any cell inside the table, click the Table Tools Design tab, then click the Total Row check box in the Table Style Options group to select it**
    A total row appears at the bottom of the table and the sum of the available seats, 1035, is displayed in cell I64. You can select other formulas in the total row.

7. **Click cell C64, then click the cell list arrow on the right side of the cell**
    The list of available functions appears, as shown in Figure G-17. You want to find the average tour length.

8. **Click Average, then save your workbook**
    The average tour length, 13 days, appears in cell C64.

	A	B	C	D	E	F	G	H	I	J
1	Tour	Depart Date	Number of Days	Seat Capacity	Seats Reserved	Price	Air Included	Meals Included	Seats Available	
2	African National Parks	4/7/2010	30	12	10	$ 4,870	Yes	Yes	=[	
3	African National Parks	10/27/2010	30	12	8	$ 4,870	Yes	Yes		
4	Amazing Amazon	2/23/2010	14	43	38	$ 2,877	No	No		
5	Amazing Amazon	4/23/2010	14	43	30	$ 2,877	No	No		
6	Amazing Amazon	8/23/2010	14	43	18	$ 2,877	No	No		
7	Catalonia Adventure	5/9/2010	14	51	30	$ 3,100	Yes	No		
8	Catalonia Adventure	6/9/2010	14	51	15	$ 3,100	Yes	No		
9	Catalonia Adventure	10/9/2010	14	51	11	$ 3,100	Yes	No		
10	Cooking in Croatia	5/23/2010	7	12	10	$ 2,110	No	No		
11	Cooking in Croatia	9/23/2010	7	12	7	$ 2,110	No	No		
12	Cooking in France	2/28/2010	7	18	15	$ 2,822	Yes	No		

Drop-down list: Tour, Depart Date, Number of Days, Seat Capacity, Seats Reserved, Price, Air Included, Meals Included, Seats Available

Table field names

FIGURE G-17: Functions in the Total Row

	Tour	Depart Date	Number of Days	Seat Capacity	Seats Reserved	Price	Air Included	Meals Included	Seats Available	J
51	Pacific Odyssey	7/7/2010	14	50	35	$ 3,105	Yes	No	15	
52	Pacific Odyssey	9/14/2010	14	50	20	$ 3,105	Yes	No	30	
53	Pacific Odyssey	12/21/2010	14	50	10	$ 3,105	Yes	No	40	
54	Panama Adventure	6/18/2010	10	50	29	$ 2,304	Yes	Yes	21	
55	Panama Adventure	12/18/2010	10	50	21	$ 2,304	Yes	Yes	29	
56	Pearls of the Orient	3/12/2010	14	50	15	$ 3,400	Yes	No	35	
57	Pearls of the Orient	9/12/2010	14	50	11	$ 3,400	Yes	No	39	
58	Silk Road Travels	3/18/2010	18	25	19	$ 2,190	Yes	Yes	6	
59	Silk Road Travels	9/18/2010	18	25	9	$ 2,190	Yes	Yes	16	
60	Treasures of Ethiopia	5/18/2010	10	41	15	$ 3,200	Yes	Yes	26	
61	Treasures of Ethiopia	11/18/2010	10	41	12	$ 3,200	Yes	Yes	29	
62	Wild River Escape	6/27/2010	10	21	21	$ 1,944	No	No	0	
63	Wild River Escape	8/27/2010	10	21	11	$ 1,944	No	No	10	
64	Total								1035	
65										
66										
67										
68										
69										
70										
71										
72										

Drop-down list: None, Average, Count, Count Numbers, Max, Min, Sum, StdDev, Var, More Functions...

Functions available in the Total Row

Using structured references

Structured references make it easier to work with formulas that use table data. You can reference all of the table, columns in the table, or specific data. What makes structured references helpful to use in formulas is that they automatically adjust as data ranges change in a table, so you don't need to edit formulas. When you create a table from worksheet data, Excel creates a default table name such as Table1. This references all of the table data but not the header row or any total rows. To refer to a table such as Table1 with its header row, you need to use the reference =Table1[#All]. Excel also names each column of a table which can be referenced in formulas. For example, in Table 1, the formula =Table1[Sales] references the data in the Sales field.

Printing a Table

You can determine the way a table will print using the Page Layout tab. Because tables often have more rows than can fit on a page, you can define the first row of the table (containing the field names) as the **print title**, which prints at the top of every page. You can also scale the table to print more or fewer rows on each page. Most tables do not have any descriptive information above the field names on the work-sheet, so to augment the field name information, you can use headers and footers to add identifying text, such as the table title or the report date. ▚▚▚▚ Kate asks you for a printout of the tour information. You begin by previewing the table.

STEPS

1. **Click the Office button ⊕, point to Print, then click Print Preview**
   The status bar reads Preview: Page 1 of 3. All of the field names in the table fit across the width of the page.

2. **In the Print Preview window, click the Next Page button in the Preview group to view the second page, then click Next Page again to view the third page**
   The third page contains only one record and the total row, so you will scale the table to print on two pages.

QUICK TIP

You can hide or print headings and grid-lines using the check boxes in the Sheet Options group on the Page Layout tab. You might want to hide a worksheet's headings if it will be displayed in a presentation.

3. **Click the Close Print Preview button, click the Page Layout tab, click the Width list arrow in the Scale to Fit group, click 1 page, click the Height list arrow, then click 2 pages**
   You decide to preview the table again to view the changes in scale.

4. **Click the Office button, point to Print, click Print Preview, then click the Next Page button in the Preview group**
   The records are scaled to fit on two pages. The status bar reads Preview: Page 2 of 2. Because the records on page 2 appear without column headings, you want to set up the first row of the table, which contains the field names, as a repeating print title.

5. **Click the Close Print Preview button, click the Print Titles button in the Page Setup group, click inside the Rows to repeat at top text box under Print titles, click any cell in row 1 on the table, then compare your Page Setup dialog box to Figure G-18**
   When you select row 1 as a print title, Excel automatically inserts an absolute reference to the row that will repeat at the top of each page.

6. **Click Print Preview, click the Next Page button to view the second page, then click the Close Print Preview button**
   Setting up a print title to repeat row 1 causes the field names to appear at the top of each printed page. The printout would be more informative with a header to identify the table information.

QUICK TIP

You can also add headers and footers by clicking the Page Layout View in the status bar.

7. **Click the Insert tab, click the Header & Footer button in the Text group, click the left header section text box, then type 2010 Tours**

8. **Select the left header section information, click the Home tab, click the Increase Font Size button Å in the Font group twice to change the font size to 14, click the Bold button B in the Font group, click any cell in the table, then click the Normal button ⊞ in the status bar**

9. **Save the table, preview then print it, close the workbook, then exit Excel**
   Compare your printed table with Figure G-19.

FIGURE G-18: Page Setup dialog box

Print title is
set to row 1

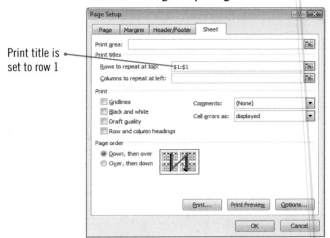

FIGURE G-19: Completed table

2010 Tours   Your Name

Tour	Depart Date	Number of Days	Seat Capacity	Seats Reserved	Price	Air Included	Meals Included	Seats Available
African National Parks	4/7/2010	30	12	10	$ 4,870	Yes	Yes	2
African National Parks	10/27/2010	30	12	8	$ 4,870	Yes	Yes	4
Amazing Amazon	2/23/2010	14	43	38	$ 2,877	No	No	5
Amazing Amazon	4/23/2010	14	43	30	$ 2,877	No	No	13
Amazing Amazon	8/23/2010	14	43	18	$ 2,877	No	No	25
Catalonia Adventure	5/9/2010	14	51	30	$ 3,100	Yes	No	21
Catalonia Adventure	6/9/2010	14	51	15	$ 3,100	Yes	No	36
Catalonia Adventure	10/9/2010	14	51	11	$ 3,100	Yes	No	40
Cooking in Croatia	5/23/2010	7	12	10	$ 2,110	No	No	2
Cooking in Croatia	9/23/2010	7	12	7	$ 2,110	No	No	5
Cooking in France	2/28/2010	7	18	15	$ 2,822	No	No	3
Cooking in France	8/29/2010	7	18	5	$ 2,822	No	No	13
Corfu Sailing Voyage	6/10/2010	21	12	10	$ 3,190	Yes	No	2
Corfu Sailing Voyage	7/9/2010	21	12	1	$ 3,190	Yes	No	11
Costa Rica Rainforests	1/30/2010	7	20	0	$ 2,590	Yes	Yes	20
Costa Rica Rainforests	3/20/2010	7	20	20	$ 2,590	Yes	Yes	0
Costa Rica Rainforests	6/20/2010	7	20	2	$ 2,590	Yes	Yes	18
Down Under Exodus	1/18/2010	10	30	28	$ 2,800	Yes	Yes	2
Down Under Exodus	4/18/2010	10	30	20	$ 2,800	Yes	Yes	10
Essential India	1/20/2010	18	51	40	$ 3,933	Yes	Yes	11
Essential India	4/20/2010	18	51	31	$ 3,933	Yes	Yes	20
Essential India	8/20/2010	18	51	20	$ 3,933	Yes	Yes	31
Essential India	9/11/2010	18	51	20	$ 3,933	Yes	Yes	31
Essential India	12/30/2010	18	51	15	$ 3,933	Yes	Yes	36
Exotic Morocco	6/12/2010	7	38	25	$ 1,900	Yes	No	13
Exotic Morocco	10/31/2010	7	38	15	$ 1,900	Yes	No	23
Experience Cambodia	4/10/2010	12	40	21	$ 2,908	Yes	No	19
Experience Cambodia	10/31/2010	12	40	2	$ 2,908	Yes	No	38
Galapagos Adventure	7/2/2010	14	15	12	$ 3,100	Yes	Yes	3
Galapagos Adventure	12/20/2010	14	15	1	$ 3,100	Yes	Yes	14
Green Adventures in Ecuador	3/23/2010	18	25	22	$ 2,450	No	No	3
Green Adventures in Ecuador	10/23/2010	18	25	12	$ 2,450	No	No	13
Ireland by Bike	6/11/2010	10	15	10	$ 2,600	Yes	No	5

			eats			Air	Meals	Seats
			served	Price		Included	Included	Available
			9	$ 2,600	Yes	No	6	
			6	$ 2,600	Yes	No	9	
			15	$ 1,970	Yes	Yes	5	
			15	$ 1,970	Yes	Yes	5	
			12	$ 1,970	Yes	Yes	8	
			4	$ 1,890	No	No	44	
			0	$ 1,890	No	No	48	
			11	$ 2,103	Yes	Yes	8	
			9	$ 2,103	Yes	Yes	10	
			0	$ 4,200	Yes	Yes	18	
			18	$ 4,200	Yes	Yes	0	
			8	$ 4,200	Yes	Yes	10	
			30	$ 2,100	Yes	No	17	
			31	$ 2,100	Yes	No	16	
			4	$ 2,100	Yes	No	43	
			50	$ 3,105	Yes	No	0	
			35	$ 3,105	Yes	No	15	
			20	$ 3,105	Yes	No	30	
			10	$ 3,105	Yes	No	40	
			29	$ 2,304	Yes	Yes	21	
			21	$ 2,304	Yes	Yes	29	
			15	$ 3,400	Yes	No	35	
			11	$ 3,400	Yes	No	39	
			19	$ 2,190	Yes	Yes	6	
			9	$ 2,190	Yes	Yes	16	
			15	$ 3,200	Yes	Yes	26	
			12	$ 3,200	Yes	Yes	29	
Wild River Escape	6/27/2010	10	21	21	$ 1,944	No	No	0
Wild River Escape	8/27/2010	10	21	11	$ 1,944	No	No	10
Total			**13**					**1035**

Setting a print area

Sometimes you will want to print only part of a worksheet. To do this, select any worksheet range, click the Office button, click Print, in the Print dialog box choose Selection under Print what, then click OK. If you want to print a selected area repeatedly, it's best to define a **print area**, which prints when you use the Quick Print feature. To set a print area, click the Page Layout tab, click the Print Area button in the Page Setup group, then click Set Print Area. You can extend the print area by selecting a range, clicking the Print Area button, then clicking Add to Print Area. If you want to print the table rather than a print area, click the Ignore print areas check box in the Print what section of the Print dialog box. To clear a print area, click the Print Area button, then click Clear Print Area.

Practice

▼ CONCEPTS REVIEW

FIGURE G-20

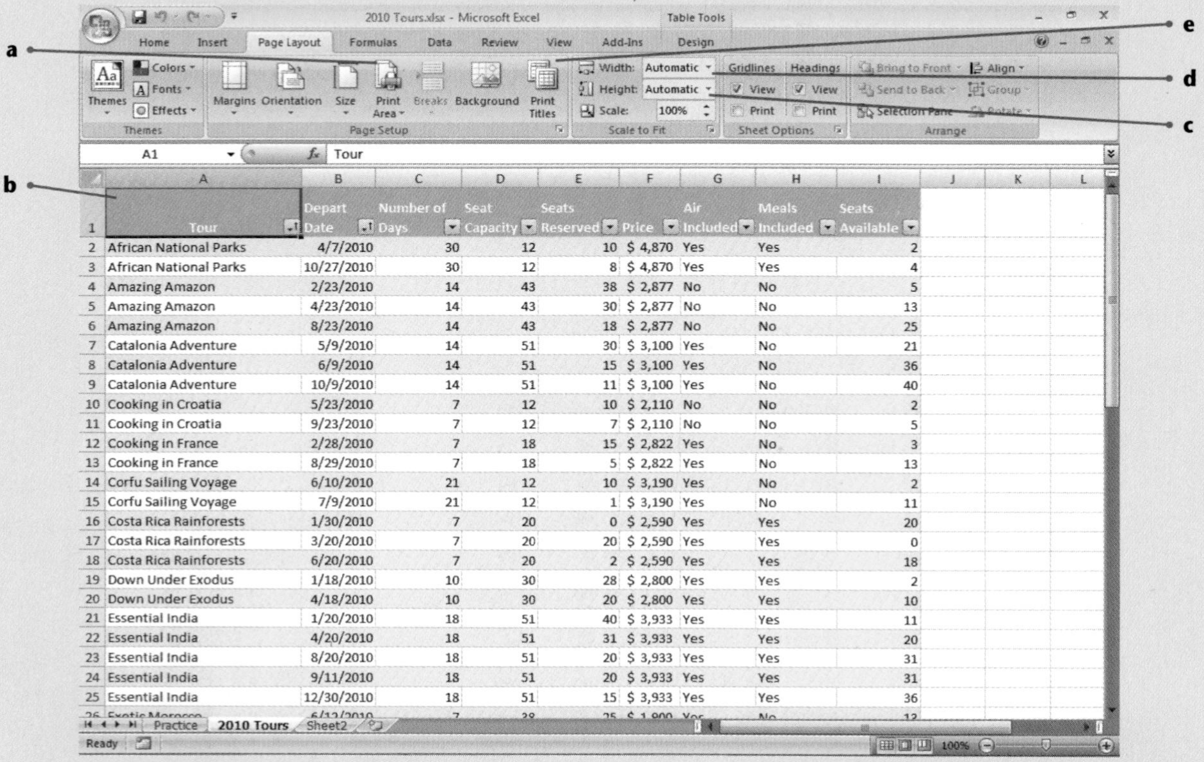

1. Which element points to a field that has been sorted in ascending order?
2. Which element do you click to adjust the number of rows printed on a page?
3. Which element do you click to adjust the number of fields printed on a page?
4. Which element do you click to print field names at the top of every page?
5. Which element do you click to set a range in a table that will print using Quick Print?

Match each term with the statement that best describes it.

6. **Header row**
7. **Record**
8. **Table**
9. **Field**
10. **Sort**

a. Organized collection of related information in Excel
b. Arrange records in a particular sequence
c. Column in an Excel table
d. First row of a table containing field names
e. Row in an Excel table

Select the best answer from the list of choices.

11. **Which of the following Excel sorting options do you use to sort a table of employee names in order from Z to A?**
    a. Absolute
    b. Ascending
    c. Alphabetic
    d. Descending

12. **Which of the following series appears in descending order?**
    a. 4, 5, 6, A, B, C
    b. 8, 6, 4, C, B, A
    c. 8, 7, 6, 5, 6, 7
    d. C, B, A, 6, 5, 4

13. **You can easily add formatting to a table by using:**
    a. Table styles.
    b. Print titles.
    c. Print areas.
    d. Calculated columns.

14. **When printing a table on multiple pages, you can define a print title to:**
    a. Include appropriate fields in the printout.
    b. Include the sheet name in table reports.
    c. Include field names at the top of each printed page.
    d. Exclude from the printout all rows under the first row.

▼ SKILLS REVIEW

1. **Create a table.**
   a. Start Excel, open the file EX G-2.xlsx from the drive and folder where you store your data files, then save it as **Employees**.
   b. Using the Practice sheet, enter the field names in the first row and the first two records in rows two and three, as shown in Table G-4. Create a table using the data you entered.

   TABLE G-4

Last Name	First Name	Years Employed	Position	Full/Part Time	Training Completed
Leone	Sally	5	Book Sales	F	Y
Mello	Donato	3	Video Sales	P	N

   c. Create a table with a header row using the data on the Staff sheet. Adjust the column widths, if necessary, to display the field names.
   d. Apply a table style of Light 12 to the table and adjust the columns widths if necessary.
   e. Enter your name in the center section of the worksheet footer, then save the workbook.

2. **Add table data.**
   a. Add a new record in row seven for **Hank Worthen**, a five-year employee in book sales. Hank works full time and has completed training. Adjust the height of the new row to match the other table rows.
   b. Insert a row above Jay Kherian's record and add a new record for **Stacy Atkins**. Stacy works full time, has worked at the company for two years in video sales, and has not completed training.
   c. Insert a new data field in cell G1 with a label **Weeks Vacation**. Adjust the column width and wrap the label in the cell to display the field name with Weeks above Vacation.
   d. Add a new column to the table by dragging the table's sizing handle and give the new field a label of **Employee #**.
   e. Save the file.

3. **Find and replace table data.**
   a. Return to cell A1.
   b. Open the Find and Replace dialog box and if necessary uncheck the Match Case option. Find the first record that contains the text **Book Sales**.
   c. Find the second record that contains the text **Book Sales**.
   d. Replace all Video text in the table with **Movie**.
   e. Save the file.

4. Delete table data.

a. Go to cell A1.

b. Delete the record for **Sally Leone**.

c. Use the Remove Duplicates button to confirm that the table does not have any duplicate records.

d. Delete the **Employee #** column from the table, then delete its column header.

e. Save the file.

5. Sort table data.

a. Sort the table by years employed in largest to smallest order.

b. Sort the table by last name in A to Z order.

c. Sort the table first by Full/Part Time in A to Z order and then by last name in A to Z order.

d. Check the table to make sure the records appear in the correct order.

e. Save the file.

6. Use formulas in a table.

a. In cell G2, enter the formula that calculates an employee's vacation time; base the formula on the company policy that employees working at the company less than three years have two weeks of vacation. At three years of employment and longer, an employee has three weeks of vacation time. Use the table's field names where appropriate. (*Hint:* The formula is: **=IF([Years Employed]<3,2,3)**)

b. Check the table to make sure the formula filled into the cells in column G and that the correct vacation time is calculated for all cells in the column.

FIGURE G-21

	A	B	C	D	E	F	G
	Last Name	First Name	Years Employed	Position	Full/Part Time	Training Completed	Weeks Vacation
2	Atkins	Stacy	2	Movie Sales	F	N	2
3	Guan	Joyce	1	Book Sales	F	N	2
4	Kherian	Jay	1	Book Sales	F	Y	2
5	Worthen	Hank	5	Book Sales	F	Y	3
6	Mello	Donato	3	Movie Sales	P	N	3
7	Rabin	Mimi	1	Movie Sales	P	Y	2
8	Total						2.333333333
9							

A1 — Last Name

c. Add a Total Row and verify the accuracy of the total number of vacation weeks.

d. Change the function in the Total Row to display the average number of vacation weeks.

e. Compare your table to Figure G-21, then save the workbook.

7. Print a table.

a. Add a header that reads **Employees** in the center section, then format the header in bold with a font size of 16.

b. Add column A as a print title that repeats at the left of each printed page.

c. Preview your table to check that the last names appear on both pages.

d. Change the page orientation to landscape, save the workbook, then print the Staff sheet.

e. Close the workbook, then exit Excel.

▼ INDEPENDENT CHALLENGE 1

You are the marketing director for a national sporting goods store. Your assistants have created an Excel worksheet with customer data including the results of an advertising survey. You will create a table using the customer data and analyze the survey results to help focus the company's advertising expenses in the most successful areas.

a. Start Excel, open the file EX G-3.xlsx from the drive and folder where you store your Data Files, then save it as **Customers**.

b. Create a table from the worksheet data and apply Table Style Light 20. Widen the columns as necessary to display the table data.

▼ INDEPENDENT CHALLENGE 1 (CONTINUED)

c. Use the data below to add the two records shown in Table G-5 to the table:

TABLE G-5

Last Name	First Name	Street Address	City	State	Zip	Area Code	Ad Source	Comments
Ross	Cathy	92 Arrow St.	Seattle	WA	98101	206	Yellow Pages	found ad informative
Janis	Steve	402 9th St.	Seattle	WA	98001	206	Newspaper	found in restaurant section

d. Find, then delete the record for Mary Ryder.

e. Click cell A1 and replace all instances of TV with WWIN TV, making sure the case is properly matched. Compare your table to Figure G-22.

f. Remove duplicate records where all fields are identical.

g. Sort the list by Last Name in A to Z order.

h. Sort the list again by Area Code in Smallest to Largest order.

i. Sort the table first by State in A to Z order, then within the state, by Zip in Smallest to Largest order.

j. Scale the table width to 1 page and the height to 2 pages.

k. Enter your name in the center section of the worksheet footer.

l. Add a centered header that reads **Customer Survey Data** in bold with a font size of 16.

m. Add print titles to repeat the first row at the top of printed pages.

n. Save the workbook, preview it, then print the table on two pages.

FIGURE G-22

	A	B	C	D	E	F	G	H	I
1	Last Name	First Name	Street Address	City	State	Zip	Area Code	Ad Source	Comments
2	Kim	Kathy	19 North St.	San Francisco	CA	94177	415	Newspaper	favorite with friends
3	Jacobs	Martha	Hamilton Park St.	San Francisco	CA	94107	415	Newspaper	no comments
4	Majors	Kathy	1 Spring St.	San Luis	CA	94018	510	Radio	loved ad voice
5	Wong	Sandy	2120 Central St.	San Francisco	CA	93772	415	Newspaper	graphics caught eye
6	Hesh	Gayle	1192 Dome St.	San Diego	CA	93303	619	Newspaper	great ads
7	Chavez	Jane	11 Northern St.	San Diego	CA	92208	619	WWIN TV	interesting ad
8	Chelly	Yvonne	900 Sola St.	San Diego	CA	92106	619	Newspaper	likes description of products
9	Smith	Carolyn	921 Lopez St.	San Diego	CA	92104	619	Newspaper	likes ad prose
10	Owen	Scott	72 Yankee St.	Brookfield	CT	06830	203	Newspaper	no comments
11	Wallace	Salvatore	100 Westside St.	Chicago	IL	60620	312	Newspaper	likes graphics
12	Roberts	Bob	56 Water St.	Chicago	IL	60618	771	Newspaper	likes ad graphic
13	Miller	Hope	111 Stratton St.	Chicago	IL	60614	773	Newspaper	likes ad in local newspaper
14	Duran	Maria	Galvin St.	Chicago	IL	60614	773	Subway	no comments
15	Roberts	Bob	56 Water St.	Chicago	IL	60614	312	Newspaper	liked photo
16	Graham	Shelley	989 26th St.	Chicago	IL	60611	773	Yellow Pages	great store description
17	Kim	Janie	9 First St.	San Francisco	CA	94177	415	Newspaper	great ads
18	Kim	Janie	9 First St.	San Francisco	CA	94177	415	Newspaper	great ads
19	Williams	Tasha	1 Spring St.	Reading	MA	03882	413	Newspaper	likes font we use
20	Julio	Manuel	544 Cameo St.	Belmont	MA	02483	617	Newspaper	no comments
21	Masters	Latrice	88 Las Puntas Rd.	Boston	MA	02205	617	Yellow Pages	likes clear store location
22	Kooper	Peter	671 Main St.	Cambridge	MA	02138	617	WWIN TV	no comments
23	Kelly	Shawn	22 Kendall St.	Cambridge	MA	02138	617	Yellow Pages	found under "cafés"
24	Rodriguez	Virginia	123 Main St.	Boston	MA	02007	617	Radio	loves radio personality
25	Frei	Carol	123 Elm St.	Salem	MA	01970	978	Newspaper	no comments
26	Stevens	Crystal	14 Waterford St.	Salem	MA	01970	508	Radio	does not like radio personality
27	Ichikawa	Pam	232 Shore Rd.	Boston	MA	01801	617	Newspaper	told friends
28	Paxton	Gail	100 Main St.	Woburn	MA	01801	508	Newspaper	no comments
29	Spencer	Robin	293 Serenity Dr.	Concord	MA	01742	508	Radio	loved radio personality
30	Lopez	Luis	1212 City St.	Kansas City	MO	64105	816	WWIN TV	liked characters
31	Nelson	Michael	229 Rally Rd.	Kansas City	MO	64105	816	Yellow Pages	found under "Compact Discs"
32	Lee	Ginny	3 Way St.	Kansas City	MO	64102	816	Radio	intrigued by announcer

Advanced Challenge Exercise

- Create a print area that prints only the first six columns of the table.
- Print the print area.
- Clear the print area

o. Save the workbook, close the workbook, then exit Excel.

▼ INDEPENDENT CHALLENGE 2

You own Around the World, a travel bookstore located in New Zealand. The store sells travel-related items such as maps, travel books, journals, and DVDs of travel destinations. Your customers are primarily tour guides who purchase items in quantities of ten or more for their tour customers. You decide to plan and build a table of sales information with eight records using the items sold.

a. Prepare a plan for a table that states your goal, outlines the data you need, and identifies the table elements.

b. Sketch a sample table on a piece of paper, indicating how the table should be built. Create a table documenting the table design including the field names, type of data, and description of the data.

▼ INDEPENDENT CHALLENGE 2 (CONTINUED)

c. Start Excel, create a new workbook, then save it as **Store Items** in the drive and folder where you store your Data Files. Enter the field names from Table G-6 in the designated cells.

d. Enter eight data records using your own data.

e. Create a table using the data in the range A1:E9. Adjust the column widths as necessary.

f. Apply the Table Style Light 4 to the table.

g. Add the following fields to the table: **Subtotal** in cell F1, and **Total** in cell G1.

h. Add the label **Tax** in cell H1 and click the first option in the AutoCorrect Options to undo the table AutoExpansion. Enter **.125** in cell I1 (the 12.5% Goods and Services tax).

i. Enter formulas to calculate the subtotal (Quantity*Cost) in cell F2 and the total (including tax) in cell G2. Check that the formulas were filled down both of the columns. (*Hint:* Remember to use an absolute reference to the tax rate cell.)

j. Format the Cost, Subtotal, and Total columns using the Accounting number format with two decimal places and the symbol $ English (New Zealand). Adjust the column widths as necessary.

k. Add a new record to your table in row 10. Add another record above row 4.

l. Sort the table in ascending order by Item.

m. Enter your name in the worksheet footer, then save the workbook.

n. Preview the worksheet, use the Scale to Fit width option to scale the worksheet to print on one page.

o. Print the worksheet, close the workbook, then exit Excel.

TABLE G-6

Cell	Field name
A1	Customer Last
B1	Customer First
C1	Item
D1	Quantity
E1	Cost

▼ INDEPENDENT CHALLENGE 3

You are the project manager at a local advertising firm. You are managing your accounts using an Excel worksheet and have decided that a table will provide additional features to help you keep track of the accounts. You will use the table sorting features and table formulas to analyze your account data.

a. Start Excel, open the file EX G-4.xlsx from the drive and folder where you store your Data Files, then save it as **Accounts**.

b. Create a table with the worksheet data and apply Table Style Light 3.

c. Sort the table on the Budget field using the Smallest to Largest order. Compare your table to Figure G-23.

d. Sort the table using two fields, by Contact in A to Z order, then by Budget in Smallest to Largest order.

e. Add the new field label **Balance** in cell G1 and adjust the column width as necessary. Format the Budget, Expenses, and Balance columns using the Accounting format with no decimal places.

FIGURE G-23

	A	B	C	D	E	F	G
1	Project	Deadline	Code	Budget	Expenses	Contact	
2	Kelly	2/1/2010	AA1	100000	30000	Connie Blake	
3	Vincent	1/15/2010	C43	100000	150000	Jane Smith	
4	Jaffrey	3/15/2010	A3A	200000	210000	Kate Jeung	
5	Karim	4/30/2010	C43	200000	170000	Connie Blake	
6	Landry	11/15/2010	V53	200000	210000	Jane Smith	
7	Kaplan	9/30/2010	V51	300000	320000	Jane Smith	
8	Graham	7/10/2010	V13	390000	400000	Charlie Katter	
9	Lannou	10/10/2010	C21	450000	400000	Connie Blake	
10	Mason	6/1/2010	AA5	500000	430210	Jane Smith	
11	Melon	12/15/2010	B12	810000	700000	Nelly Atli	
12							

f. Enter a formula in cell G2 that uses structured references to table fields to calculate the balance on an account as the Budget minus the Expenses.

g. Add a new record for a project named **Franklin** with a deadline of **2/15/2010**, a code of **AB2**, a budget of **200000**, expenses of **150000**, and a contact of **Connie Blake**.

h. Verify that the formula accurately calculated the balance for the new record.

i. Replace all of the Jane Smith data with **Jane Jacobson** and adjust the column width as necessary.

j. Enter your name in the center section of the worksheet footer, add a center section header of **Accounts** using formatting of your choice, then save the workbook.

▼ INDEPENDENT CHALLENGE 3 (CONTINUED)

Advanced Challenge Exercise

- Sort the table on the Balance field using the smallest to largest order.
- Use conditional formatting to format the cells of the table containing negative balances with a dark green text on a green fill.
- Sort the table using the order of no cell color on top.
- Format the table to emphasize the Balance column and turn off the banded rows. (*Hint*: Use the Table Style Options on the Table Tools Design tab.)
- Compare your table with Figure G-24.

FIGURE G-24

	A	B	C	D	E	F	G	H
1	Project	Deadline	Code	Budget	Expenses	Contact	Balance	
2	Karim	4/30/2010	C43	$ 200,000	$ 170,000	Connie Blake	$ 30,000	
3	Lannou	10/10/2010	C21	$ 450,000	$ 400,000	Connie Blake	$ 50,000	
4	Franklin	2/15/2010	AB2	$ 200,000	$ 150,000	Connie Blake	$ 50,000	
5	Mason	6/1/2010	AA5	$ 500,000	$ 430,210	Jane Jacobson	$ 69,790	
6	Kelly	2/1/2010	AA1	$ 100,000	$ 30,000	Connie Blake	$ 70,000	
7	Melon	12/15/2010	B12	$ 810,000	$ 700,000	Nelly Atli	$ 110,000	
8	Vincent	1/15/2010	C43	$ 100,000	$ 150,000	Jane Jacobson	$ (50,000)	
9	Kaplan	9/30/2010	V51	$ 300,000	$ 320,000	Jane Jacobson	$ (20,000)	
10	Graham	7/10/2010	V13	$ 390,000	$ 400,000	Charlie Katter	$ (10,000)	
11	Landry	11/15/2010	V53	$ 200,000	$ 210,000	Jane Jacobson	$ (10,000)	
12	Jaffrey	3/15/2010	A3A	$ 200,000	$ 210,000	Kate Jeung	$ (10,000)	
13								
14								

k. Save the workbook, print the table, close the workbook, then exit Excel.

▼ REAL LIFE INDEPENDENT CHALLENGE

You have decided to organize your recording collection using a table in Excel. This will enable you to easily find songs in your music library. You will add records as you purchase new music and delete records if you discard a recording.

a. Use the fields Title, Artist, Genre, and Format and prepare a diagram of your table structure.

b. Document the table design by detailing the type of data that will be in each field and a description of the data. For example, in the Format field you may have mp3, aac, wma, or other formats.

c. Start Excel, create a new workbook, then save it as **Music Titles** in the drive and folder where you store your Data Files.

d. Enter the field names into the worksheet, enter the records for seven of your music recordings, then save the workbook.

e. Create a table that contains your music information. Resize the columns as necessary.

f. Choose a Table Style and apply it to your table.

g. Add a new field with a label of Comments. Enter information in the new table column describing the setting in which you listen to the title, such as driving, exercising, entertaining, or relaxing.

h. Sort the records by the Format field using A to Z order.

i. Add a record to the table for the next recording you will purchase.

j. Add a Total row to your table and verify that the Count function accurately calculated the number of your recordings.

k. Enter your name in the worksheet footer, then save the workbook.

l. Print the table, close the workbook, then exit Excel.

▼ VISUAL WORKSHOP

Start Excel, open the file EX G-5.xlsx from the drive and folder where you store your Data Files, then save it as **Products**. Sort the data as shown in Figure G-25. The table is formatted using Table Style Light 3. Add a header with the file name that is centered and formatted in bold with a size of 18. Enter your name in the worksheet footer. Save the workbook, preview and print the table, close the workbook, then exit Excel.

FIGURE G-25

Products.xlsx

Order Number	Order date	Amount	Shipping	Sales Rep
1134	4/30/2010	$ 200,000	Air	Edward Callegy
1465	11/15/2010	$ 210,000	Air	Edward Callegy
7733	3/15/2010	$ 230,000	Air	Edward Callegy
2889	2/15/2010	$ 300,000	Air	Edward Callegy
1532	10/10/2010	$ 450,000	Air	Edward Callegy
9345	1/15/2010	$ 100,000	Ground	Gary Clarkson
5623	2/1/2010	$ 130,000	Air	Gary Clarkson
1112	9/30/2010	$ 300,000	Ground	Gary Clarkson
2156	6/1/2010	$ 500,000	Ground	Gary Clarkson
2134	7/10/2010	$ 390,000	Ground	Ned Blair
2144	12/15/2010	$ 810,000	Ground	Ned Blair

Analyzing Table Data

Excel data tables let you manipulate and analyze data in many ways. One way is to filter a table so that it displays only the rows that meet certain criteria. In this unit, you will display selected records using the filter feature, create a custom filter, and filter a table using an Advanced Filter. In addition, you will learn to insert automatic subtotals, use lookup functions to locate table entries, and apply database functions to summarize table data that meet specific criteria. You'll also learn how to restrict entries in a column by using data validation. The vice president of sales, Kate Morgan, asks you to extract information from a table of the 2010 scheduled tours to help the sales representatives with customer inquiries. She also asks you to prepare summaries of the tour sales for a presentation at the international sales meeting.

OBJECTIVES

Filter a table

Create a custom filter

Filter a table with Advanced Filter

Extract table data

Look up values in a table

Summarize table data

Validate table data

Create subtotals

Filtering a Table

When you create a table, arrows automatically appear next to each column header. These arrows are called **filter list arrows**, or **list arrows**, and you can use them to **filter** a table to display only the records that meet criteria you specify, temporarily hiding records that do not meet those criteria. For example, you can use the filter list arrow next to the Tour field header to display only records that contain Nepal Trekking in the Tour field. Once you filter data, you can copy, chart, and print the displayed records. You can easily clear a filter to redisplay all the records. Kate asks you to display only the records for the Pacific Odyssey tours. She also asks for information about the tours that sell the most seats and the tours that depart in March.

STEPS

1. **Start Excel, open the file EX H-1.xlsx from the drive and folder where you save your Data Files, then save it as Tours**

2. **Click the Tour list arrow**

   Sort options appear at the top of the menu, advanced filtering options appear in the middle, and at the bottom is a list of the tour data from column A, as shown in Figure H-1. Because you want to display data for only the Pacific Odyssey tours, your **search criterion** (the text you are searching for) is Pacific Odyssey. You can select one of the Tour data options in the menu, which acts as your search criterion.

   > **QUICK TIP**
   > You can also filter or sort a table by the color of the cells if conditional formatting has been applied.

3. **In the list of tours for the Tour field, click Select All to clear the checks from the tours, scroll down the list of tours, click the Pacific Odyssey check box, then click OK**

   Only those records containing Pacific Odyssey in the Tour field appear, as shown in Figure H-2. The row numbers for the matching records change to blue, and the list arrow for the filtered field has a filter icon. Both indicate that there is a filter in effect and that some of the records are temporarily hidden.

4. **Move the pointer over the Tour list arrow**

   The ScreenTip (Tour: Equals "Pacific Odyssey") describes the filter for the field, meaning that only the Pacific Odyssey records appear. You decide to remove the filter to redisplay all of the table data.

5. **Click the Tour list arrow, then click Clear Filter From "Tour"**

   You have cleared the Pacific Odyssey filter, and all the records reappear. You want to display the most popular tours, those that are in the top five percent of seats reserved.

6. **Click the Seats Reserved list arrow, point to Number Filters, click Top 10, select 10 in the middle box, type 5, click the Items list arrow, click Percent, then click OK**

   Excel displays the records for the top five percent in the number of Seats Reserved field, as shown in Figure H-3. You decide to clear the filter to redisplay all the records.

   > **TROUBLE**
   > If the Clear command is not available, check to be sure the active cell is inside the table.

7. **Click the Home tab, click the Sort & Filter button in the Editing group, then click Clear**

   You have cleared the filter and all the records reappear. You want to find all of the tours that depart in March.

8. **Click the Depart Date list arrow, point to Date Filters, point to All Dates in the Period, then click March**

   Excel displays the records for the four tours that leave in March. You decide to clear the filter and display all of the records.

   > **QUICK TIP**
   > You can also clear a filter by clicking the Clear button in the Sort & Filter group on the Data tab.

9. **Click Sort & Filter button in the Editing group, click Clear, then save the workbook**

Analyzing Table Data

FIGURE H-1: Worksheet showing filter options

Tour filter list arrow

Sort Options

Advanced filtering options

List of tours

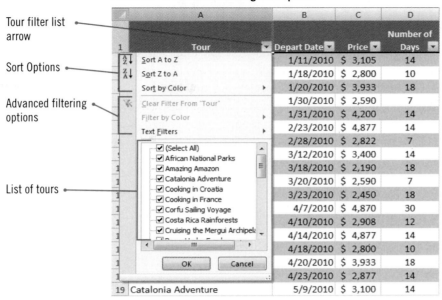

	A	B	C	D
1	Tour	Depart Date	Price	Number of Days
		1/11/2010	$ 3,105	14
Sort A to Z		1/18/2010	$ 2,800	10
Sort Z to A		1/20/2010	$ 3,933	18
Sort by Color		1/30/2010	$ 2,590	7
Clear Filter From "Tour"		1/31/2010	$ 4,200	14
Filter by Color		2/23/2010	$ 4,877	14
Text Filters		2/28/2010	$ 2,822	7
☑ (Select All)		3/12/2010	$ 3,400	14
☑ African National Parks		3/18/2010	$ 2,190	18
☑ Amazing Amazon		3/20/2010	$ 2,590	7
☑ Catalonia Adventure		3/23/2010	$ 2,450	18
☑ Cooking in Croatia		4/7/2010	$ 4,870	30
☑ Cooking in France		4/10/2010	$ 2,908	12
☑ Corfu Sailing Voyage		4/14/2010	$ 4,877	14
☑ Costa Rica Rainforests		4/18/2010	$ 2,800	10
☑ Cruising the Mergui Archipela		4/20/2010	$ 3,933	18
OK Cancel		4/23/2010	$ 2,877	14
19	Catalonia Adventure	5/9/2010	$ 3,100	14

FIGURE H-2: Table filtered to show Pacific Odyssey tours

	A	B	C	D	E	F	G	H	I
1	Tour	Depart Date	Price	Number of Days	Seat Capacity	Seats Reserved	Seats Available	Air Included	Meals Included
2	Pacific Odyssey	1/11/2010	$ 3,105	14	50	30	20	Yes	No
34	Pacific Odyssey	7/7/2010	$ 3,105	14	50	32	18	Yes	No
48	Pacific Odyssey	9/14/2010	$ 3,105	14	50	26	24	Yes	No
61	Pacific Odyssey	12/21/2010	$ 3,105	14	50	50	0	Yes	No
64									

Matching row numbers are blue and sequence indicates that not all rows appear

Filter displays only Pacific Odyssey tours

Filter icon

FIGURE H-3: Table filtered with top 5% of Seats Reserved

	A	B	C	D	E	F	G	H	I
1	Tour	Depart Date	Price	Number of Days	Seat Capacity	Seats Reserved	Seats Available	Air Included	Meals Included
18	Amazing Amazon	4/23/2010	$ 2,877	14	50	48	2	No	No
37	Kayak Newfoundland	7/12/2010	$ 1,970	7	50	49	1	Yes	Yes
45	Cooking in France	8/29/2010	$ 2,822	7	50	48	2	Yes	No
61	Pacific Odyssey	12/21/2010	$ 3,105	14	50	50	0	Yes	No
64									

Table filtered with top 5% in this field

Creating a Custom Filter

So far, you have filtered rows based on an entry in a single column. You can perform more complex filters by using options in the Custom Filter dialog box. For example, your criteria can contain comparison operators such as "greater than" or "less than" that let you display values above or below a certain amount. You can also use **logical conditions** like And and Or to narrow a search even further. You can have Excel display records that meet a criterion in a field *and* another criterion in that same field. This is often used to find records between two values. For example, by specifying an And logical condition, you can display records for customers with incomes between $40,000 *and* $70,000. You can also have Excel display records that meet either criterion in a field by specifying an Or condition. The Or condition is used to find records that satisfy either of two values. For example, in a table of book data you can use the Or condition to find records that contain either Beginning *or* Introduction in the title name. ⬛⬛⬛ Kate wants to locate water tours for customers who like boating adventures. She also wants to find tours that depart between February 15, 2010 and April 15, 2010. She asks you to create custom filters to find the tours satisfying these criteria.

STEPS

1. **Click the Tour list arrow, point to Text Filters, then click Contains**

   The Custom AutoFilter dialog box opens. You enter your criteria in the text boxes. The left text box on the first line currently displays "contains." You want to display tours that contain the word sailing in their names.

2. **Type sailing in the right text box on the first line**

   You want to see entries that contain either sailing or cruising.

QUICK TIP
When specifying criteria in the Custom AutoFilter dialog box, you can use the ? wildcard to represent any single character and the * wildcard to represent any series of characters.

3. **Click the Or option button to select it, click the left text box list arrow on the second line, select contains, then type cruising in the right text box on the second line**

   Your completed Custom AutoFilter dialog box should match Figure H-4.

4. **Click OK**

   The dialog box closes, and only those records having sailing or cruising in the Tour field appear in the worksheet. You want to find all tours that depart between February 15, 2010 and April 15, 2010.

5. **Click the Tour list arrow, click Clear Filter From "Tour", click the Depart Date list arrow, point to Date Filters, then click Custom Filter**

   The Custom AutoFilter dialog box opens. The word "equals" appears in the left text box on the first line. You want to find the departure dates that are between February 15, 2010 and April 15, 2010 (that is, after February 15th *and* before April 15th).

6. **Click the left text box list arrow on the first line, click is after, then type 2/15/2010 in the right text box on the first line**

   The And condition is selected, which is correct.

7. **Click the left text box list arrow on the second line, select is before, type 4/15/2010 in the right text box on the second line, then click OK**

   The records displayed have departing dates between February 15, 2010 and April 15, 2010. Compare your records to those shown in Figure H-5.

8. **Add your name to the center section of the footer, scale the page width to one page, then preview and print the filtered table**

   The worksheet prints using the existing landscape orientation, on one page with your name in the footer.

9. **Click the Depart Date list arrow, then click Clear Filter From "Depart Date"**

   You have cleared the filter, and all the tour records reappear.

FIGURE H-4: Custom AutoFilter dialog box

FIGURE H-5: Results of custom filter

	A	B	C	D	E	F	G	H	I
1	Tour	Depart Date	Price	Number of Days	Seat Capacity	Seats Reserved	Seats Available	Air Included	Meals Included
7	Cruising the Mergui Archipelago	2/23/2010	$ 4,877	14	50	42	8	No	No
8	Cooking in France	2/28/2010	$ 2,822	7	50	18	32	Yes	No
9	Pearls of the Orient	3/12/2010	$ 3,400	14	50	22	28	Yes	No
10	Silk Road Travels	3/18/2010	$ 2,190	18	50	44	6	Yes	Yes
11	Costa Rica Rainforests	3/20/2010	$ 2,590	7	50	32	18	Yes	Yes
12	Green Adventures in Ecuador	3/23/2010	$ 2,450	18	50	45	5	No	No
13	African National Parks	4/7/2010	$ 4,870	30	50	18	32	Yes	Yes
14	Experience Cambodia	4/10/2010	$ 2,908	12	50	29	21	Yes	No
15	Cruising the Mergui Archipelago	4/14/2010	$ 4,877	14	50	20	30	No	No
64									

Depature dates are
between 2/15 and 4/15

Using more than one rule when conditionally formatting data

You can apply conditional formatting to table cells in the same way that you can format a range of worksheet data. You can add multiple rules by clicking the Home tab, clicking the Conditional Formatting button in the Styles group, then clicking New Rule for each additional rule that you want to apply. You can also add rules using the Conditional Formatting Rules Manager, which displays all of the rules for a data range. To use the Rules Manager, click the Home tab, click the Conditional Formatting button in the Styles group, click Manage Rules, then click New Rule for each rule that you want to apply to the data range.

Filtering a Table with Advanced Filter

The Advanced Filter command lets you search for data that matches criteria in more than one column, using And and Or conditions. For example, you can use Advanced Filter to find Tours that leave before a certain date *and* have meals included. To use advanced filtering, you must create a criteria range. A **criteria range** is a cell range containing one row of labels (usually a copy of the column labels) and at least one additional row underneath the row of labels that contains the criteria you want to match. Placing the criteria in the same row indicates that the records you are searching for must match both criteria; that is, it specifies an **And condition**. Placing the criteria in the different rows indicates that the records you are searching for must match only one of the criterion; that is, it specifies an **Or condition**. ▓▓▓▓ Kate wants to identify tours that depart after 6/1/2010 and that cost less than $2000. She asks you to use the Advanced Filter to retrieve these records. You begin by defining the criteria range.

STEPS

1. **Select table rows 1 through 6, click the Insert list arrow in the Cells group, click Insert Sheet Rows; click cell A1, type Criteria Range, then click the Enter button ✓ on the Formula bar**

   Six blank rows are added above the table. Excel does not require the label Criteria Range, but it is useful in organizing the worksheet. It is also helpful to see the column labels.

2. **Select the range A7:I7, click the Copy button 📋 in the Clipboard group, click cell A2, click the Paste button in the Clipboard group, then press [Esc]**

   Next, you want to list records for only those tours that depart after June 1, 2010 and that cost under $2000.

3. **Click cell B3, type >6/1/2010, click cell C3, type <2000, then click ✓**

   You have entered the criteria in the cells directly beneath the Criteria Range labels, as shown in Figure H-6.

4. **Click any cell in the table, click the Data tab, then click the Advanced button in the Sort & Filter group**

   The Advanced Filter dialog box opens, with the table range already entered. The default setting under Action is to filter the table in its current location ("in-place") rather than copy it to another location.

TROUBLE

If your filtered records don't match Figure H-7, make sure there are no spaces between the > symbol and the 6 in cell B3 and the < symbol and the 2 in cell C3.

5. **Click the Criteria range text box, select range A2:I3 in the worksheet, then click OK**

   You have specified the criteria range and performed the filter. The filtered table contains eight records that match both criteria—the departure date is after 6/1/2010 and the price is less than $2000, as shown in Figure H-7. You'll filter this table even further in the next lesson.

FIGURE H-6: Criteria in the same row

	A	B	C	D	E	F	G	H	I
1	Criteria Range								
2	Tour	Depart Date	Price	Number of Days	Seat Capacity	Seats Reserved	Seats Available	Air Included	Meals Included
3		>6/1/2010	<2000						
4									
5									
6									
7	Tour	Depart Date	Price	Number of Days	Seat Capacity	Seats Reserved	Seats Available	Air Included	Meals Included
8	Pacific Odyssey	1/11/2010	$ 3,105	14	50	30	20	Yes	No
9	Down Under Exodus	1/18/2010	$ 2,800	10	50	39	11	Yes	Yes

Filtered records will match these criteria

FIGURE H-7: Filtered table

	A	B	C	D	E	F	G	H	I
1	Criteria Range								
2	Tour	Depart Date	Price	Number of Days	Seat Capacity	Seats Reserved	Seats Available	Air Included	Meals Included
3		>6/1/2010	<2000						
4									
5									
6									
7	Tour	Depart Date	Price	Number of Days	Seat Capacity	Seats Reserved	Seats Available	Air Included	Meals Included
34	Exotic Morocco	6/12/2010	$ 1,900	7	50	34	16	Yes	No
35	Kayak Newfoundland	6/12/2010	$ 1,970	7	50	41	9	Yes	Yes
38	Wild River Escape	6/27/2010	$ 1,944	10	50	1	49	No	No
43	Kayak Newfoundland	7/12/2010	$ 1,970	7	50	49	1	Yes	Yes
45	Magnificent Montenegro	7/27/2010	$ 1,890	10	50	11	39	No	No
47	Kayak Newfoundland	8/12/2010	$ 1,970	7	50	2	48	Yes	Yes
50	Wild River Escape	8/27/2010	$ 1,944	10	50	18	32	No	No
62	Exotic Morocco	10/31/2010	$ 1,900	7	50	18	32	Yes	No
70									

Dates are after 6/1/2010

Prices are less than $2,000

Using advanced conditional formatting options

You can emphasize top or bottom ranked values in a field using conditional formatting. To highlight the top or bottom values in a field, select the field data, click the Conditional Formatting button on the Home tab, point to Top/Bottom Rules, select a Top or Bottom rule, if necessary enter the percentage or number of cells in the selected range that you want to format, select the format for the cells that meet the top or bottom criteria, then click OK. You can also format your worksheet or table data using icon sets and color scales based on the cell values. A **color scale** uses a set of two, three, or four fill colors to convey relative values. For example, red could fill cells to indicate they have higher values and green could signify lower values. To add a color scale, select a data range, click the Home tab, click the Conditional Formatting button in the Styles group, then point to Color Scales. On the submenu, you can select preformatted color sets or click More Rules to create your own color sets. **Icon sets** let you visually communicate relative cell values by adding icons to cells based on the values they contain. An upward-pointing green arrow might represent the highest values, and downward-pointing red arrows could represent lower values. To add an icon set to a data range, select a data range, click the Conditional Formatting button in the Styles group, then point to Icon Sets. You can customize the values that are used as thresholds for color scales and icon sets by clicking the Conditional Formatting button in the Styles group, clicking Manage Rules, clicking the rule in the Conditional Formatting Rules Manager dialog box, then clicking Edit Rule.

Extracting Table Data

Whenever you take the time to specify a complicated set of search criteria, it's a good idea to extract the matching records, rather than filtering it in-place. When you **extract** data, you place a copy of a filtered table in a range that you specify in the Advanced Filter dialog box. This way, you won't accidentally clear the filter or lose track of the records you spent time compiling. To extract data, you use an advanced filter and enter the criteria beneath the copied field names, as you did in the previous lesson. ▰▰▰▰ Kate needs to filter the table one step further to reflect only the Exotic Morocco or Kayak Newfoundland tours in the current filtered table. She asks you to complete this filter by specifying an Or condition, which you will do by entering two sets of criteria in two separate rows. You decide to save the filtered records by extracting them to a different location in the worksheet.

STEPS

1. **In cell A3, enter Exotic Morocco, then in cell A4, enter Kayak Newfoundland**

   The new sets of criteria need to appear in two separate rows, so you need to copy the previous filter criteria to the second row.

2. **Copy the criteria in B3:C3 to B4:C4**

   The criteria are shown in Figure H-8. When you perform the advanced filter this time, you indicate that you want to copy the filtered table to a range beginning in cell A75, so that Kate can easily refer to the data, even if you perform more filters later.

3. **Click the Data tab if necessary, then click Advanced in the Sort & Filter group**

4. **Under Action, click the Copy to another location option button to select it, click the Copy to text box, then type A75**

   The last time you filtered the table, the criteria range included only rows 2 and 3, and now you have criteria in row 4.

TROUBLE

Make sure the criteria range in the Advanced Filter dialog box includes the field names and the number of rows underneath the names that contain criteria. If you leave a blank row in the criteria range, Excel filters nothing and shows all records.

5. **Edit the contents of the Criteria range text box to show the range $A$2:$I$4, click OK, then if necessary scroll down until row 75 is visible**

   The matching records appear in the range beginning in cell A75, as shown in Figure H-9. The original table, starting in cell A7, contains the records filtered in the previous lesson.

6. **Select the range A75:I80, click the Office button 📄, click Print, under Print what click the Selection option button, click Preview, then click Print**

   The selected area prints.

7. **Press [Ctrl][Home], then click the Clear button in the Sort & Filter group**

   The original table is displayed starting in cell A7, and the extracted table remains in A75:I80.

8. **Save the workbook**

FIGURE H-8: Criteria in separate rows

	A	B	C	D	E	F	G	H	I
1	Criteria Range								
2	Tour	Depart Date	Price	Number of Days	Seat Capacity	Seats Reserved	Seats Available	Air Included	Meals Included
3	Exotic Morocco	>6/1/2010	<2000						
4	Kayak Newfoundland	>6/1/2010	<2000						
5									

Two sets of criteria on separate lines indicates an OR condition

FIGURE H-9: Extracted data records

	Tour	Depart Date	Price	Number of Days	Seat Capacity	Seats Reserved	Seats Available	Air Included	Meals Included
73									
74									
75	Tour	Depart Date	Price	Number of Days	Seat Capacity	Seats Reserved	Seats Available	Air Included	Meals Included
76	Exotic Morocco	6/12/2010	$ 1,900	7	50	34	16	Yes	No
77	Kayak Newfoundland	6/12/2010	$ 1,970	7	50	41	9	Yes	Yes
78	Kayak Newfoundland	7/12/2010	$ 1,970	7	50	49	1	Yes	Yes
79	Kayak Newfoundland	8/12/2010	$ 1,970	7	50	2	48	Yes	Yes
80	Exotic Morocco	10/31/2010	$ 1,900	7	50	18	32	Yes	No
81									

Only Exotic Morocco and Kayak Newfoundland tours appear

Departure date after 6/1/2010

Price is less than $2000

Understanding the criteria range and the copy-to location

When you define the criteria range and the copy-to location in the Advanced Filter dialog box, Excel automatically creates the names Criteria and Extract for these ranges in the worksheet. The criteria range includes the field names and any criteria rows underneath them. The extract range includes just the field names above the extracted table. You can select these ranges by clicking the Name box list arrow, then clicking the range name. If you click the Name Manager button in the Defined Names group on the Formulas tab, you will see these new names and the ranges associated with the names.

Looking Up Values in a Table

The Excel VLOOKUP function helps you locate specific values in a table. VLOOKUP searches vertically (V) down the far left column of a table, then reads across the row to find the value in the column you specify, much as you might look up a number in a phone book: You locate a person's name, then read across the row to find the phone number you want. Kate wants to be able to find a tour destination by entering the tour code. You will use the VLOOKUP function to accomplish this task. You begin by viewing the table name so you can refer to it in a Lookup function.

STEPS

QUICK TIP

You can change table names to better represent their content so they are easier to use in formulas. Click the table in the list of names in the Name Manager text box, click Edit, type the new table name in the Name text box, then click OK.

1. **Click the Lookup sheet tab, click the Formulas tab, then click the Name Manager button in the Defined Names group**

   The named ranges for the workbook appear in the Name Manager dialog box, as shown in Figure H-10. The Criteria and Extract ranges appear at the top of the range name list. At the bottom of the list is information about the three tables in the workbook. Table1 refers to the table on the Tours sheet, Table2 refers to the table on the Lookup sheet, and Table3 refers to the table on the Subtotals worksheet. These table names were automatically generated when the table was created by the Excel structured reference feature.

2. **Click Close**

   You want to find the tour represented by the code 675Y. The VLOOKUP function lets you find the tour name for any trip code. You will enter a trip code in cell L2 and a VLOOKUP function in cell M2.

3. **Click cell L2, enter 675Y, click cell M2, click the Lookup & Reference button in the Function Library group, then click VLOOKUP**

   The Function Arguments dialog box opens, with boxes for each of the VLOOKUP arguments. Because the value you want to find is in cell L2, L2 is the Lookup_value. The table you want to search is the table on the Lookup sheet, so its assigned name, Table2, is the Table_array.

QUICK TIP

If you want to find only the closest match for a value, enter TRUE in the Range_lookup text box. However, this can give misleading results if you are looking for an exact match. If you use FALSE and Excel can't find the value, you see an error message.

4. **With the insertion point in the Lookup_value text box, click cell L2, click the Table_array text box, then type Table2**

   The column containing the information that you want to find and display in cell M2 is the second column from the left in the table range, so the Col_index_num is 2. Because you want to find an exact match for the value in cell L1, the Range_lookup argument is FALSE.

5. **Click the Col_index_num text box, type 2, click the Range_lookup text box, then enter FALSE**

   Your completed Function Arguments dialog box should match Figure H-11.

6. **Click OK**

   Excel searches down the leftmost column of the table until it finds a value matching the one in cell L2. It finds the tour for that record, Catalonia Adventure, then displays it in cell M2. You use this function to determine the tour for one other trip code.

7. **Click cell L2, type 439U, then click the Enter button ✔ on the formula bar**

   The VLOOKUP function returns the value of Cooking in France in cell M2.

8. **Press [Ctrl][Home], then save the workbook**

Finding records using the DGET function

You can also use the DGET function to find a record in a table that matches specified criteria. For example, you could use the criteria of L1:L2 in the DGET function. When using DGET, you need to include [#All] after your table name in the formula to include the column labels that are used for the criteria range.

FIGURE H-10: Named ranges in the workbook

Created by
Advanced
Filter

Tables in the
workbook

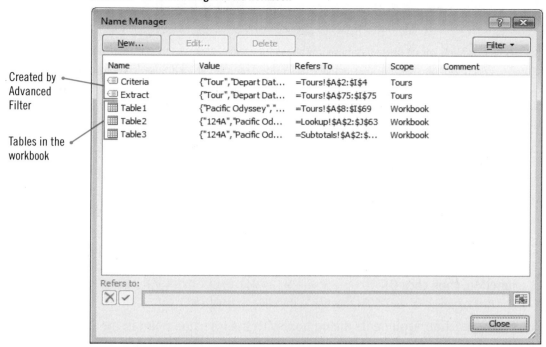

FIGURE H-11: Completed Function Arguments dialog box for VLOOKUP

Range name of
table to search

Finds exact
match

Location of
value you want
to search for

Number of
column to
search

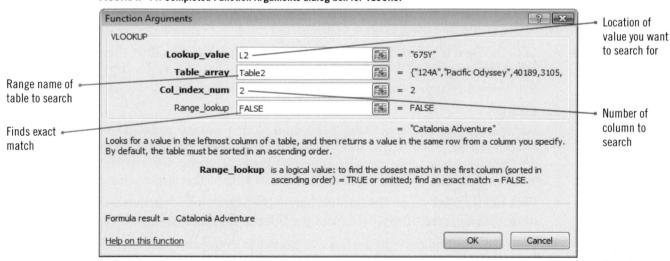

Using the HLOOKUP and MATCH functions

The VLOOKUP (Vertical Lookup) function is useful when your data is arranged vertically, in columns. The HLOOKUP (Horizontal Lookup) function is useful when your data is arranged horizontally, in rows. HLOOKUP searches horizontally across the upper row of a table until it finds the matching value, then looks down the number of rows you specify. The arguments for this function are identical to those for the VLOOKUP function, with one exception. Instead of a Col_index_number, HLOOKUP uses a Row_index_number, which indicates the location of the row you want to search. For example, if you want to search the fourth row from the top, the Row_index_number should be 4. You can use the MATCH function when you want the position of an item in a range. The MATCH function uses the syntax: MATCH (lookup_value,lookup_array,match_ type) where lookup_value is the value you want to match in the lookup_array range. The match_type can be 0 for an exact match, 1 for matching the largest value that is less than or equal to lookup_value, or –1 for matching the smallest value that is greater than or equal to lookup_value.

Summarizing Table Data

Because a table acts much like a database, database functions allow you to summarize table data in a variety of ways. When working with a sales activity table, for example, you can use Excel to count the number of client contacts by sales representative or to total the amount sold to specific accounts by month. Table H-1 lists database functions commonly used to summarize table data. ⬛⬛⬛ Kate is considering adding tours for the 2010 schedule. She needs your help in evaluating the number of seats available for scheduled tours.

STEPS

1. **Review the criteria range for the Pacific Odyssey tour in the range L6:L7**

   The criteria range in L6:L7 tells Excel to summarize records with the entry Pacific Odyssey in the Tour column. The functions will be in cells N6 and N7. You use this criteria range in a DSUM function to sum the seats available for only the Pacific Odyssey tours.

2. **Click cell N6, click the Insert Function button in the Function Library group, in the Search for a function text box type database, click Go, click DSUM under Select a function, then click OK**

   The first argument of the DSUM function is the table, or database.

3. **In the Function Arguments dialog box, with the insertion point in the Database text box, move the pointer over the upper-left corner of the Trip Code column header until the pointer becomes ⬊, click once, then click again**

   The first click selects the table's data range and the second click selects the entire table, including the header row. The second argument of the DSUM function is the label for the column that you want to sum. You want to total the number of available seats. The last argument for the DSUM function is the criteria that will be used to determine which values to total.

4. **Click the Field text box, then click cell H1, Seats Available; click the Criteria text box and select the range L6:L7**

   Your completed Function Arguments dialog box should match Figure H-12.

5. **Click OK**

   The result in cell N6 is 62. Excel totaled the information in the column Seats Available for those records that meet the criterion of Tour equals Pacific Odyssey. The DCOUNT and the DCOUNTA functions can help you determine the number of records meeting specified criteria in a database field. DCOUNTA counts the number of nonblank cells. You will use DCOUNTA to determine the number of tours scheduled

6. **Click cell N7, click 𝑓𝑥 on the formula bar, in the Search for a function text box type database, click Go, select DCOUNTA from the Select a function list, then click OK**

7. **With the insertion point in the Database text box, move the pointer over the upper-left corner of the Trip Code column header until the pointer becomes ⬊, click once, click again to, click the Field text box and click cell B1, click the Criteria text box and select the range L6:L7, then click OK**

   The result in cell N7 is 4, meaning that there are four Pacific Odyssey tours scheduled for the year. You also want to display the number of seats available for the Cooking in France tours.

8. **Click cell L7, type Cooking in France, then click the Enter button ✓ on the formula bar**

   Figure H-13 shows that only three seats are available in the Cooking in France tours.

FIGURE H-12: Completed Function Arguments dialog box for DSUM

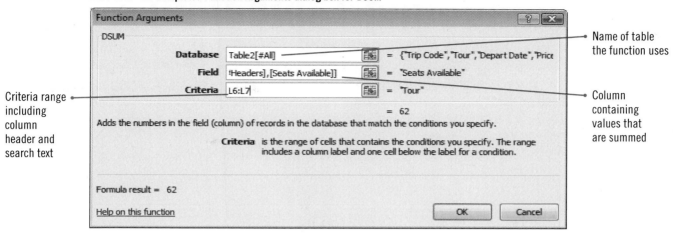

Criteria range including column header and search text

Name of table the function uses

Column containing values that are summed

FIGURE H-13: Result generated by database functions

	D	E	F	G	H	I	J	K	L	M	N
1	Price	Number of Days	Seat Capacity	Seats Reserved	Seats Available	Air Included	Meals Included		Trip Code	Tour	
2	$ 3,105	14	50	30	20	Yes	No		439U	Cooking in France	
3	$ 2,800	10	50	39	11	Yes	Yes				
4	$ 3,933	18	50	45	5	Yes	Yes				
5	$ 2,590	7	50	30	20	Yes	Yes		Criteria		
6	$ 4,200	14	50	38	12	Yes	Yes		Tour	Seats Available	3
7	$ 4,877	14	50	42	8	No	No		Cooking in France	Number of tours scheduled	2
8	$ 2,822	7	50	48	2	Yes	No				

TABLE H-1: Common database functions

function	result
DGET	Extracts a single record from a table that matches criteria you specify
DSUM	Totals numbers in a given table column that match criteria you specify
DAVERAGE	Averages numbers in a given table column that match criteria you specify
DCOUNT	Counts the cells that contain numbers in a given table column that match criteria you specify
DCOUNTA	Counts the cells that contain nonblank data in a given table column that match criteria you specify

Validating Table Data

When setting up data tables, you want to help ensure accuracy when you or others enter data. The Excel data validation feature allows you to do this by specifying what data users can enter in a range of cells. You can restrict data to whole numbers, decimal numbers, or text. You can also specify a list of acceptable entries. Once you've specified what data the program should consider valid for that cell, Excel displays an error message when invalid data is entered and can prevent users from entering any other data that it considers to be invalid.  Kate wants to make sure that information in the Air Included column is entered consistently in the future. She asks you to restrict the entries in that column to two options: Yes and No. First, you select the table column you want to restrict.

STEPS

1. **Click the top edge of the Air Included column header**

   The column data is selected.

2. **Click the Data tab, click the Data Validation button in the Data Tools group, click the Settings tab if necessary, click the Allow list arrow, then click List**

   Selecting the List option lets you type a list of specific options.

3. **Click the Source text box, then type Yes, No**

   You have entered the list of acceptable entries, separated by commas, as shown in Figure H-14. You want the data entry person to be able to select a valid entry from a drop-down list.

4. **Click the In-cell dropdown check box to select it if necessary, then click OK**

   The dialog box closes, and you return to the worksheet.

5. **Click the Home tab, click any cell in the last table row, click the Insert list arrow in the Cells group, click Insert Table Row Below, click cell I64, then click the list arrow to display the list of valid entries**

   The dropdown list is shown in Figure H-15. You could click an item in the list to have it entered in the cell, but you want to test the data restriction by entering an invalid entry.

6. **Click the list arrow to close the list, type Maybe, then press [Enter]**

   A warning dialog box appears to prevent you from entering the invalid data, as shown in Figure H-16.

7. **Click Cancel, click the list arrow, then click Yes**

   The cell accepts the valid entry. The data restriction ensures that records contain only one of the two correct entries in the Air Included column. The table is ready for future data entry.

8. **Delete the last table row, then save the workbook**

9. **Add your name to the center section of the footer, select the range L1:N7, click the Office button ⊙, click Print, under Print what, click the Selection option button, click Preview, then click Print**

Restricting cell values and data length

In addition to providing an in-cell drop-down list for data entry, you can use data validation to restrict the values that are entered into cells. For example, if you want to restrict cells to values less than a certain number, date, or time, click the Data tab, click the Data Validation button in the Data Tools group, and on the Settings tab, click the Allow list arrow, select Whole number, Decimal, Date, or Time, click the Data list arrow, select less than, then in the bottom text box, enter the maximum value. You can also limit the length of data entered into cells by choosing Text length in the Allow list, clicking the Data list arrow and selecting less than, then entering the maximum length in the Maximum text box.

FIGURE H-14: Creating data restrictions

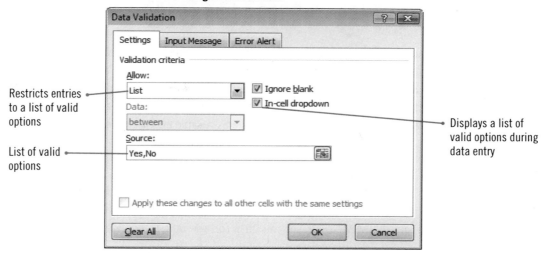

Restricts entries to a list of valid options

List of valid options

Displays a list of valid options during data entry

FIGURE H-15: Entering data in restricted cells

61	307R	Pacific Odyssey		12/21/2010	$ 3,105	14	50	50	0	Yes	No
62	927F	Essential India		12/30/2010	$ 3,933	18	50	31	19	Yes	Yes
63	448G	Old Japan		12/31/2010	$ 2,100	21	50	44	6	Yes	No
64									0		
65										Yes	
66										No	

Dropdown list

FIGURE H-16: Invalid data warning

Microsoft Office Excel

The value you entered is not valid.

A user has restricted values that can be entered into this cell.

Retry   Cancel   Help

Adding input messages and error alerts

You can customize the way data validation works by using the two other tabs in the Data Validation dialog box: Input Message and Error Alert. The Input Message tab lets you set a message that appears when the user selects that cell; for example, the message might contain instructions about what type of data to enter. On the Input Message tab, enter a message title and message, then click OK. The Error Alert tab lets you set one of three alert levels if a user enters invalid data. The Information level displays your message with the information icon but allows the user to proceed with data entry. The Warning level displays your information with the warning icon and gives the user the option to proceed with data entry or not. The Stop level, which you used in this lesson, displays your message and only lets the user retry or cancel data entry for that cell.

Creating Subtotals

The Excel Subtotals feature provides a quick, easy way to group and summarize a range of data. Usually, you create subtotals with the SUM function, but you can also summarize data groups with functions such as COUNT, AVERAGE, MAX, and MIN. Subtotals cannot be used in a table structure. Before you can add subtotals to a table, you must first convert the data to a range and sort it. ▄▄▄▄▄▄ Kate wants you to group data by tours, with subtotals for the number of seats available and the number of seats reserved. You begin by converting the table to a range.

STEPS

1. **Click the** Subtotals sheet tab, **click any cell inside the table, click the** Table Tools Design tab, **click the** Convert to Range button **in the Tools group, then click** Yes

    Before you can add the subtotals, you must first sort the data. You decide to sort it in ascending order, first by tour and then by departure date.

2. **Click the** Data tab, **click the** Sort button **in the Sort & Filter group, in the Sort dialog box click the** Sort by list arrow, **click** Tour, **then click the** Add Level button, **click the** Then by list arrow, **click** Depart Date, **verify that the order is** Oldest to Newest, **then click** OK

    You have sorted the range in ascending order, first by tour, then by departure date.

3. **Click any cell in the data range, then click the** Subtotal button **in the Outline group**

    The Subtotal dialog box opens. Here you specify the items you want subtotaled, the function you want to apply to the values, and the fields you want to summarize.

4. **Click the** At each change in list arrow, **click Tour, click the** Use function list arrow, **click** Sum; **in the Add subtotal to list, click the** Seats Reserved **and** Seats Available **check boxes to select them, if necessary, then click the** Meals Included **check box to deselect it**

5. **If necessary, click the** Replace current subtotals **and** Summary below data **check boxes to select them**

    Your completed Subtotal dialog box should match Figure H-17.

6. **Click OK, then scroll down so row 90 is visible**

    The subtotaled data appears, showing the calculated subtotals and grand total in columns G and H, as shown in Figure H-18. Notice that Excel displays an outline to the left of the worksheet, with outline buttons to control the level of detail that appears. The button number corresponds to the detail level that is displayed. You want to show the second level of detail, the subtotals and the grand total.

7. **Click the** outline symbol ⌷2⌷

    The subtotals and the grand totals appear.

8. **Add your name to the center section of the footer, scale the worksheet width to print on one page, save, preview the worksheet, then print it**

9. **Close the workbook and exit Excel**

> **QUICK TIP**
> You can click the
> [−] button to hide
> or the [+] button to
> show a group of
> records in the subto-
> taled structure.

> **QUICK TIP**
> You can remove
> subtotals in a work-
> sheet by clicking the
> Subtotal button and
> clicking Remove All.
> The subtotals no
> longer appear, and
> the Outline feature
> is turned off
> automatically.

FIGURE H-17: Completed Subtotal dialog box

Field to use in grouping data

Function to apply to groups

Subtotal these fields

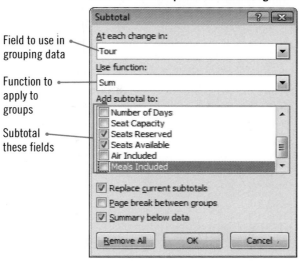

FIGURE H-18: Portion of subtotaled table

Outline symbols

	A	B	C	D	E	F	G	H	I	J
66		**Nepal Trekking Total**					94	56		
67	622V	Old Japan	7/12/2010	$ 2,100	21	50	33	17	Yes	No
68	448G	Old Japan	12/31/2010	$ 2,100	21	50	44	6	Yes	No
69		**Old Japan Total**					77	23		
70	124A	Pacific Odyssey	1/11/2010	$ 3,105	14	50	30	20	Yes	No
71	133E	Pacific Odyssey	7/7/2010	$ 3,105	14	50	32	18	Yes	No
72	698N	Pacific Odyssey	9/14/2010	$ 3,105	14	50	26	24	Yes	No
73	307R	Pacific Odyssey	12/21/2010	$ 3,105	14	50	50	0	Yes	No
74		**Pacific Odyssey Total**					138	62		
75	467B	Panama Adventure	6/18/2010	$ 2,304	10	50	22	28	Yes	Yes
76	793T	Panama Adventure	12/18/2010	$ 2,304	10	50	30	20	Yes	Yes
77		**Panama Adventure Total**					52	48		
78	966W	Pearls of the Orient	3/12/2010	$ 3,400	14	50	22	28	Yes	No
79	572D	Pearls of the Orient	9/12/2010	$ 3,400	14	50	19	31	Yes	No
80		**Pearls of the Orient Total**					41	59		
81	653S	Silk Road Travels	3/18/2010	$ 2,190	18	50	44	6	Yes	Yes
82	724D	Silk Road Travels	9/18/2010	$ 2,190	18	50	18	32	Yes	Yes
83		**Silk Road Travels Total**					62	38		
84	544T	Treasures of Ethiopia	5/18/2010	$ 3,200	10	50	18	32	Yes	Yes
85	621R	Treasures of Ethiopia	11/18/2010	$ 3,200	10	50	46	4	Yes	Yes
86		**Treasures of Ethiopia Total**					64	36		
87	558B	Wild River Escape	6/27/2010	$ 1,944	10	50	1	49	No	No
88	923Q	Wild River Escape	8/27/2010	$ 1,944	10	50	18	32	No	No
89		**Wild River Escape Total**					19	81		
90		**Grand Total**					1817	1283		

Subtotals

Grand totals

Practice

If you have a SAM user profile, you may have access to hands-on instruction, practice, and assessment of the skills covered in this unit. Log in to your SAM account (http://sam2007.course.com/) to launch any assigned training activities or exams that relate to the skills covered in this unit.

▼ CONCEPTS REVIEW

FIGURE H–19

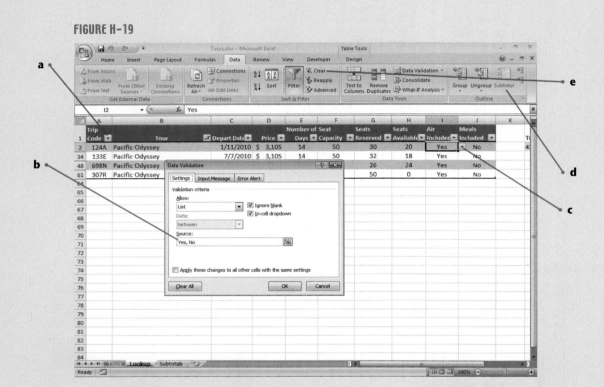

1. **Which element do you click to specify acceptable data entries for a table?**
2. **Which element points to a field's list arrow?**
3. **Which element do you click to group data and summarize data in a table?**
4. **Which element would you click to remove a filter?**
5. **Which element points to an In-cell dropdown list arrow?**

Match each term with the statement that best describes it.

6. **DSUM**	**a.** Cell range when Advanced Filter results are copied to another location
7. **Data validation**	**b.** Range in which search conditions are set
8. **Criteria range**	**c.** Restricts table entries to specified options
9. **Extracted table**	**d.** Name of the table searched in a VLOOKUP function
10. **Table_array**	**e.** Function used to total table values that meet specified criteria

Select the best answer from the list of choices.

11. **The _____ logical condition finds records matching both listed criteria.**
   - **a.** Or
   - **b.** And
   - **c.** True
   - **d.** False

12. **What does it mean when you select the Or option when creating a custom filter?**
   - **a.** Both criteria must be true to find a match.
   - **b.** Neither criterion has to be 100% true.
   - **c.** Either criterion can be true to find a match.
   - **d.** A custom filter requires a criteria range.

13. What must a data range have before subtotals can be inserted?

   a. Enough records to show multiple subtotals   **c.** Formatted cells

   b. Grand totals   **d.** Sorted data

14. Which function finds the position of an item in a table?

   a. MATCH   **c.** DGET

   b. VLOOKUP   **d.** HLOOKUP

▼ SKILLS REVIEW

1. Filter a table.

   a. Start Excel, open the file EX H-2.xlsx from the drive and folder where you store your Data Files, then save it as **Salary Summary**.

   b. With the Compensation sheet active, filter the table to list only records for employees in the Boston branch.

   c. Clear the filter, then add a filter that displays the records for employees in the Boston and Philadelphia branches.

   d. Redisplay all employees, then use a filter to show the three employees with the highest annual salary.

   e. Redisplay all the records, then save the workbook.

2. Create a custom filter.

   a. Create a custom filter showing employees hired before 1/1/2007 or after 12/31/2007.

   b. Create a custom filter showing employees hired between 1/1/2007 and 12/31/2007.

   c. Enter your name in the worksheet footer, save the workbook, then preview and print the filtered worksheet.

   d. Redisplay all records.

   e. Save the workbook.

3. Filter and extract a table with Advanced Filter.

   a. You want to retrieve a list of employees who were hired before 1/1/2008 and who have an annual salary of more than $80,000 a year. Define a criteria range by inserting six new rows above the table on the worksheet and copying the field names into the first row.

   b. In cell D2, enter the criterion **<1/1/2008**, then in cell G2 enter **>80000**.

   c. Click any cell in the table.

   d. Open the Advanced Filter dialog box.

   e. Indicate that you want to copy to another location, enter the criteria range **A1:J2**, verify that the List range is $A$7:$J$17, then indicate that you want to place the extracted list in the range starting at cell **A20**.

   f. Confirm that the retrieved list meets the criteria as shown in Figure H-20.

   g. Save the workbook, then preview and print the worksheet.

FIGURE H-20

4. Look up values in a table.

   a. Click the Summary sheet tab. Use the Name Manager to view the table names in the workbook, then close the dialog box.

   b. You will use a lookup function to locate an employee's annual compensation; enter the Employee Number **2214** in cell A17.

   c. In cell B17, use the VLOOKUP function and enter **A17** as the Lookup_value, **Table2** as the Table_array, **10** as the Col_index_num, and **FALSE** as the Range_lookup; observe the compensation displayed for that employee number, then check it against the table to make sure it is correct.

   d. Enter another Employee Number, **4177**, in cell A17 and view the annual compensation for that employee.

   e. Format cell B17 with the Accounting format with no decimal places and the $ symbol.

   f. Save the workbook.

	A	B	C	D	E	F	G	H	I	J
1	Employee Number	First Name	Last Name	Hire Date	Branch	Monthly Salary	Annual Salary	Annual Bonus	Benefits Dollars	Annual Compensation
2				<1/1/2008			>80000			
3										
4										
5										
6										
7	Employee Number	First Name	Last Name	Hire Date	Branch	Monthly Salary	Annual Salary	Annual Bonus	Benefits Dollars	Annual Compensation
8	1311	Mary	Lawson	2/12/2007	NY	$ 4,500	$ 54,000	$ 1,200	$ 12,420	$ 67,620
9	4522	Laurie	Wales	4/1/2008	Boston	$ 5,800	$ 69,600	$ 5,400	$ 16,008	$ 91,008
10	4177	Donna	Dahar	5/6/2006	Philadelphia	$ 7,500	$ 90,000	$ 16,000	$ 20,700	$ 126,700
11	2571	Mary	Marlin	12/10/2007	Boston	$ 8,000	$ 96,000	$ 18,000	$ 22,080	$ 136,080
12	2214	Paul	Gamache	2/15/2009	Boston	$ 2,900	$ 34,800	$ 570	$ 8,004	$ 43,374
13	6587	Peter	Erickson	3/25/2007	NY	$ 2,775	$ 33,300	$ 770	$ 7,659	$ 41,729
14	2123	Erin	Mallo	6/23/2006	NY	$ 3,990	$ 47,880	$ 2,500	$ 11,012	$ 61,392
15	4439	Mark	Merry	8/3/2009	Philadelphia	$ 6,770	$ 81,240	$ 5,000	$ 18,685	$ 104,925
16	9807	Hailey	Reed	9/29/2008	Philadelphia	$ 8,600	$103,200	$ 14,000	$ 23,736	$ 140,936
17	3944	Joyce	Roy	5/12/2007	Boston	$ 3,500	$ 42,000	$ 900	$ 9,660	$ 52,560
18										
19										
20	Employee Number	First Name	Last Name	Hire Date	Branch	Monthly Salary	Annual Salary	Annual Bonus	Benefits Dollars	Annual Compensation
21	4177	Donna	Dahar	5/6/2006	Philadelphia	$ 7,500	$ 90,000	$ 16,000	$ 20,700	$ 126,700
22	2571	Mary	Marlin	12/10/2007	Boston	$ 8,000	$ 96,000	$ 18,000	$ 22,080	$ 136,080
23										

5. **Summarize table data.**

   a. You want to enter a database function to average the annual salaries by branch, using the NY branch as the initial criterion. In cell E17, use the DAVERAGE function and click the top left corner of cell A1 twice to select the table and its header row as the Database, select cell G1 for the Field and select the range D16:D17 for the Criteria.

   b. Test the function further by entering the text **Philadelphia** in cell D17. When the criterion is entered, cell E17 should display 91480.

   c. Format cell E17 in Accounting format with no decimal places and the $ symbol.

   d. Save the workbook.

6. **Validation table data.**

   a. Select the data in column E of the table and set a validation criterion specifying that you want to allow a list of valid options.

   b. Enter a list of valid options that restricts the entries to **NY**, **Boston**, and **Philadelphia**. Remember to use a comma between each item in the list.

   c. Indicate that you want the options to appear in an in-cell dropdown list, then close the dialog box.

   d. Add a row to the table. Go to cell E12, then select Boston in the dropdown list.

   e. Select column F in the table and indicate that you want to restrict the data entered to only whole numbers. In the Minimum text box, enter **1000**; in the Maximum text box, enter **20000**. Close the dialog box.

   f. Click cell F12, enter **25000**, then press [Enter]. You should get an error message.

   g. Click Cancel, then enter **17000**.

   h. Complete the new record by adding an Employee Number of 1112, a First Name of Caroline, a Last Name of Dow, a Hire Date of 2/1/2010, and an Annual Bonus of $1000. Format the range F12:J12 as Accounting with no decimal places and using the $ symbol. Compare your screen to Figure H-21.

   i. Add your name to the center section of the footer, save, preview the worksheet and fit it to one page if necessary, then print it.

FIGURE H-21

	A	B	C	D	E	F	G	H	I	J
1	Employee Number	First Name	Last Name	Hire Date	Branch	Monthly Salary	Annual Salary	Annual Bonus	Benefits Dollars	Annual Compensation
2	1311	Mary	Lawson	2/12/2007	NY	$ 4,500	$ 54,000	$ 1,200	$ 12,420	$ 67,620
3	4522	Laurie	Wales	4/1/2008	Boston	$ 5,800	$ 69,600	$ 5,400	$ 16,008	$ 91,008
4	4177	Donna	Dahar	5/6/2006	Philadelphia	$ 7,500	$ 90,000	$ 16,000	$ 20,700	$ 126,700
5	2571	Mary	Marlin	12/10/2007	Boston	$ 8,000	$ 96,000	$ 18,000	$ 22,080	$ 136,080
6	2214	Paul	Gamache	2/15/2009	Boston	$ 2,900	$ 34,800	$ 570	$ 8,004	$ 43,374
7	6587	Peter	Erickson	3/25/2007	NY	$ 2,775	$ 33,300	$ 770	$ 7,659	$ 41,729
8	2123	Erin	Mallo	6/23/2006	NY	$ 3,990	$ 47,880	$ 2,500	$ 11,012	$ 61,392
9	4439	Mark	Merry	8/3/2009	Philadelphia	$ 6,770	$ 81,240	$ 5,000	$ 18,685	$ 104,925
10	9807	Hailey	Reed	9/29/2008	Philadelphia	$ 8,600	$ 103,200	$ 14,000	$ 23,736	$ 140,936
11	3944	Joyce	Roy	5/12/2007	Boston	$ 3,500	$ 42,000	$ 900	$ 9,660	$ 52,560
12	1112	Caroline	Dow	2/1/2010	Boston	$ 17,000	$ 204,000	$ 1,000	$ 46,920	$ 251,920
13										
14										
15										
16	Employee Number	Annual Compensation			Branch	Average Annual Salary				
17	4177	$ 126,700			Philadelphia	$ 91,480				

7. **Create subtotals using grouping and outlines.**

   a. Click the Subtotals sheet tab.

   b. Use the Department field list arrow to sort the table in ascending order by department.

   c. Convert the table to a range.

   d. Group and create subtotals by department, using the SUM function, then click the AnnualCompensation checkbox if necessary in the Add Subtotal to list.

   e. Click the 2 outline button on the outline to display only the subtotals and the grand total. Compare your screen to Figure H-22.

   f. Enter your name in the worksheet footer, save the workbook, preview, then print the subtotals and grand total.

   g. Save the workbook, close the workbook, then exit Excel.

FIGURE H-22

	A	B	C	D	E	F	G	H	I	J
1	Employee Number	First Name	Last Name	Hire Date	Department	Monthly Salary	Annual Salary	Annual Bonus	Benefits Dollars	Annual Compensation
6					Boston Total					$ 323,022
10					NY Total					$ 170,741
14					Philadelphia Total					$ 372,561
15					Grand Total					$ 866,325
16										

▼ INDEPENDENT CHALLENGE 1

As the owner of Preserves, a gourmet food store located in Dublin, Ireland, you spend a lot of time managing your inventory. To help with this task, you have created an Excel table of your jam inventory. You want to filter the table and add subtotals and a grand total to the table. You also need to add data validation and summary information to the table.

▼ INDEPENDENT CHALLENGE 1 (CONTINUED)

a. Start Excel, open the file EX H-3.xlsx from the drive and folder where you store your Data Files, then save it as **Jams**.

b. Using the table data on the Inventory sheet, create a filter to generate a list of rhubarb jams. Enter your name in the worksheet footer, save the workbook, then preview and print the table. Clear the filter.

c. Use a Custom Filter to generate a list of jams with a quantity greater than 20. Preview, then print the table. Clear the filter.

d. Copy the labels in cells A1:F1 into A16:F16. Type **Gooseberry** in cell B17 and type **Small** in cell C17. Use the Advanced Filter with a criteria range of A16:F17 to extract a table of small gooseberry jams to the range of cells beginning in cell A20. Save the workbook, preview, then print the table with the extracted information.

e. Click the Summary sheet tab, select the table data in column B. Open the Data Validation dialog box, then indicate you want to use a validation list with the acceptable entries of **Gooseberry, Blackberry, Rhubarb**. Make sure the In-cell dropdown check box is selected.

f. Test the data validation by trying to change a cell in column B of the table to Strawberry.

g. Using Figure H-23 as a guide, enter a function in cell G18 that calculates the total quantity of blackberry jam in your store. Enter your name in the worksheet footer, save the workbook, then preview and print the worksheet.

FIGURE H-23

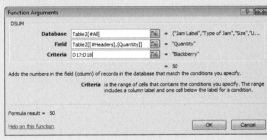

h. Use the filter list arrow for the Type of Jam field to sort the table in ascending order by type of jam. Convert the table to a range. Insert subtotals by type of jam using the SUM function, then select Quantity in the Add Subtotal to table box. Use the appropriate button on the outline to display only the subtotals and grand total. (Note that the number of Blackberry Jams calculated in cell G22 is incorrect after subtotals are added because the subtotals are included in the database calculation.) Save the workbook, preview, then print the range containing the subtotals and grand total.

FIGURE H-24

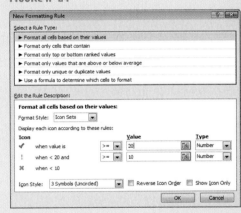

Advanced Challenge Exercise

- Clear the subtotals from the worksheet.
- Use conditional formatting to add icons to the quantity field using the following criteria: quantities greater than or equal to 20 are formatted with a green check mark, quantities greater than or equal to 10 but less than 20 are formatted with a yellow exclamation point, and quantities less than 10 are formatted with a red x. Use Figure H-24 as a guide to adding the formatting rule, then compare your Quantity values to Figure H-25. (*Hint*: You may need to click in the top Value text box for the correct value to display for the red x.)
- Save the workbook, preview then print the worksheet.

i. Close the workbook, then exit Excel.

FIGURE H-25

	A	B	C	D	E	F
1	Jam Label	Type of Jam	Size	Unit Price	Quantity	Total
2	Tipperary Ranch	Blackberry	Medium	6.00	! 11	66.00
3	Galway Estate	Blackberry	Small	5.25	! 12	63.00
4	Wexford Hills	Blackberry	Medium	5.75	! 15	86.25
5	Kerry Lane	Blackberry	Small	6.55	! 12	78.60
6	Tipperary Ranch	Gooseberry	Small	5.75	✖ 6	34.50
7	Cork Estate	Gooseberry	Small	5.75	✖ 8	46.00
8	Wexford Hills	Gooseberry	Small	5.75	✔ 21	120.75
9	Kerry Lane	Gooseberry	Medium	7.25	! 18	130.50
10	Tipperary Ranch	Rhubarb	Small	6.50	✖ 5	32.50
11	Galway Estate	Rhubarb	Small	6.25	! 11	68.75
12	Wexford Hills	Rhubarb	Small	5.25	✔ 31	162.75
13	Kerry Lane	Rhubarb	Medium	7.55	✔ 24	181.20
14						

▼ INDEPENDENT CHALLENGE 2

You recently started a personalized pet tag business, called Paw Tags. The business sells engraved cat and dog tags. Customers order tags for their cat or dog and provide you with the name of the pet and whether they want engraving on one or both sides of the tag. You have put together an invoice table to track sales for the month of October. Now that you have this table, you would like to manipulate it in several ways. First, you want to filter the table to retrieve only tags retailing for more than a particular price and ordered during a particular part of the month. You also want to subtotal the unit price and total cost columns by tag and restrict entries in the Order Date column. Finally, you would like to add database and lookup functions to your worksheet to efficiently retrieve data from the table.

▼ INDEPENDENT CHALLENGE 2 (CONTINUED)

a. Start Excel, open the file EX H-4.xlsx from the drive and folder where you store your Data Files, then save it as **Paw Tags**.

b. Use the Advanced Filter to show tags with a price of $12.99 ordered before 10/15/2010, using cells A27:B28 to enter your criteria and filtering the table in place. (*Hint*: You don't need to specify an entire row as the criteria range.) Enter your name in the worksheet footer, save the workbook, then print the filtered table. Clear the filter, then save your work again.

c. Use the Data Validation dialog box to restrict entries to those with order dates on or after 10/1/2010 and before or on 10/31/2010. Test the data restrictions by attempting to enter an invalid date in cell D25.

d. Enter **23721** in cell F28. Enter a VLOOKUP function in cell G28 to retrieve the total based on the invoice number entered in cell F28. Make sure you have an exact match with the invoice number. Test the function with the invoice number 23718.

e. Enter the date **10/1/2010** in cell I28. Use the database function, DCOUNT, in cell J28 to count the number of invoices for the date in cell I28. Save the workbook.

f. Sort the table in ascending order by Tag, then convert the table to a range. Create subtotals showing the number of cat and dog tags in the Invoice Number column. Save your subtotaled data, then preview and print the Invoice worksheet.

Advanced Challenge Exercise

■ Clear the subtotals and create a table using the data in the range A1:J25. Change the font color of the column headers to white. If the font headers are not visible, change the font color to one that contrasts with the fill color of your headers.

■ Use the filtering feature to display only the Cat tags, then add a total row to display the number of cat tags in cell E26. Change the font color in cells A26 and E26 to white. If the contents of cells A26 and E26 are not visible, change the font color to one that contrasts with the fill color for those cells. Delete the total in cell J26.

■ Use conditional formatting to format the cells where the Total is greater than $12.00 with light red fill and dark red text.

■ Using the Total Filter arrow, sort the table by color to display the totals exceeding $12.00 on top. Filter the table by color to display only the rows with totals greater than $12.00.

g. Save the workbook, print the Invoice worksheet, close the workbook, then exit Excel.

▼ INDEPENDENT CHALLENGE 3

You are the manager of Green Mountain, a gift shop in Burlington, Vermont. You have created an Excel table that contains your order data, along with the amounts for each item ordered and the date the order was placed. You would like to manipulate this table to display product categories and ordered items meeting specific criteria. You would also like to add subtotals to the table and add database functions to total orders. Finally, you want to restrict entries in the Category column.

a. Start Excel, open the file EX H-5.xlsx from the drive and folder where you store your Data Files, then save it as **Gifts**.

b. Using the table data, create an advanced filter that retrieves, to its current location, records with dates before 9/10/2010 and whose orders were greater than $1000, using cells A37:E38 to enter your criteria for the filter. Clear the filter.

c. Create an advanced filter that extracts records with the following criteria to cell A42: orders greater than $1000 having dates either before 9/10/2010 or after 9/24/2010. (*Hint*: Recall that when you want records to meet one criterion or another, you need to place the criteria on separate lines.) Enter your name in the worksheet footer, then preview and print the worksheet.

d. Use the DSUM function in cell H2 to let worksheet users find the total order amounts for the category entered in cell G2. Format the cell containing the total order using the Accounting format with the $ symbol and no decimals. Test the DSUM function using the Food category name. (The sum for the Food category should be $5,998.) Print the worksheet.

e. Use data validation to create an in-cell drop-down that restricts category entries to Food, Clothing, Book, Personal. Use the Error Alert tab of the Data Validation dialog box to set the alert level to the Warning style with the message "Data is not valid." Test the validation in the table with valid and invalid entries.

▼ INDEPENDENT CHALLENGE 3 (CONTINUED)

f. Sort the table by category in ascending order. Add Subtotals to the order amounts by category. The total order amount in cell H2 will be incorrect after adding subtotals because the subtotals will be included in the database calculation.

g. Use the outline to display only category names with subtotals and the grand total.

Advanced Challenge Exercise

- Clear the subtotals from the worksheet.
- Conditionally format the 1-Month Order data using Top/Bottom Rules to emphasize the cells containing the top 10 percent with yellow fill and dark yellow text.
- Add another rule to format the bottom 10 percent in the 1-Month Order column with a light blue fill.

h. Save the workbook, preview, then print the worksheet.

i. Close the workbook, then exit Excel.

▼ REAL LIFE INDEPENDENT CHALLENGE

You decide to organize your business and personal contacts using the Excel table format. You want to use the table to look up cell, home, and work phone numbers. You also want to include addresses and a field documenting whether the contact relationship is personal or business. You enter your contact information in an Excel worksheet that you will convert to a table so you can easily filter the data. You also use lookup functions to locate phone numbers when you provide a last name in your table. Finally, you restrict the entries in one of the fields to values in drop-down lists to simplify future data entry and reduce errors.

a. Start Excel, open a new workbook, then save it as **Contacts** in the drive and folder where you store your Data Files.

b. Use the structure of Table H-2 to enter at least six of your personal and business contacts into a worksheet. (*Hint*: You will need to format the Zip column using the Zip Code type of the Special category.) In the Relationship field, enter either Business or Personal. If you don't have phone numbers for all the phone fields, leave them blank.

TABLE H-2

Last name	First name	Cell phone	Home phone	Work phone	Street address	City	State	Zip	Relationship

c. Use the worksheet information to create a table. Use the Name Manager dialog box to edit the table name to Contacts.

d. Create a filter that retrieves records of personal contacts. Clear the filter.

e. Create a filter that retrieves records of business contacts. Clear the filter.

f. Restrict the Relationship field entries to Business or Personal. Provide an in-cell drop-down list allowing the selection of these two options. Add an input message of **Select from the dropdown list**. Add an Information level error message of **Choose Business or Personal**. Test the validation by adding a new record to your table.

g. Below your table, create a phone lookup area with the following labels in adjacent cells: **Last name**, **Cell phone**, **Home phone**, **Work phone**.

h. Enter one of the last names from your table under the label Last Name in your phone lookup area.

i. In the phone lookup area, enter lookup functions to locate the cell phone, home phone, and work phone numbers for the contact last name that you entered in the previous step. Make sure you match the last name exactly.

j. Enter your name in the center section of the worksheet footer, save the workbook, preview, then print the worksheet on one page.

k. Close the workbook, then exit Excel.

▼ VISUAL WORKSHOP

Open the file EX H-6.xlsx from the drive and folder where you save your Data Files, then save it as **Schedule**. Complete the worksheet as shown in Figure H-26. Cells B18:E18 contain lookup functions that find the instructor, day, time, and room for the course entered in cell A18. Use HIS101 in cell A18 to test your lookup functions. The range A22:G27 is extracted from the table using the criteria in cells A20:A21. Add your name to the worksheet footer, save the workbook, then preview and print the worksheet.

FIGURE H-26

	A	B	C	D	E	F	G
1	Spring 2011 Schedule of History Classes						
2							
3	Course number	ID #	Time	Day	Room	Credits	Instructor
4	HIS100	1245	8:00 - 9:00	M,W,F	126	3	Walsh
5	HIS101	1356	8:00 - 9:30	T,TH	136	3	Guan
6	HIS102	1567	9:00 - 10:00	M,W,F	150	3	Marshall
7	HIS103	1897	10:00 - 11:30	T,TH	226	3	Benson
8	HIS104	3456	2:00 - 3:30	M,W,F	129	4	Paulson
9	HIS200	4678	12:00 - 1:30	T,TH	156	3	Dash
10	HIS300	7562	3:00 - 4:30	M,W,F	228	4	Christopher
11	HIS400	9823	11:00 - 12:00	M,W,F	103	3	Robbinson
12	HIS500	7123	3:00 - 4:30	T,TH	214	3	Matthews
13							
14							
15							
16							
17	Course Number	Instructor	Day	Time	Room		
18	HIS101	Guan	T,TH	8:00 - 9:30	136		
19							
20	Day						
21	M,W,F						
22	Course number	ID #	Time	Day	Room	Credits	Instructor
23	HIS100	1245	8:00 - 9:00	M,W,F	126	3	Walsh
24	HIS102	1567	9:00 - 10:00	M,W,F	150	3	Marshall
25	HIS104	3456	2:00 - 3:30	M,W,F	129	4	Paulson
26	HIS300	7562	3:00 - 4:30	M,W,F	228	4	Christopher
27	HIS400	9823	11:00 - 12:00	M,W,F	103	3	Robbinson
28							

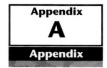
Restoring Defaults in Windows Vista and Disabling and Enabling Windows Aero

Windows Vista is the most recent version of the Windows operating system. An operating system controls the way you work with your computer, supervises running programs, and provides tools for completing your computing tasks. After surveying millions of computer users, Microsoft incorporated their suggestions to make Windows Vista secure, reliable, and easy to use. In fact, Windows Vista is considered the most secure version of Windows yet. Other improvements include a powerful new search feature that lets you quickly search for files and programs from the Start menu and most windows, tools that simplify accessing the Internet, especially with a wireless connection, and multimedia programs that let you enjoy, share, and organize music, photos, and recorded TV. Finally, Windows Vista offers lots of visual appeal with its transparent, three-dimensional design in the Aero experience. This appendix explains how to make sure you are using the Windows Vista default settings for appearance, personalization, security, hardware, and sound and to enable and disable Windows Aero. For more information on Windows Aero, go to *www.microsoft.com/windowsvista/experiences/aero.mspx*.

OBJECTIVES

Restore the defaults in the Appearance and Personalization section

Restore the defaults in the Security section

Restore the defaults in the Hardware and Sound section

Disable Windows Aero

Enable Windows Aero

Restoring the Defaults in the Appearance and Personalization Section

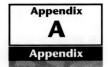

The following instructions require a default Windows Vista Ultimate installation and the student logged in with an Administrator account. All of the following settings can be changed by accessing the Control Panel.

STEPS

- To restore the defaults in the Personalization section

    1. **Click** Start, **and then click** Control Panel. **Click** Appearance and Personalization, **click** Personalization, **and then compare your screen to Figure A-1**

    2. **In the Personalization window, click** Windows Color and Appearance, **select the Default color, and then click** OK

    3. **In the Personalization window, click** Mouse Pointers. **In the Mouse Properties dialog box, on the Pointers tab, select** Windows Aero (system scheme) **in the Scheme drop-down list, and then click** OK

    4. **In the Personalization window, click** Theme. **Select** Windows Vista **from the Theme drop-down list, and then click** OK

    5. **In the Personalization window, click** Display Settings. **In the Display Settings dialog box, drag the Resolution bar to 1024 by 768 pixels, and then click** OK

FIGURE A-1

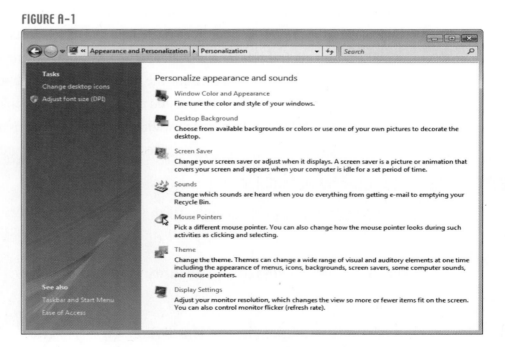

- To restore the defaults in the Taskbar and Start Menu section

  1. Click Start, and then click Control Panel. Click Appearance and Personalization, click Taskbar and Start Menu, and then compare your screen to Figure A-2

  2. In the Taskbar and Start Menu Properties dialog box, on the Taskbar tab, click to select all checkboxes except for "Auto-hide the taskbar"

  3. On the Start Menu tab, click to select the Start menu radio button and check all items in the Privacy section

  4. In the System icons section on the Notification Area tab, click to select all of the checkboxes except for "Power"

  5. On the Toolbars tab, click to select Quick Launch, none of the other items should be checked

  6. Click OK to close the Taskbar and Start Menu Properties dialog box

- To restore the defaults in the Folder Options section

  1. Click Start, and then click Control Panel. Click Appearance and Personalization, click Folder Options, and then compare your screen to Figure A-3

  2. In the Folder Options dialog box, on the General tab, click to select Show preview and filters in the Tasks section, click to select Open each folder in the same window in the Browse folders section, and click to select Double-click to open an item (single-click to select) in the Click items as follows section

  3. On the View tab, click the Reset Folders button, and then click Yes in the Folder views dialog box. Then click the Restore Defaults button

  4. On the Search tab, click the Restore Defaults button

  5. Click OK to close the Folder Options dialog box

- To restore the defaults in the Windows Sidebar Properties section

  1. Click Start, and then click Control Panel. Click Appearance and Personalization, click Windows Sidebar Properties, and then compare your screen to Figure A-4

  2. In the Windows Sidebar Properties dialog box, on the Sidebar tab, click to select Start Sidebar when Windows starts. In the Arrangement section, click to select Right, and then click to select 1 in the Display Sidebar on monitor drop-down list

  3. Click OK to close the Windows Sidebar Properties dialog box

FIGURE A-3

FIGURE A-4

FIGURE A-2

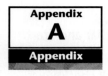

Restoring the Defaults in the Security Section

The following instructions require a default Windows Vista Ultimate installation and the student logged in with an Administrator account. All of the following settings can be changed by accessing the Control Panel.

STEPS

- To restore the defaults in the Windows Firewall section
    1. Click Start, and then click Control Panel. Click Security, click Windows Firewall, and then compare your screen to Figure A-5
    2. In the Windows Firewall dialog box, click Change settings. If the User Account Control dialog box appears, click Continue
    3. In the Windows Firewall Settings dialog box, click the Advanced tab. Click Restore Defaults, then click Yes in the Restore Defaults Confirmation dialog box
    4. Click OK to close the Windows Firewall Settings dialog box, and then close the Windows Firewall window

- To restore the defaults in the Internet Options section
    1. Click Start, and then click Control Panel. Click Security, click Internet Options, and then compare your screen to Figure A-6
    2. In the Internet Properties dialog box, on the General tab, click the Use default button. Click the Settings button in the Tabs section, and then click the Restore defaults button in the Tabbed Browsing Settings dialog box. Click OK to close the Tabbed Browsing Settings dialog box
    3. On the Security tab of the Internet Properties dialog box, click to uncheck the Enable Protected Mode checkbox, if necessary. Click the Default level button in the Security level for this zone section. If possible, click the Reset all zones to default level button
    4. On the Programs tab, click the Make default button in the Default web browser button for Internet Explorer, if possible. If Office is installed, Microsoft Office Word should be selected in the HTML editor drop-down list
    5. On the Advanced tab, click the Restore advanced settings button in the Settings section. Click the Reset button in the Reset Internet Explorer settings section, and then click Reset in the Reset Internet Explorer Settings dialog box
    6. Click Close to close the Reset Internet Explorer Settings dialog box, and then click OK to close the Internet Properties dialog box

FIGURE A-5

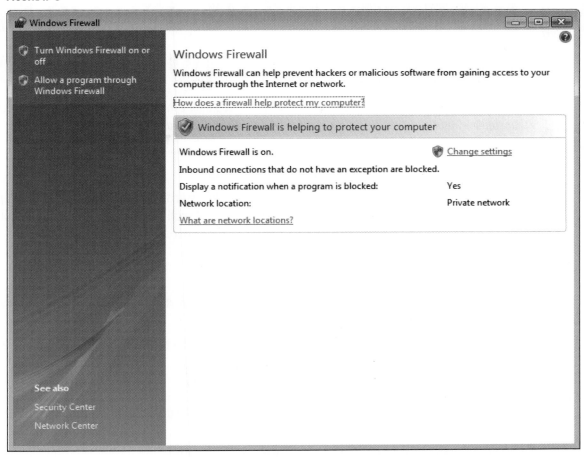

FIGURE A-6

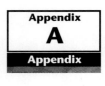

Restoring the Defaults in the Hardware and Sound Section

The following instructions require a default Windows Vista Ultimate installation and the student logged in with an Administrator account. All of the following settings can be changed by accessing the Control Panel.

STEPS

- To restore the defaults in the Autoplay section

  1. Click Start, and then click Control Panel. Click Hardware and Sound, click Autoplay, and then compare your screen to Figure A-7. Scroll down and click the Reset all defaults button in the Devices section at the bottom of the window, and then click Save

- To restore the defaults in the Sound section

  1. Click Start, and then click Control Panel. Click Hardware and Sound, click Sound, and then compare your screen to Figure A-8

  2. In the Sound dialog box, on the Sounds tab, select Windows Default from the Sound Scheme drop-down list, and then click OK

- To restore the defaults in the Mouse section

  1. Click Start, and then click Control Panel. Click Hardware and Sound, click Mouse, and then compare your screen to Figure A-9

  2. In the Mouse Properties dialog box, on the Pointers tab, select Windows Aero (system scheme) from the Scheme drop-down list

  3. Click OK to close the Mouse Properties dialog box

FIGURE A-7

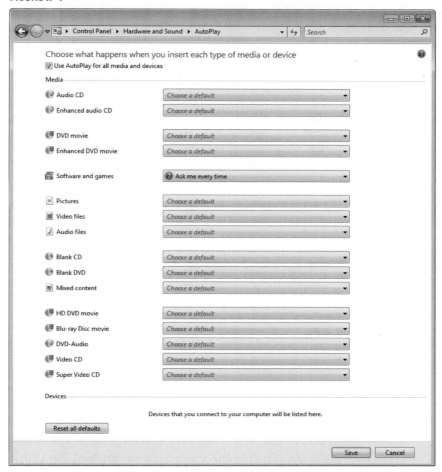

FIGURE A-8

FIGURE A-9

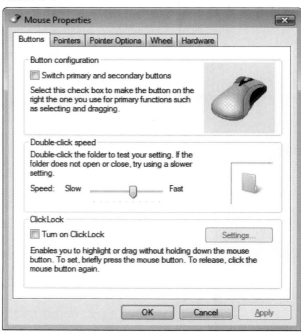

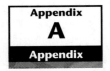
Disabling and Enabling Windows Aero

Unlike prior versions of Windows, Windows Vista provides two distinct user interface experiences: a "basic" experience for entry-level systems and more visually dynamic experience called Windows Aero. Both offer a new and intuitive navigation experience that helps you more easily find and organize your applications and files, but Aero goes further by delivering a truly next-generation desktop experience.

Windows Aero builds on the basic Windows Vista user experience and offers Microsoft's best-designed, highest-performing desktop experience. Using Aero requires a PC with compatible graphics adapter and running a Premium or Business edition of Windows Vista.

The following instructions require a computer capable of running Windows Aero, with a default Windows Vista Ultimate installation and student logged in with an Administrator account.

STEPS

- **To Disable Windows Aero**

We recommend that students using this book disable Windows Aero and restore their operating systems default settings (instructions to follow).

1. **Right-click the desktop, select Personalize, and then compare your screen in Figure A-10. Select Window Color and Appearance, and then select Open classic appeareance properties for more color options. In Appearance Settings dialog box, on the Appearance tab, select any non-Aero scheme (such as Windows Vista Basic or Windows Vista Standard) in the Color Scheme list, and then click OK. Figure A-11 compares Windows Aero to other color schemes. Note that this book uses Windows Vista Basic as the color scheme**

- **To Enable Windows Aero**

1. **Right-click the desktop, and then select Personalize. Select Window Color and Appearance, then select Windows Aero in the Color scheme list, and then click OK in the Appearance Settings dialog box**

FIGURE A-10

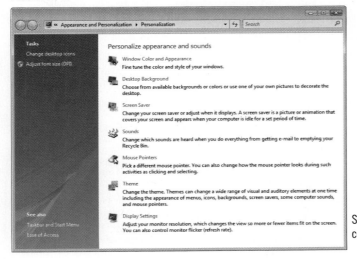

FIGURE A-11

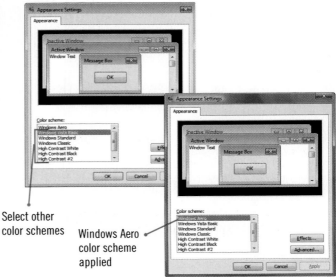

Select other
color schemes

Windows Aero
color scheme
applied

Glossary

3-D reference A worksheet reference that uses values on other sheets or workbooks, effectively creating another dimension to a workbook.

Absolute cell reference In a formula, type of cell address that does not change when you copy the formula; indicated by a dollar sign before the column letter and/or row number. *See also* Relative cell reference.

Active cell The cell in which you are currently working.

Add-in An extra program, such as Solver and the Analysis ToolPak, that provides optional Excel features. To activate an add-in, click the Office button, click Excel options, click Add-Ins, then click Go. Select or deselect add-ins from the list.

Alignment The placement of cell contents; for example, left, center, or right.

AND condition A filtering feature that searches for records by specifying that all entered criteria must be matched.

Arithmetic operators In a formula, symbols that perform mathematical calculations, such as plus (+), minus (–), multiplication (*), divide (/), or exponentiation (^).

Ascending order In sorting worksheet records, the lowest value (the beginning of the alphabet, or the earliest date) appears at the beginning of the sorted data.

Attributes Styling characteristics such as bold, italics, and underlining that you can apply to change the way text and numbers look in a worksheet or chart.

AutoFill Options button Feature that lets you fill cells with specific elements (such as formatting) of the copied cell.

AutoFilter A table feature that lets you click a list arrow and select criteria by which to display certain types of records; *also called* filter.

AutoFilter list arrows List arrows that appear next to field names in an Excel table; used to display portions of your data. *Also called* filter list arrows.

AutoFit A feature that automatically adjusts the width of a column or the height of a row to accommodate its widest or tallest entry.

Banding Worksheet formatting in which adjacent rows and columns are formatted differently.

Calculated columns In a table, a column that uses one formula that automatically adjusts to accommodate additional rows.

Calculation operators Symbols that indicate what type of calculation to perform on the cells, ranges or values.

Category axis Horizontal axis of a chart, usually containing the names of data groups; in a 2-dimensional chart, also known as the x-axis.

Cell The intersection of a column and a row in a worksheet, datasheet, or table.

Cell address The location of a cell, expressed by cell coordinates; for example, the cell address of the cell in column A, row 1 is A1.

Cell pointer Dark rectangle that outlines the active cell.

Cell styles Predesigned combinations of formatting attributes that can be applied to selected cells, to enhance the look of a worksheet.

Chart sheet A separate sheet in a workbook that contains only a chart, which is linked to the workbook data.

Charts Pictorial representations of worksheet data that make it easier to see patterns, trends, and relationships; *also called* graphs.

Clip A media file, such as art, sound, animation, or a movie.

Clip art A graphic image, such as a corporate logo, a picture, or a photo, that can be inserted into a document.

Color scale In conditional formatting, a formatting scheme that uses a set of two, three, or four fill colors to convey relative values of data.

Column heading Identifies the column letter, such as A, B, etc.; located above each column in a worksheet.

Comparison operators In a calculation, symbols that compare values for the purpose of true/false results.

Conditional format A type of cell formatting that changes based on the cell's value or the outcome of a formula.

Consolidate To combine data on multiple worksheets and display the result on another worksheet.

Criteria range In advanced filtering, a cell range containing one row of labels (usually a copy of column labels) and at least one additional row underneath it that contains the criteria you want to match.

Data entry area The unlocked portion of a worksheet where users are able to enter and change data.

Data marker A graphical representation of a data point, such as a bar or column.

Data point Individual piece of data plotted in a chart.

Data series A column or row in a datasheet. Also, the selected range in a worksheet that Excel converts into a chart.

Delimiter A separator such as a space, comma, or semicolon between elements in imported data.

Descending order In sorting an Excel field (column), the order that begins with the letter Z or the highest number of the values in the field.

Dynamic page breaks In a larger workbook, horizontal or vertical dashed lines that represent the place where pages print separately. They also adjust automatically when you insert or delete rows or columns, or change column widths or row heights.

Edit To make a change to the contents of an active cell.

Electronic spreadsheet A computer program that performs calculations and presents numeric data.

Embedded chart A chart displayed as an object in a worksheet.

Exploding pie slice A slice of a pie chart that has been pulled away from the whole pie, in order to add emphasis.

External reference indicator The exclamation point (!) used in a formula to indicate that a referenced cell is outside the active sheet.

Extract To place a copy of a filtered table in a range you specify in the Advanced Filter dialog box.

Field In a table (an Excel database), a column that describes a characteristic about records, such as first name or city.

Field name A column label that describes a field.

Filter To display data in an Excel table that meet specified criteria. *See also* AutoFilter.

Filter arrows *See* AutoFilter list arrows.

Font The typeface or design of a set of characters (letters, numerals, symbols, and punctuation marks).

Font size The size of characters, measured in units called points (pts).

Format The appearance of text and numbers, including color, font, attributes, borders, and shading. *See also* Number format.

Formula bar The area above the worksheet grid where you enter or edit data in the active cell.

Formula prefix An arithmetic symbol, such as the equal sign (=), used to start a formula.

Formulas A set of instructions used to perform one or more numeric calculations, such as adding, multiplying, or averaging, on values or cells.

Freeze To hold in place selected columns or rows when scrolling in a worksheet that is divided in panes. *See also* Panes.

Functions A special, predefined formula that provides a shortcut for a commonly used or complex calculation, for example, SUM (for calculating a sum) or FV (for calculating the future value of an investment).

Gridlines Evenly spaced horizontal and/or vertical lines used in a worksheet or chart to make it easier to read.

Header row In a table, the first row that contains the field names.

HTML Hypertext Markup Language, the format of pages that a Web browser can read.

Hyperlink An object (a filename, a word, a phrase, or a graphic) in a worksheet that, when you click it, displays another worksheet or a Web page called the target. *See also* Target.

Icon sets In conditional formatting, groups of images that are used to visually communicate relative cell values based on the values they contain.

Insertion point A blinking vertical line that appears when you click in the formula bar; indicates where new text will be inserted.

Instance A worksheet in its own workbook window.

Intranet An internal network site used by a group of people who work together.

Keywords Terms added to a workbook's Document Properties that help locate the file in a search.

Labels Descriptive text or other information that identifies rows, columns, or chart data, but are not included in calculations.

Landscape orientation Print setting that positions a document so it spans the widest margins of the page, making the page wider than it is tall.

Legend In a chart, information that explains how data is represented by colors or patterns.

Linking The dynamic referencing of data in the same or in other workbooks, so that when data in the other location is changed, the references in the current location are automatically updated.

List arrows *See* AutoFilter list arrows.

Lock To secure a row, column, or sheet so that data in that location cannot be changed.

Logical conditions Using the operators And and Or to narrow a custom filter criteria.

Logical formula A formula with calculations that are based on stated conditions.

Logical test The first part of an IF function; if the logical test is true, then the second part of the function is applied, and if it is false, then the third part of the function is applied.

Metadata Information that describes data and is used in Microsoft Windows document searches.

Mixed reference Cell reference that combines both absolute and relative addressing.

Mode indicator An area in the lower-left corner of the status bar that informs you of a program's status. For example, when you are changing the contents of a cell, the word 'Edit' appears.

Multilevel sort A reordering of table data using more than one column at a time.

Name box Left most area of the formula bar that shows the cell reference or name of the active cell.

Named range A range of cells with a meaningful name such as "July Sales" instead of simply the range coordinates such as "C7:G7"; used to make it easier to reference data in a worksheet.

Navigate To move around in a worksheet; for example, you can use the arrow keys on the keyboard to navigate from cell to cell, or press [Page Up] or [Page Down] to move a screen at a time.

Normal view Default worksheet view that shows the worksheet without features such as headers and footers; ideal for creating and editing a worksheet, but may not be detailed enough when formatting a document.

Number format A format applied to values to express numeric concepts, such as currency, date, and percentage.

Object A chart or graphic image that can be moved and resized; displays handles when selected.

Or condition The records in a search must match only one of the criterion.

Page Break Preview A worksheet view that shows page break indicators that you can drag to include more or less information on each page in a worksheet.

Page Layout View Provides an accurate view of how a worksheet will look when printed, including headers and footers.

Panes Sections into which you can divide a worksheet when you want to work on separate parts of the worksheet at the same time; one pane freezes, or remains in place, while you scroll in another pane until you see the desired information.

Paste Options button Allows you to paste only specific elements of the copied selection, such as the formatting or values.

Plot area In a chart, the area inside the horizontal and vertical axes.

Point A unit of measure used for fonts and row height. One inch equals 72 points, or a point is equal to 1/72nd of an inch.

Portrait orientation A print setting that positions the document on the page so the page is taller than it is wide.

Print area A portion of a worksheet that you can define using the Print Area button on the Page Layout tab; after you select and define a print area, the Quick Print feature prints only that worksheet area.

Print title In a table that spans more than one page, the field names that print at the top of every printed page.

Properties File characteristics, such as the author's name, keywords, or the title, that help others understand, identify, and locate the file.

Publish To place an Excel workbook or worksheet on a Web site or an intranet in HTML format so that others can access it using their Web browsers.

Range A selection of two or more cells, such as B5:B14.

Read-only format Data that users can view but not change.

Record In a table (an Excel database), data about an object or a person.

Reference operators Mathematical calculations which enable you to use ranges in calculations.

Relative cell reference In a formula, type of cell addressing that automatically changes when the formula is copied or moved, to reflect the new location; default type of referencing used in Excel worksheets. *See also* Absolute cell referencing.

Return In a function, to display a result.

Scope In a named cell or range, the worksheets where the name can be used.

Scroll bars Bars on the right edge (vertical scroll bar) and bottom edge (horizontal scroll bar) of the document window that allow you to move around in a document that is too large to fit on the screen at once.

Search criterion In a workbook or table search, the text you are searching for.

Shared workbook An Excel workbook that several users can open and modify.

Sheet tab Identifies sheets in a workbook and lets you switch between sheets; sheet tabs are located below the worksheet grid.

Single-file Web page A Web page that integrates all of the worksheets and graphical elements from a workbook into a single file in the MHTML file format, making it easier to publish to the Web.

Sizing handles Small dots at the corners and edges of a chart, indicating that the chart is selected.

SmartArt Predesigned diagram types for the following types of data: List, Process, Cycle, Hierarchy, Relationship, Matrix, and Pyramid.

Sort To change the order of records in a table according to one or more fields, such as Last Name.

Sort keys Criteria on which a sort, or a reordering of data, is based.

Stated conditions In a logical formula, criteria you create.

Status bar Bar at the bottom of the Excel window that provides information about various keys, commands, and processes.

Structured reference Allows table formulas to refer to table columns by names that are automatically generated when the table is created.

Table An organized collection of rows and columns of similarly structured data on a worksheet.

Table styles Preset formatting combinations for a table.

Table total row A row you can add to the bottom of a table for calculations with the data in the table columns.

Target The location that a hyperlink displays after you click it.

Template A file whose content or formatting serves as the basis for a new workbook; Excel template files have the file extension .xltx.

Text annotations Labels added to a chart to draw attention to a particular area.

Text concatenation operators Mathematical calculations that join strings of text in different cells.

Theme A predefined set of colors, fonts, and line and fill effects that can easily be applied to an Excel worksheet and give it a consistent, professional look.

Tick marks Notations of a scale of measure on a chart axis.

Tiled Repeated, like a graphic in a worksheet background.

Track To identify and keep a record of who makes which changes to a workbook.

Value axis In a chart, vertical axis that contains numerical values; in a 2-dimensional chart, also known as the y-axis.

Values Numbers, formulas, and functions used in calculations.

View A set of display or print settings that you can name and save for access at another time. You can save multiple views of a worksheet.

Watermark A translucent background design on a worksheet that is displayed when the worksheet is printed. Watermarks are graphic files that are inserted into the document header.

What-if analysis A decision-making tool in which data is changed and formulas are recalculated, in order to predict various possible outcomes.

Wildcard A special symbol that substitutes for unknown characters in defining search criteria in the Find and Replace dialog box. The most common types of wildcards are the question mark (?), which stands for any single character, and the asterisk (*), which represents any group of characters.

Workbook A collection of related worksheets contained within a single file.

Worksheet A single sheet within a workbook file; also, the entire area within an electronic spreadsheet that contains a grid of columns and rows.

Worksheet background A background design on a worksheet; created with the background button on the Page Layout tab. Visible on the screen only, it does not print with the worksheet.

Worksheet window Area of the program window that displays part of the current worksheet; the worksheet window displays only a small fraction of the worksheet, which can contain a total of 1,048,576 rows and 16,384 columns.

Workspace An Excel file with an .xlw extension containing information about the identity, view, and placement of a set of open workbooks. Instead of opening each workbook individually, you can open the workspace file instead.

X-axis The horizontal axis in a chart; because it often shows data categories, such as months, *also called* the Category axis.

Y-axis The vertical axis in a chart; because it often shows numerical values in a 2-dimensional chart, *also called* the Value axis.

Z-axis The third axis in a true 3-D chart, lets you compare data points across both categories and values.

Index